Twentieth Century Architecture 2

Twentieth Century
Architecture 2

THE MODERN HOUSE REVISITED

The Twentieth Century Society
1996

TWENTIETH CENTURY ARCHITECTURE
is published by the Twentieth Century Society
70 Cowcross Street, London ECIM 6BP

NUMBER 2 · 1996 · ISSN 1353–1964

The Twentieth Century Society was founded in 1979
as the Thirties Society to protect British architecture and
design after 1914.
Registered Charity No. 326746

Seven numbers of *Thirties Society Journal* were published
between 1981 and 1991. *Twentieth Century Architecture* is the
continuation of *Thirties Society Journal*.

 The Twentieth Century Society
acknowledges the support of the
Arts Council of England for this
publication.

Generous support has also been given by:
Michael Schofield.
The Trustees of Mike Davies.

Editorial Committee:
Gavin Stamp, Jill Lever and Alan Powers.
Guest editor: Neil Bingham.

Designed and typeset in Quadraat
and Festival Titling by Dalrymple.
Printed by BAS Printers Ltd.

Contents

1 Harbour Meadow, Birdham, Sussex

PETER MORO

Harbour Meadow, Birdham, Sussex

PETER MORO

AFTER collaborating with Sir Leslie Martin on the design of the Royal Festival Hall (1948–51), Peter Moro started his own practice, the Peter Moro Partnership with a mixed workload of local authority housing, schools, university buildings and private houses including his own at 20 Blackheath Park (1956), now listed. After a commission to design the Nottingham Playhouse (1963), the practice tended to specialise in theatre design and at its dissolution, eight theatres had been built.

Moro was born in Heidelberg in 1911. He studied architecture for a year at the Technische Hochschule in Stuttgart transferring in 1931 to Berlin Charlottenburg. In Berlin he witnessed with extreme distaste the rise of the Nazis, and although raised a Catholic, was brought before a disciplinary committee of the Technische Hochschule for having a Jewish grandmother and was asked to leave. Moro chose to move to Zurich and complete his training at the Eidgenössische Technische Hochschule. In 1936, he qualified and returned to Germany, but found the atmosphere intolerable. Moving to London, he obtained a position with Lubetkin's firm of Tecton and worked on Highpoint II.

In 1937 he took a room in the Brunswick Square flat of his friend Richard Llewelyn-Davies (later Lord Llewelyn-Davies), who was a student at the Architectural Association. They formed a partnership to design a large country house at Birdham, Sussex. This commission saved Moro from being deported. The house was barely finished when, in 1940, Moro was interned. He was released after six months and for the next seven years he taught at the Regent Street Polytechnic School of Architecture. In his spare time he designed many exhibitions for the Central Office of Information mostly in partnership with Robin Day.

The following is an extract from Peter Moro's unpublished autobiography A Sense of Proportion: Memoirs of an Architect (1990).

One evening Richard came home having worked rather later than usual at the Architectural Association. 'Guess what happened? I was just about to leave the building when I ran into a lady in a fur coat obviously searching for something. "Tell me young man", she said, "this is the Architectural Association? I want to build a house and I'm looking for an architect."' She mistakenly thought that the AA was a sort of labour exchange for architects. He told her that unfortunately

figure 1
The front entrance and hall.
(Dell & Wainwright/Architectural Review)

figure 2
The entrance to the courtyard is approached through a framed opening in a rubble wall.
(Dell & Wainwright/Architectural Review)

figure 3
The west front over Birdham Creek.

he was only a student. 'Richard, for heaven's sake, have you forgotten me!' I asked. Although I was not at that time a member of the RIBA, I was a fully qualified architect. However, all was not lost. Richard had told the lady that he could give her some useful advice about the choice of architects as he knew the scene well.

Richard had taken her address and a few days later a meeting was arranged with her and her husband in their London flat. Mr Tawse was a wealthy Scotsman, a steel manufacturer. Mrs Tawse, who was younger than her husband, was keen to have a new house built on a 15-acre site they owned at Birdham, near Chichester, in Sussex. We presented them with a list of leading architects: Wells Coates, Serge Chermayeff, Maxwell Fry, Lubetkin, and so forth, and explained: 'This one is good but rather expensive, that one excellent but not very interested in doing one-off houses, this one is perhaps the most talented but unlikely to take much notice of the client's special requirements,' etc.

Having thus eliminated the lot, Mr Tawse said, 'This doesn't help us very much does it?' Richard with his enormous charm said, 'Well, how about us?' The inevitable question at this juncture was, 'And what have you chaps built so far?' Our reply was honest, 'Nothing.' After a few moments thought, Mr Tawse said, 'Alright, you've got the job.' This courageous decision by an extraordinary man changed my life and was the start of my architectural career.

However, just at that time, I received a deportation order. I was in despair. Richard, with his considerable connections, made arrangements through a solicitor for me to receive a one year extension to my work permit.

Although like a fairy tale commission, there were problems. In spite of the client being very wealthy, the budget of £5000 was tight. But even worse, they wanted a house in the Neo-Georgian style. At the risk of losing this once-in-a-lifetime opportunity, we did not for one moment consider producing anything but a modern building. However, we did not argue the point at the meeting, knowing that we had to tread very carefully. Our idea was to produce a vaguely traditional design to start with in order to get a foot in the door and as a basis for further discussion.

To our horror, they quite liked our first scheme but made several detailed suggestions. They wanted a balcony and expressed a desire to be able to see the spire of Chichester Cathedral from their bed. We told them that we thought these splendid requirements but explained that they had far-reaching design implications and conceptual repercussions requiring a new design. Thus, in the process, the roof got imperceptibly flatter and the windows a bit larger and more horizontal in proportion. The revised design was accepted, but more separation between parents, children and servants was requested. We agreed that this was an excellent recommendation and went back to the drawing board and prepared an articulated design accommodating parents and children in separate blocks with a Z-shaped plan of linked wings.

The clients were delighted with the new scheme as it satisfied all their wishes. In their excitement they seem not to have noticed the large glass areas, the flat roof and the fact that they were looking at a modern house.

The basis of a modern design having thus been gradually introduced and accepted, the possibility of developing the whole thing into an uncompromisingly contemporary house without further interference seemed assured. Although the design had developed from a single block into a spread out and articulated one, we felt that more had still to be done to make the house sit comfortably on the rather characterless flat meadow. There was also the need to screen and enclose part of the garden and the projected swimming pool from the drive. To do this we placed the 3-car garage some distance from the house and connected it with a covered way which formed the desired screen. While this solved the problem of siting to our satisfaction, we still had to convince Mr Tawse that the inconven-

figure 4
The south entrance front.
(Sydney W. Newbery)

figure 5
The fireplace area of the living room.
(Sydney W. Newbery)

figure 6
The elliptical staircase in the entrance
hall. (Sydney W. Newbery)

figure 7
The sun lounge overlooking Birdham
Creek. (Sydney W. Newbery)

ience of walking 100 feet to his car was worth it for reasons of aesthetics.

During our dealings with the client, we had observed a childlike obsession with gadgets, a weakness we decided to exploit on the day when we presented our final scheme in the form of a scale model. We placed the model on the floor, took the lid off, and positioned three Dinky cars on the drive. Mr Tawse immediately went down on his knees and began to move the little cars up and down the drive and eventually into the garage. Just in case it dawned on him that the garage was a fair distance from the house, we explained that under the engine of each car would be installed an electric heater controlled from the house. Each individual car could thus be warmed from a small control panel which had three indicator lights in different colours. This did the trick and no more was requested, but looking at the model Mr Tawse said, 'It's very nice but it looks rather pricey. How much?' Richard replied, '£15,000'. Still playing with the cars, Mr Tawse did not seem to be too bothered about the threefold increase.

Once the job got underway, Mr Tawse faded into the background and his wife took on the role of client. The house had really been her idea in the first place. He seemed to enjoy immensely her personal involvement and was passionately interested in every single detail. As I gained her confidence she would consult me on everything right down to the parlourmaid's dress. I shall never forget meeting her one day at Fortnum and Mason's when the snooty doorman, looking at my shabby mac, tried to direct me to the tradesmen's entrance.

I designed many of the light fittings and furniture including her dressing table which looked rather like a cinema organ. We had wallpaper printed from original William Morris blocks but in my own special colourways.

Richard and I did all the drawings and Pat (later his wife), did our secretarial work. Our office was a room in my new flat in Woburn Square; my landlady was Jane Drew. Two flush doors across the room formed a worktop with a drawing board behind each of the two Georgian sash windows. While drawing thus side-by-side I got to know Richard well and learned a great deal from him. He was a true intellectual and had a fund of knowledge on many subjects.

When the War broke out in September 1939, the house was nearing completion. The Swiss windows came across on the last boat from Boulogne as France fell. Richard, who was half Irish, left for Ireland, his second home. I moved into his new flat in Highpoint I and from the window could see the barrage balloons going up all over London. Needing some help, I persuaded my friend from Tecton days, Gordon Cullen, to work with me. Gordon was not only an architectural draughtsman of genius who later became an urbanist responsive to environmental context, but was also progressive in spirit. He contributed much to the interior design of the house including, as an architectural joke, a Neo-Classical surround for a small yellow-glazed picture window which framed the view of Birdham Creek.

figure 8
The dressing table with pivoting drawer.
(Sydney W. Newbery)

Being near Portsmouth, the house was in a restricted zone which made supervision of me as an alien difficult and on every visit I had to report to the police at Chichester. When the photographer from the *Architectural Review* arrived in kneebreeches, black pelerine and large floppy hat, looking like a spy in a third-rate play, he promptly was arrested while taking pictures. A few months later when a landmine dropped near the house and blew in all the windows, rumours were rife that the house had been designed in the shape of half a swastika as a landmark for the Luftwaffe on their way to Portsmouth.

Finally, having persuaded the client to have a modern rather than a Neo-Georgian house, at the risk of losing the job, we successfully passed the first test of professional integrity.

J. M. Richards, whom I had met as a member of the MARS Group, was editor of the *Architectural Review*, and featured the house extensively in the April 1941 issue. This publicity helped me on my way as an architect. But more important than all this was the fact that the client and his children loved the house beyond all expectations.

figure 9
Gordon Cullen's Neo-Classical picture window. *(Sydney W. Newbery)*

figure 10
Plans. *(Architectural Review)*

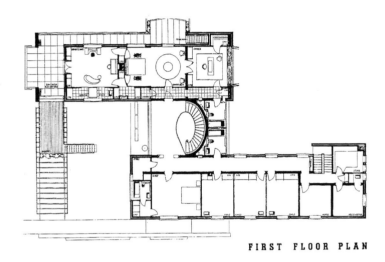

FIRST FLOOR PLAN

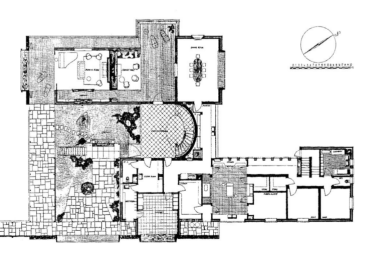

GROUND FLOOR PLAN

2 A Zebra at Villa Savoye: interpreting the Modern House

ALAN POWERS

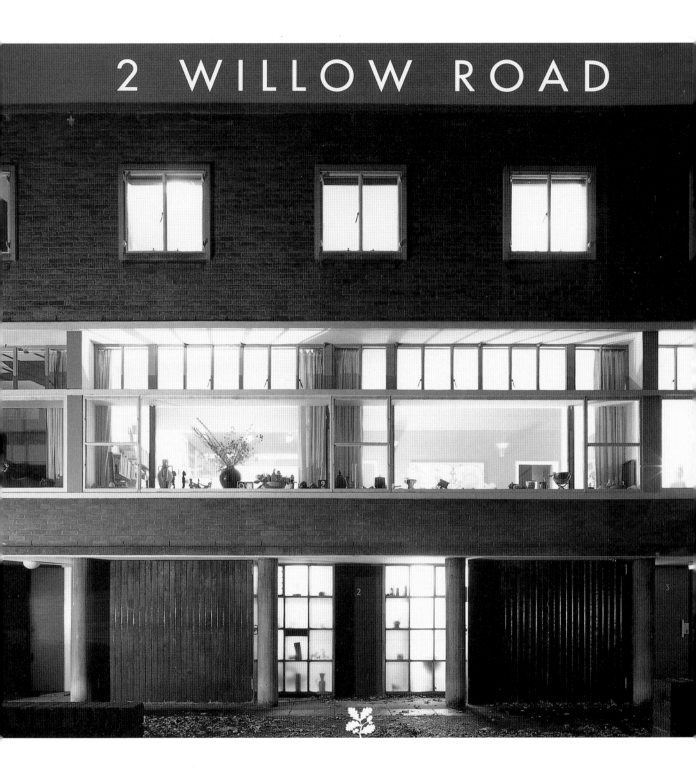

figure 1
Guidebook cover, 2 Willow Road, 1996.
(Photo NTPL/Angelo Hornak)

figure 2
'Save Monkton' poster 1985.
(Design Peter Campbell, photos Country Life.)

A Zebra at Villa Savoye:
interpreting the Modern House

ALAN POWERS

I N April 1996, the house at No 2 Willow Road, Hampstead, designed by Ernö Goldfinger and occupied by his family from 1939 onwards opened to the public under the ownership of the National Trust. In September 1995 English Heritage announced its intention to manage Eltham Palace, including granting public access to the 1935 wing designed by Seely and Paget for Stephen and Virginia Courtauld. This is a dual recognition of the importance of 1930s houses, the first categorically "modern", the second equivocally pluralist. These events come ten years after The Thirties Society (the Twentieth Century under its former name) and SAVE tried and failed to ensure the preservation of Monkton House, West Sussex, the home of Edward James as an ensemble of house and contents, either at the hands of the National Trust or English Heritage.

Conservation is linked to research, and this in turn is communicated through writing. When the National Trust began to explain Willow Road to journalists, potential benefactors and it members, nothing of substance had been written on

SAVE MONKTON
THE LAST SURREALIST DREAM

Design Peter Campbell. Photograph: Country Life

£1.6 million is urgently needed by June 1986 to prevent the break up of Monkton House in Sussex, with its sensational and unique 1930s interiors. Built by the great Lutyens, Monkton was transformed into an unforgettable masterpiece of Surrealist decoration by the colourful Edward James, international art patron and friend of such diverse figures as Dali, Magritte, Poulenc, John Betjeman and Evelyn Waugh. The Thirties Society and Save Britain's Heritage ask for your donation or pledge to help save Monkton and its contents for the nation. Once sold up this amazing ensemble could never be recreated. There is nothing else like it left in the world.
Write now to: The Monkton Appeal, 68 Battersea High Street, London SW11 3HX

the modern house in England since Jeremy Gould's excellent but brief monograph for the Society of Architectural Historians of Great Britain in 1977. Although the subject once seemed overworked, it has actually been surprisingly neglected. This collection of essays attempts to bring new interpretations to the subject and to explore aspects of these houses that most historians now expect to consider, such as patronage, the dissemination and reception of the work and, of particular concern with the history of the house, its furnishings and equipment. An essay on gardening was sought but proved impossible to find, and would have gone further to provide the context for these very distinctive houses.

Modern houses of the 1930s still create great excitement, not only among architects but among non-specialists and the in the press. Because of their inability to confront social issues directly the houses of the period were once considered a weak point in modernism's ideological front. Instead they have potentially become the means of its acceptance by a broader public, specially through the National Trust's timely action in buying No 2 Willow Road and the Trust's agreement to accept The Homewood, Esher, the house designed by Patrick Gwynne for his parents in 1937. We have to ask why this excitement should focus on houses. What is the aesthetic quality in these houses? To what extent is it dependant on the defining factor of the flat roof, and does it have any particular meaning in respect of English houses rather than those of any other country? The answers have to be found beyond the primary documents relating to the houses themselves, published statments, letters and recollections of architects or clients, in broader fields of architectural theory and in the cultural context of Britain in the 1930s.

Modernists of the 1930s in all countries presented their work in entirely material terms, as F. R. S. Yorke did in his books on the modern house. The pictures supplied the imaginative material. Their polemic presented the modern house as the shape of normality to come, its deviation from previous norms being a matter of improved comfort or convenience. This type of explanation supported the architect's competence as a technician. Scientific explanations were considered the most valid in all fields of human activity and any other kind of interpretation threatened the rational world-view on which Modernism was based. At the same time, the potency of Le Corbusier's images, as drawings and photographs, has long been acknowledged.

Monkton House, transformed in 1936 and 1937 from a small Lutyens house of 1902 into a major monument of built Surrealism, involved no significant use of modern structural materials or forms. The designers were Christopher Nicholson with his assistant Hugh Casson, advised at intervals by Salvador Dali. In Nicholson's *oeuvre* and in the history of the modern house it has been written off as an uncanonic eccentricity that challenges taste as well as categories of style.[1]

Monkton is an extreme case but a useful one in stating the problem of interpreting the modern house. Willow Road apparently represents the rationalist opposite of Monkton–a *machine à habiter* to be loved or hated according to taste– but Ernö and Ursula Goldfinger were perhaps second only to Edward James among those building houses in the thirties in Britain in their involvement in the Surrealist movement, as the works in the house by Max Ernst, Roland Penrose and other artists testify. Monkton fits to perfection the popular image of Surrealist strangeness cultivated by Salvador Dali, in this case literally applied from outside, while at Willow Road the surrealist theme is so subtly developed that its existence has been entirely overlooked. But is the claim to find it there an unwarrantable assumption?

Statements of intention in architecture are rare, and often focus only on one part of the design process. Modern architects, particularly in England, seem to have been shy of appearing in the role of artist, preferring something more inconspicuous in the technical line. This was surely a defence against hostile criticism rather than a denial of their role as creators of works of the imagination. The architectural culture of the time reflected the widespread belief in objectivity and science, factual description and mechanistic explanation. We are obliged to reconstruct the imaginative aspect of the modern house using our own observation of the houses and whatever techniques of interpretation seem sustainable and verifiable in terms of the houses and their cultural context.

The reaction of many planning authorities in the 1930s demonstrated that for the uninitiated, the modern house was an incomprehensible and threatening idea although they could not find adequate means to explain why. The polemic for the modern house in the 1930s depended on presenting it as normal, but was its true, if unstated, intention to provoke? The functional demands of the Modernist programme could be satisfied with less controversial aesthetic consequences and the means selected instead by architects, particularly monolithic reinforced concrete which was the ideal of the first half of the 1930s, were clearly in contradiction to commonsense. As Ove Arup wrote in 1968,

They were in love with an architectural style, with the aesthetic feel of the kind of building they admired; and so they were prepared and indeed determined to design their buildings in reinforced concrete–a material they knew next to nothing about–even if it meant using the concrete to do things that could be done better or more cheaply in another material.[2]

What was so appealing about the image of the modern house? Arup's commentary reveals the emotional and subconscious factors which, far from being peripheral, may be claimed as central to the whole business. In this light of emotional conflict, incapable of articulation by either side, the famous battles of the modern house begin to make sense. But how can we begin to understand these houses better than their own authors?

Through studying the poetics (by which I mean a standard set of creative and compositional devices) of the modern house, a logical explanation can be found. Metaphor is one of the fundamental devices of western literature, defined by Aristotle as a bringing together of two things – one of which acts to create strangeness in the other. As the linguistic philosopher Paul Ricoeur describes the process, 'the use of metaphor is close to the use of strange, ornamental, coined, lengthened and shortened terms.'[3] Metaphor disorders the scheme of classification and as opposed to passive conventional ornament, it bears meaning because it 'redescribes' reality.

The modern house makes its metaphorical statement by the introduction of imagery derived from alien building types such as industrial buildings or hospitals to take the place of conventional ornament. It inverts the expected signals of a house, particularly of an English house, such as local materials, the pitched roof, the central entrance, small windows and smoking chimney. This identity had been actively reasserted through the Arts and Crafts period and reinvested with national feeling to the point where it had become a cliché, hardly capable any longer of serious artistic development. Looking at the published collections of houses of the 1920s in England, one can see why the modern house of the Continent was attractive. The old type had lost the ability to excite an aesthetic response, even when pushed into the knowing ultra-picturesque of Oliver Hill.

The modern house, despite its wide-ranging intentions of reform in constructional practice, planning and building economics, would not interest us now were it not for its poetic appeal through its strangeness. There is no other explanation for the wide divergence between those stated intentions which were achieved only in part if at all and the actuality of the buildings which made their revolutionary impact through their appearance. Most Modernist architects, aware that the aesthetic aims of a previous generation had apparently led them into a cul-de-sac, would have echoed Eric Gill's words, "Beauty looks after herself." Serge

1. For a more sympathetic interpretation see Neil Bingham, *Christopher Nicholson*, (London: Academy Editions, 1996).
2. Ove Arup 'The World of the Structural Engineer' 1968, repr. *Arup Journal* XX, No.1, Spring 1985, p.5.
3. Paul Ricoeur *The Rule of Metaphor*, (London: Routledge, 1978), p.18.

Chermayeff, for one, was fond of quoting them. This absence of conscious aesthetic self-control was a perfect condition for the development of the subconscious. The modern house is a work of the imagination, for the imagination.

As Le Corbusier had shown, photography could create the dreamlike quality of the modern house, but this also gives a clue to the continuity between the Edwardian "Dream House"–archly camera-conscious and transforming the reality of regional style or tradition into a fantasy–and the modern house with its complete separation from reality. No figures ever populate its spaces and the evidence of daily life is reduced to stylised objects that could be stage props. The houses exist ideally without a context of locality or neighbouring buildings. They are

figure 3
Denys Lasdun. 32 Newton Road,
London, 1938.
(Photo Cracknell, courtesy Architectural Press)

lightly connected with the earth and their flat roofs bring them closer to the sky, the immaterial element that metaphorically contradicts their materiality.

Although the modern house is normally associated with abstract art of the 1930s, its essential characteristics as a work of art are better understood through Surrealism, the movement which links the two houses discussed at the beginning of this article. Surrealists were active in painting, poetry and film but their concern with architecture was largely related to the city rather than to the design of new buildings. An exception to this is André Breton's essay "Situation surréaliste de l'objet" where, in the words of a summary by Stuart Knight, 'Breton observes that there is no collective dream so pure and disturbing as the buildings of the "modern style"'. These he regards as 'the solidification of desire in the most violent and cruel automatism that indicates the disgust of the real world.'[4] The buildings admired by surrealists included fantasy structures such as the Palais Idéal du Facteur Cheval, built between 1890 and 1924, seen by Breton as the antithesis of modern architecture. The connection between Surrealism and modern architecture was therefore one which neither side was eager to acknowledge but which, with a new generation of critical history of surrealism and investigation of its ideas, needs to be reassessed.

Surrealism gave primacy to dream states such as the modern house, part of the 'collective dream' that Breton recognised, was designed to create. This goal was achieved by various means, literary and visual. Max Ernst's description of collage as 'the coupling of two realities, irreconcilable in appearance, upon a plane which apparently does not suit them'[5] corresponds to the understanding of metaphor proposed earlier. The modern house is fundamentally irreconcilable to its landscape, appearing not even as a man-made object but as a work without any human touch or effect of time. This could be inferred, not only from architects who typically made no explicit statements on the matter, but from painters, particularly Paul Nash in whose works of the 1920s and 30s smooth geometrical objects appear in open landscape to memorable effect. The importance of this effect, and its historical basis, was recognised by Patrick Abercrombie, a well-informed writer with no *parti-pris* in the debate for or against Modernism, when he wrote in 1939, 'there are the opposed effects of a building in harmony or in contrast with its surroundings; and it is surprising how often it is the contrast that gives the especial pleasure.'[6]

Perhaps the only relevant statement of intention by a modern house architect (and one, as John Allan recognises in his Lubetkin monograph, that is bursting with aggressive irony against uncomprehending colleagues and critics), is that in the *Architectural Review* of 1937 by Berthold Lubetkin concerning his Bungalow A at Whipsnade,

The flat roof is not a sign of exhibitionist tendencies of nudist inhabitants; the bathroom is not top lit in order that the bather may be more jealously guarded; the cornices are not specially designed for the local cats or for sleepwalkers; and the dish-washer in the kitchen has never been in working order.

On the contrary, the designer admits that there is, on the walls of the W.C., a collection of cold-blooded tropical butterflies; while the bedspreads have little bells sewn on them to brighten the dreams of the occupants.

The designer admits also that he has not capitulated to the accidents of a site which was forced on him; he excavated 800 cubic yards of dazzling white chalk full of megalithic fossils, to make a flat lawn and a flat house—where any Czech would have made a house in steps with a roof garden.[7]

This could not be clearer in its denial of pure functionalism and its affirmation of the imaginative and expressive character of the architecture.

Other aspects of Surrealism can be recognised in the modern house. 'The Outmoded' (an irrational attraction to obsolete, out-of-fashion objects) was recognised by Surrealists in France as an essential part of their revolutionary repertoire. The pages of the *Architectural Review* in the early 1930s were full of graphic versions of the same thing, and even the revival of interest in its pages in the pioneers of Modernism (articles by John Betjeman and P. Morton Shand on Voysey, Mackintosh and George Walton) could be a polite parallel to Dali's obsession with Gaudi and Art Nouveau. In actual architecture, the outmoded played a lesser role, although Le Corbusier had shown its potential in the apartment for Charles de Bestegui, an example followed with every appearance of innocence by Denys Lasdun in presenting alternative furnishings for the main living room at 32 Newton Road in modern and traditional styles, in the process undermining the authenticity of both, and leaving a very curly French-style fireplace as a permanent feature. The same shock value can be found in the coloured glass Rococo chandelier which has hung over the spiral staircase at Patrick Gwynne's The Homewood, Esher, since the completion of the house in 1938.

The most explicitly surrealistic modern house in this respect is Harbour Meadow, Birdham, by Llewelyn Davies and Moro which expanded on Lubetkin's repertory of metaphorical devices with its single window surrounded by false picture frame, its collage-like mixture of materials and complex plan. The care-

4. Stuart Knight 'Observations on Dada and Surrealism' in *Architectural Design*, Surrealism and Architecture Special Issue, vol.XLVIII, 1978, No.2–3, p.108.

5. Max Ernst, *Beyond Painting*, p.177, quoted in Hal Foster *Compulsive Beauty*, (Cambridge & London: MIT Press, 1993), p.81.

6. Patrick Abercombie, *The Book of the Modern House*, (London: Hodder & Stoughton,1939), p.xvii.

7. *Architectural Review*, vol.LXXXI, 1937, p.60.

ful placing of an opening to frame a view became more important in an architecture that had lost conventional means of emphasis through ornament as well as the spatial progression offered by compartmentalised planning. At Little Winch by Maxwell Fry the window beside the front door aligns with the garden window to give a transparent cut through the house. Framing devices, a prominent feature of the work of Max Ernst, are a conspicuous theme of Goldfinger's houses at Willow Road and at Broxted, Essex. The approach to the latter, through a narrow door in a garden wall, giving access to a covered way which in turn offers a view right through the house to the garden beyond, was the only moment in his architecture that Goldfinger was prepared to accept as being directly influenced by Surrealism.[8] These were admittedly small gestures, because they were subver-

 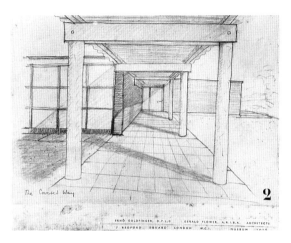

figures 4 & 5
Ernö Goldfinger. Hill Farm, Broxted.
Drawings of door in garden wall
and entrance pergola, 1937.
(photos courtesy of John Stubbington)

sive in a climate where Modernism was desperately seeking approval as an orthodoxy. Besides, to exaggerate the obsolete and bizarre, as Edward James instructed his architects to do at Monkton, is to diminish its effectiveness.

A major aspect of the Surrealist exploration of the subconscious was the erotic, presented as a route to political liberation but also closely linked to ideas of death. As André Breton wrote in *L'Amour Fou*, 'Convulsive Beauty will be veiled-erotic, fixed-explosive, magical-circumstantial or will not be.'[9]

The veiled erotic aspect of the modern house may be hard to demonstrate, but the propaganda against it reveals more than the writing promoting it. Opponents regularly assumed that the house-owners were nudists, and some of them were. Even if they were not, the flat roofs for sunbathing celebrated the body in a suggestive way. The circular house at St Ann's Hill, Chertsey by Raymond McGrath was built for a homosexual couple whose living arrangements are reflected in its plan. Sketches by Goldfinger for No 2 Willow Road mingle architectural ideas with sexual desire, notably a tender sketch of the proposed bedroom, already occupied by a standing female figure who is approached by a male figure from outside this serene nesting-box. Within these houses, surrealist emblems of the feminine are found, notably furs. In Chermayeff's Bentley Wood and No 2 Willow Road white polar bear rugs emphasise virginal softness, the opposite extreme of the hard-edged architecture. To develop his definition, Breton offered images, such as a limestone deposit shaped like an egg, which transfer imagery from one life form to another and often refer to geology and objects associated with early stages of evolution. Flints were used by Lubetkin in his conversion of West Grove, Mill Hill and by Samuel and Harding in a fire surround at No 13A Arkwright Road and random rubble appears in modern houses, following the lead given by Le Corbusier.

Against these images of life and generation are counterposed images of death, the "fixed-explosive" with its suspended motion. Paul Nash used the image of a Modernist grid of open square forms to illustrate "The soul visiting the Mansions of the Dead" from Sir Thomas Browne's *Urne Buriall* in 1932. In later paintings by Nash flowers float in the sky as an image of death. The Surrealist interest in primitive culture is displayed in certain objects found within houses, such as the Navaho rugs which furnished Sir Arthur Bliss's Pen Pits (where Nash stayed as a guest and painted), or the African and oriental masks at Willow Road.

Architectural forms may be considered to have specific meanings that do not apply to other building types when they appear in houses, since houses are the most direct extension of inner psychological states. In C. G. Jung's *Modern Man*

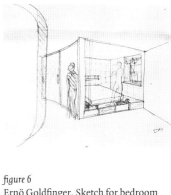

figure 6
Ernö Goldfinger. Sketch for bedroom at 2 Willow Road, *c.*1937.
(*RIBA* Drawings Collection)

figure 7
Paul Nash. 'The Soul Visiting the Mansions of the Dead' (illustration to *Urne Buriall* and *The Garden of Cyrus* by Sir Thomas Browne) 1932.

in *Search of a Soul*, 1933, the attic is portrayed, on the basis of dream analysis, as the symbol of the conscious mind, the cellar of the unconscious. Extrapolating from this, the habitable flat roof could well be seen as an extreme form of conscious compensation–a place of safety where the super-ego touches the sky, the culmination of the stairs that Gaston Bachelard saw as 'the mark of ascension to a more tranquil solitude'[10] – the ultimate image of peaceful death. Psychology

8. Information from James Dunnett.

9. Andre Breton, *L'Amour Fou*, 1937, quoted in Foster op. cit p.23.

10. Gaston Bachelard, *The Poetics of Space*, (Boston: Beacon Press, 1969), p.26.

figure 8
Raymond McGrath. St Ann's Hill,
Chertsey, 1936 *(Architectural Press).*

(from which Surrealism derived much of its theoretical grounding) was also introducing men and women of the 1930s to the idea that tranquillity is only won after confronting the dark forces.

The garden and landscape were more readily admitted as the proper area for poetic expression in the modern house, although few of these houses had elaborate gardens. They tended to be placed in lawn, often with pre-existing trees very close to the house. Examples include Oliver Hill's Landfall and Connell Ward and Lucas's No 6 Temple Drive, Moor Park. The houses most often considered in relation to landscape are those where Christopher Tunnard was involved as garden designer, notably Raymond McGrath's two houses at St Ann's Hill, Chertsey, 1936 and Carrygate, Galby, 1940, Chermayeff's Bentley Wood 1938 and Oliver Hill's Hill House, Hampstead, 1937. Tunnard's reputation rests chiefly on his writings, collected as *Gardens in the Modern Landscape*, 1938, a book which is reticent on aesthetic matters, although the illustrations included quasi-surrealist images such as the grottos at Painshill and Oatlands which Tunnard had researched yet seemed unwilling to admit as influences. Nonetheless on his home ground at St Ann's Hill Tunnard, playing part-role as architectural patron as well as landscape designer, assisted in the creation of one of the best house and garden ensembles. McGrath's house, inside and out, has a controlled stream of fantasy which lives up to the promise of his conversion of Finella, Cambridge for Mansfield Forbes in 1928–29. It is unlike any other modern house in Europe and plays most successfully with ambiguities of internal and external space, framed by flying beams and walls.

If we accept that the white modern house had a special meaning in an English context because the established image of the house had acquired such strong nationalistic overtones, then the developments towards the end of the 1930s can also be seen to have a special meaning in England. The period of shock was short-lived and by around 1936 brick, timber and stone were increasingly used. Was this a return to tradition or primarily a practical response to issues of weathering? These explanations need not be discounted in adding the speculation that after the tabula rasa of the early thirties, these materials had regained a poetic quality. One must refer to the presentations of texture as primary subject matter in surrealist and related art to understand the impact, still hardly explicable in words, that they must have had.

The second volume of Le Corbusier's *Oeuvre Complète*, published in 1935, included not only the rampantly Surrealist Bestegui appartment (1930–31) but also the Villa of Madame de Mandrot near Toulon (1930–31) with its contrasts of rough stone walling and smooth rendered surfaces. The *Architect and Building News* published his house at Mathès and the Petite Maison de Weekend at Celle St Cloud in December 1935, the year of their completion, both powerful images in which the emphasis is on texture and contrast. In his contribution to *The Arts To-Day* (1935) edited by Geoffrey Grigson, John Summerson wrote,

The machine, scientific building, mass-production, these are Le Corbusier's anchors to the world of commonsense, while he explores the underworld of form. His taste is exquisite, as unerring as Paul Klee, an artist with whom he has definite affinities.[11]

Writing in 1986, William Curtis recognised the links between these houses and Surrealism, including their play on gender and eroticism, quoting Le Corbusier's own comment on the contrast of angles and curves, 'in the one, strong objectivity of forms ... *male* architecture; in the other, limitless subjectivity ... *female* architecture.'[12] Le Corbusier had himself modified his own most infamous saying when he wrote in 1925 that a house was not just a machine for living in, but also 'le lieu utile pour la meditation.'[13]

This makes an interesting parallel with Elisabeth Benjamin's East Wall at Gerrards Cross and its half-joking narrative title of the "St George and Dragon House" derived from its contrast of brick and concrete.[14] The techniques of montage developed in Le Corbusier's paintings and applied to his architecture encouraged architects in England to draw on the abstract and Surrealist art of their English contemporaries to harness the expressive power of locality and tradition to the Modernist cause.[15] Although at the time there was a divergence between the "constructive" group which produced the *Circle* anthology in 1937 and the Surrealists, whose major London exhibition had been held the previous year, in reality there was a crossing of the lines by such major figures as Henry Moore, Paul Nash and John Piper. Moore wrote in 1937,

the violent quarrel between the abstractionists and the surrealists seems to me quite unnecessary. All good art has contained both abstract and surrealist elements, just as it has contained both classical and romantic elements – order and surprise, intellect and imagination, conscious and unconscious.[16]

Even Leslie Martin, editor of *Circle* with Ben Nicholson and Naum Gabo, mixed stone, brick and concrete, curved and straight forms at Brackenfell near Carlisle, the house he built for the painter and textile producer Alistair Morton in 1938.

11. John Summerson, 'Architecture' in G. Grigson, ed. *The Arts To-Day*, (London: John Lane, The Bodley Head, 1935), p.282.

12. Le Corbusier, *The Modulor*, (London: Faber & Faber, 1954), p.224, quoted in William J. R. Curtis, *Le Corbusier, Ideas and Forms*, (London: Phaidon Press, 1986), p.115.

13. Le Corbusier, *Almanach de l'Architecture Moderne*, (Paris: G. Crès & Cie, 1925), p.29.

14. See Lynne Walker's interview with Elisabeth Benjamin in this journal.

15. See Alan Powers, 'The Reconditioned Eye, architects and artists in English Modernism', *AA Files* xxv, 1993, pp.54-62. David Mellor of Sussex University has written, '[Graham Sutherland and Paul Nash] had endeavoured to disclose a specifically national Heimat, a British counterpart to the painted locations of international modernism – the South of France for example.', see 'Sketch for a Historical Portrait of Humphrey Jennings' in Mary-Lou Jennings, ed. *Humphrey Jennings, film-maker, painter, poet*, (London: British Film Institute 1981).

16. Henry Moore, 'Notes on Sculpture' in Myfanwy Evans ed. *The Painter's Object*, (London: Gerald Howe, 1937), p.28.

figure 9
Le Corbusier. Petite Maison de Weekend, La Celle St Cloud, 1935 (*from Le Corbusier & P Jeanneret, Septième série, Paris: Editions Albert Morance, 1936*).

This period was complex in its sense of haste before the threatened disaster of European war and it is not surprising that its architectural expression became increasingly plural and multi-layered, self-conscious and ironical. There is still a reluctance among historians to admit these aspects of the modern house, still more to make them the central theme of its story as I have attempted to do here. At least one advantage of considering houses in terms of architectural poetics is that it allows for the inclusion of all styles without implying a relativistic pluralism in which no criteria of quality can be established. As considered at the outset, this is a preferable precondition for effective conservation than the inherited paradigm of a battle of the styles.

figure 10
Christopher Wood, 'Zebra and Parachute'
(from *Christopher Wood 1901–1930*,
London Redfern Gallery 1938)

Christopher Wood's painting "Zebra and Parachute" (July 1930) shows the roof terrace of the Villa Savoye inhabited by the zebra while in the background a limply hanging man descends by parachute. It was probably his last painting, since he died in mysterious circumstances falling under a train at Salisbury Station a month later. The painting has eluded explanation, but may help to focus the problem of the meaning of the modern house for us. The roof terrace is disturbed by the incongruity of the zebra, yet this primitive and exotic animal is its necessary counterpart, like the animal hide furnishings found in so many modern houses. It has the tranquillity of a sacrificial beast, suggesting the suspended time of surrealism. Who knows how it connects with the parachute man, equally suspended in time? Stephen Gardiner writes

the idea of the painting is the same as the idea that Le Corbusier captured in his sun-terrace—the remembered pleasure, if you like, of a single timeless moment in the sun one afternoon—and the peculiar presence of the zebra catches, as somehow no human figure could, the mood of that moment.[17]

But the zebra is an extreme form of metaphor, the thing you would least expect and therefore the one that brings insight and understanding, the necessary confrontation prior to release. Christopher Wood shows us how every modern house has its zebra, its inner contradiction, visible or unseen, through which it is not just a machine but a work of art and a place of meditation.

17. Stephen Gardiner, *Le Corbusier*,
(London: Fontana/Collins, 1974), p.33.

3 F. R. S. Yorke and *The Modern House*

JEREMY MELVIN AND DAVID ALLFORD

THE MODERN HOUSE

F R S YORKE

F. R. S. Yorke and *The Modern House*

JEREMY MELVIN AND DAVID ALLFORD

I F a year had to be chosen when the introduction of European Modernism into Britain became irreversible, it would be 1934. During that year several established but loose threads began to draw together, weaving the social and intellectual fabric from which Modernism in Britain would take its distinctive course. It may not have been apparent at the time, but by the end of 1934 the seeds which shaped Modernism had firmly taken root.

The publication of F. R. S. Yorke's book *The Modern House* [1] was one reason why 1934 was such an important year. Its success was huge. Three editions appeared before 1939, two during the war, and three after the War. It remained in print until his death in 1962. It was the first introduction to European Modernism for many people. Widely reviewed on publication, its reputation endured. Writing in the *Spectator*, G. M. Boumphrey advised,

Mr Yorke's book is by far the best on its subject [ie modern architecture] that has yet appeared ... it would be expensive folly for any layman to think of building a house today without first reading this book – or seeing that his architect had done so. [2]

Much later, in an appreciation of Yorke written after his death, Maxwell Fry recalled,

The Modern House ... showed us where we stood, introduced us to architects ... acted as an open sesame for a new type of continental tour ... set standards of excellence by which we could measure ourselves ... I find it hard to overestimate the value of that book. [3]

At either end of its published life, *The Modern House* was recognised as one of the most important documents of its time.

There are many reasons why *The Modern House* made such an impression. Clearly it appeared at a propitious moment, when people were hungry for a book on modern architecture and just as the conditions for practicing architecture were irrevocably changing. *The Modern House*, although not the first work on the subject, was easily the most digestible, with striking graphic design and relatively unencumbered by text.[4] It could be read purely as a picture book with 128 pages devoted to illustrations of 57 house designs from 14 countries, while a more literary reader could plough through the written chapters at the beginning and end. These give a clear, if somewhat limited and not entirely original, account of the nature of modern architecture. As Fry implies, an impoverished, inexperienced architect could turn to *The Modern House* as a source book, almost even, a religious text.

Yorke's selection of examples may seem more original than his written sentiments. But in reality both his manifesto and his selection are and were fundamental to the book's appeal. Each shows how an aspect of Yorke's experience conveniently meshed with the publisher's programme. Together they are a touchstone of progressive architectural thought of the 1930s, as the book was to some extent at least a collaborative effort between Yorke, and his publishers and advisers. It is in this sense that *The Modern House* is a critical event in the architec-

1. *The Modern House* by F. R. S. Yorke was published by The Architectural Press, London, 1934. Subsequent editions were 1935, 1937, 1943, 1944, 1948, 1951 and 1956.

2. *Spectator*, 17 August 1934, p.231.

3. *Architectural Review*, vol.CXXXII, October 1962, pp.279–80.

4. Le Corbusier's *Vers Une Architecture* (1924) had, for example, been translated by Frederick Etchells in 1927 as *Towards a New Architecture*. Bruno Taut's *Modern Architecture*. published by Studio in 1929 is another early publication on modernism. It was simultaneously published in German as *Die Neue Baukunst*.

figure 1
Book jacket for The Modern House, 1934. Drawing by H. T. Fisher.

figure 2
Sieldung Siemensstadt, Berlin.
Walter Gropius 1929–30.

figure 3
Haus Haeffuer, Pichelsdorf, Berlin, 1928.
Adolf Rading (photo Köster, Berlin).

figure 4
Haus Hasek, Gablonz, 1931.
Heinrich Lauterbach.

tural maelstrom of the 1934. His ideas, derived from background and education, were moulded by subsequent experiences and contacts, and in *The Modern House*, by a publishing policy which tempered enlightenment with commercial shrewdness. Although the book appropriated an established genre of books about domestic architecture, it was refreshingly cosmopolitan and introduced new graphics and buildings to British readers; many of the architects and more of their houses had never been published in the UK before. *The Modern House* was as much a publishing achievement as an architectural one. Its triumph was that the strictures of publishing, its mode of production, did not absolutely dominate reader's perceptions. The skills and experiences of an individual meshed with the context of architectural practice, theory and publishing to shape a uniquely influential document in the early development of Modern architecture in Britain – a subject which still awaits a definitive historical study.

But *The Modern House* is not without its flaws. The book uniquely combines three themes which could be described as the bane of later architectural thought: determinism of two varieties, historical and materialist, and a subliminal acknowledgement of the picturesque attitude that architecture is about skilful composition of form and little more. That this combination of apparently contradictory ideas could exist says almost as much about publishing as about architecture. *The Modern House* is a document of its time, and as the outcome of collaboration between publisher, author and several other contemporaries it has extra piquancy. Looking into the book's origin, from the point of view of its author, publishers, and the context into which it was received is no less than a dissection of the architectural attitudes of its generation.[5] Both a recipient and contributor to historical circumstances, it is influenced as much by the exigencies of experience as by a grand vision of the future.

Francis Reginald Stevens Yorke brought a unique series of influences to bear in his conception of *The Modern House*. Born in 1906, by 1934 he was already established as an advocate of contemporary architecture. At the recommendation of P. Morton Shand – whose enthusiasm for things Continental and knowledge of languages put him in the first rank of British commentators on European modernism – Yorke became secretary of the MARS group, established in 1932 as the British branch of the *Congrès Internationale d'Architecture Moderne* (CIAM) following an approach to Shand from CIAM's redoubtable secretary Siegfried Giedion. In 1933, the *Architects' Journal* described Yorke as '… well-known as one of the most progressive younger architects'.[6] Yorke's reputation rested almost entirely on publishing as at this stage his credentials to be an experienced architect were tenuous: the few buildings to which his name can be attached were designed in partnership and are undistinguished.

But Yorke's background was actually far more interesting and complex than his reputation as a young expert on modern architecture suggests. From an early

 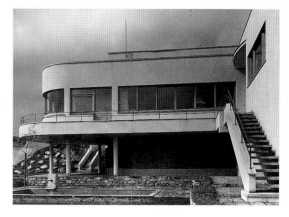

age he was immersed in the influences which shaped the Arts and Crafts architects. He was born in Stratford-upon-Avon, the son of a proficient architect, F. W. B. Yorke, whose work veered gently between neo-Georgian and Arts & Crafts and was occasionally published in architectural periodicals. [7] The younger Yorke went to school in Chipping Camden, a hotbed of Arts & Crafts thinking, and a town with buildings which appealed to Arts & Crafts architects. Later he studied at Birmingham School of Art (1924–30), whose principal in architecture, George Drysdale, had studied at the Ecole des Beaux Arts in Paris. [8] Despite the formal classical basis of the course, there was also an Arts and Crafts influence through tenuous links with W. R. Lethaby. Throughout his life, Yorke retained an interest in craft, although it is more visually obvious in work of the late 1930s and post-war period. [9]

On leaving Birmingham in February 1930 Yorke came to London where he began to direct these interests to fit in an embryonic avant garde enthusiasm for modern architecture. After a year with the architects Campbell-Jones Son & Smithers, he quickly established a relationship with the Architectural Press, the leading but not the only publishers of modernism; his first traceable publication was a measured drawing of the Landor House, an attractive 18th century building on Leamington Road, Warwick, in the *Architects' Journal* of 8 April 1931. [10] The following year Yorke and the engineer W. E. J. Budgen provided primers for architectural students sitting their intermediate and final structures exams set by the RIBA. [11] Yorke was acquiring the reputation of a technical expert, to the extent that on 22 March 1933, the *AJ* was able to announce that he would write the weekly 'Trade Notes' column – a review of new materials and products – as he was 'well-known as one of the most progressive younger architects', and had a 'unique knowledge of materials and is in close contact with the work of British manufacturers'. [12]

Within three years Yorke had modernised, or at least industrialised his knowledge of materials. Retaining an essentially Arts and Crafts view that architecture derived from components, their manufacture and assembly, he had also embraced the process of industrial production and its products. As the *AJ* implied, his understanding of modernism depended on knowledge of materials.

This was fundamental to his interpretation of modern architecture, and to the formation of *The Modern House*. Sir James Richards, who joined the Architectural Press in 1933, remembered Yorke's role there primarily as a technical expert, seeking this knowledge from him rather than his opinion as a straightforward critic. [13] Technical expertise, particularly relating to industrialised production of building components, is one aspect of *The Modern House* where Yorke's skills neatly matched the Architectural Press's programme. [14] Chapter titles like 'Wall and window', and 'Roof', as well as a section on 'Experimental and pre-fabricated houses', suggest Yorke's approach was to present modern houses through

5. Roy Landau, in 'The History of Modern Architecture which has yet to be Written', *AA Files*, Spring 1991 No.21, pp.49–54, suggested a Foucauldian approach to studying architecture of the 1930s might advance the subject.

6. *Architects' Journal*, vol.LXXVII, 22 March 1933, p.408.

7. See for example, *Architects' Journal*, vol.LXXI, 1930, p.108.

8. For information about the character of Birmingham School of Architecture and early formal architectural education in Britain, see Alan Powers, *Architectural Education in Britain 1880–1914* (PhD thesis, University of Cambridge 1982). For a picture of the Arts and Crafts movement in Chipping Campden see Alan Crawford, *C. R. Ashbee*, (London: Yale University Press 1985). Crawford notes that there was a revival at Chipping Campden in 1924, 'Quite a colony of craftsmen was growing up in the town and that Summer there was a big Arts and Crafts exhibition'. pp.171 & 200.

9. See Alan Powers, *In the Line of Development, F. R. S. Yorke, E. Rosenberg and C. S. Mardall to YRM 1930–1992*, (London: Heinz Gallery 1992), p.19.

10. Architectural Press lore has it that Yorke was 'discovered' by an advertisement manager. This is possible as advertisement managers would be likely to court specifiers who have an interest in materials and products. Another entrée could have come from his father, whose work had already been published by the AP.

11. See *Architects' Journal*, vol.LXXV, 11 & 18 March 1933, pp.639 & 665.

12. *Architects' Journal*, vol.LXXVII, 22 March 1933, p.408. Previously 'Trade Notes' had been an irregular column.

13. Sir James Richards, in conversation with Jeremy Melvin, 28 November 1991.

14. *The Modern House* was not the only place where the AP put Yorke's knowledge to sound commercial use. From 1935 until his death in 1962 Yorke edited the annual *Specification*.

figure 5
Haus Loosen, Cologne, 1931.
Hans Schumacher.
(photo H. Schmölx, Cologne).

their construction, rather than as the dynamic play of platonic solids in light, or even first and foremost as the path to social amelioration. It is here that a trace of materialist determinism can be detected. Variously Yorke wrote, 'The new materials are light, strong, mobile; their aesthetic is other than that of piled-up mass masonry'; 'Modern materials and construction and the shapes produced by them have an intrinsic beauty which needs no embellishment'. There is plenty of ammunition in the book for a critic who wants to accuse Yorke of simple, reductivist and derivative arguments.[15] For Yorke, the starting point is '*the new functional plan*' (his italics). 'There is only one law for [the typical form of an industrial product]; that it shall be entirely appropriate to its purpose', he trilled, to the accompaniment of pictures of North Michigan Avenue in Chicago and the liner Europa.[16] He had learnt his lessons and sources well. Knowing about the products on the market did not necessarily give him license to transcend the received wisdom of progressive architecture of the time, although it gave weight to his unlikely claims for the influence of materials on architecture.

Yorke had another value to the Architectural Press – international contacts. Between 1929 and 1932 he spent a total of five months travelling on the European mainland, visiting Italy, Germany and Czechoslovakia.[17] That these voyages began before he arrived in London suggests some shrewd self motivation on his part. Contacts with architects in these countries were facilitated after he joined the Architectural Press, especially through Morton Shand. Their fruits occasionally became apparent in the company's flagship publication, the *Architectural Review*. In February 1932, for example, Lois Welzenbacher's House Rosenbauer overlooking the Danube valley was illustrated; it was included in the book two years later.[18] This feature makes a change from most of Yorke's other contributions to the *Architectural Review*, which started in the second half of 1931 and tended to be on craft and trade matters. Again the Architectural Press exploited Yorke's particular interests.[19]

Arguably Yorke's most important foreign contact in the book's production was Karel Honzik, of the Prague firm Havlicek & Honzik. In his Acknowledgements, Yorke placed on record his 'indebtedness to ... Honzik, who has supplied me with much of the material that has made the production of this book possible'. Havlicek & Honzik were among the good second division architects who were first published in Britain in *The Modern House*. Yorke also showed enthusiasm for developments in America although he did not visit the United States until after the War. Lawrence Kocher, editor of the *Architectural Record*, also received a generous acknowledgement from Yorke. Yorke was attracted to America more by its technical prowess, as the predominance of American examples in the section on 'Experimental and pre-fabricated houses' shows. He also favoured European immigrants such as Richard Neutra, William Lescaze and Kocher's partner Albert Frey rather than native Americans. Kocher & Frey, for example, have four full examples to one small illustration of Frank Lloyd Wright.

Yorke's combination of Arts and Crafts and Modernist influences shaped the book's structure and selection. He drew heavily on his knowledge of material and travel experience. He virtually introduced Czech Modernism to Britain, and showed that German modernism was deeper than Gropius and Mendelsohn. Of the 57 house designs featured in the first edition, 39 come from the European continent including one from the USSR. A house by Heinrich Lauterbach rubs shoulders with one by Mies, Ladislav Zak's work with Le Corbusier's. Although paying lip service to the CIAMesque view of modern architecture – already firmly established by 1934 when political circumstances in Germany ended any real debate about the nature of Modernism and Siegfried Giedion's deft handling had more or less elided the so-called 'other tradition' represented by Scharoun and Haring – Yorke did retain a catholic range of examples.[20] Blaksted & Munthe Kaas's house, for example, would hardly make a conventional CIAM text book.

But the main departure from a CIAMesque line is again informed by Yorke's interest in construction. Each architect was asked to supply details of: type of construction and general structural materials; walls – filling walls and partitions; insulation against sound, weather, heat, roof construction and insulation; heating and ventilation systems; water heating in kitchen and bathroom, type of kitchen range; windows; doors, handles, frames etc; floor and pavings; furniture if built-in type and material; internal/external wall finish; and special arrangements.[21] In this definition through materials lurked both the ghost of the Arts and Crafts movement, and the embryo of materialist determinism.

These tastes led Yorke to favour pre-fabricated houses, and were gratified by his contacts with Lawrence Kocher. American examples dominate the section on 'Pre-fabricated and experimental houses'. Through Kocher he had access to work by Buckminster Fuller, Kocher & Frey and especially General Houses, one of whose examples graced the dust jacket. This is a significant decision, for Yorke could easily have chosen the Villa Savoye or the Haus Tugendhat, both of which were included in the book. Either would have been in line with the CIAM version of modernism. But for the principle image of *The Modern House*, he selected a drawing by the almost unknown H. T. Fisher, founder of General Houses be-

15. *The Modern House*, pp.12 & 14.

16. The quote is from page 14, and the pictures are on pages 13 and 15 of *The Modern House*.

17. See Yorke's nomination papers for his fellowship of the RIBA, held at the RIBA. There are also a large number of post cards in the possession of David Allford from Yorke to his parents which give some indication of his travels.

18. 'Three new houses' in *Architectural Review*, vol.LXXII, February 1932, pp.266–8. Yorke only described the Haus Rosenbauer. The other two houses are a vaguely 'moderne' example by Oliver Hill, and a thatched-cottage style one by T. Cecil Howitt.

19. Maxwell Fry, *op cit* p.280 mentions how he lacked the money to travel.

20. Giorgio Ciucci, in 'The Invention of the Modern Movement' in *Oppositions* 25, argued that 'Modernism' was essentially invented as a coherent body of ideas from a disparate bundle of approaches between the first and second meetings of CIAM in 1927 and 1928. The term 'the other tradition', was used by Colin St John Wilson in 'The Other Tradition', *AA Files*, Autumn 1992, No.24, pp.3–6.

21. This list is published at the end of the review of *The Modern House* in *Architects' Journal*, vol.CXXX, 12 July 1934, p.60.

figure 6
Architect's own house, Prague, 1926–8.
Eugen Linhart.

figure 7
House for a doctor, Ullern, Oslo.
Blakstad & Munthe
(photo O. Vaering, Olso).

22. *Architects' Journal*, vol.LXXVII, 29 June 1933, p.875.

23. *Architects' Journal*, vol.LXXVII, 12 April 1933, p.506.

24. Ludwig Hilberseimer, 'Die Wohnung Unserer Zeit', in *Die Form* vol. 6, 15 July 1931, pp.249–70.

25. *The Modern House*, p.1.

26. Ibid. p.2.

27. Ibid. p.4.

28. Herman Muthesius, *Das Englische Haus*, 1904–5. The genre of books on house design could be said to go back to J. J. Stevenson, *House Architecture*, 1877.

29. B. Weinreb Architectural Books Ltd, *The Small English House*, 1977, is a catalogue with 29 pages of mainly early 20th century books on domestic architecture.

30. Hubert de Cronin Hastings, *Recent English Domestic Architecture*, 1929.

31. Raymond McGrath's book, *Twentieth Century Houses*, (London: Faber & Faber 1934), was published shortly after *The Modern House*. and consequently had no effect on it. That another publisher should be seeking to produce a book on an outwardly theme suggests its commercial viability.

32. F. R. Yerbury, *Modern European Buildings*, (London: Gollancz, 1928).

33. *The Modern House*, p.1.

34. Ibid, p.5.

35. Sir James Richards suggested this in discussion with Jeremy Melvin in a discussion on 28 November 1991. No definitive evidence has come to light, but even if Hastings did not originate the idea, he must have known about it from an early stage. In the acknowledgments Yorke wrote 'Two years ago, when the project was originally contemplated', so there was plenty of time for various views to contribute to the book's formation.

36. Nathaniel Lloyd, *A History of the English House*, (London: Architectural Press, 1931).

cause it was the apogee of his reading of modern architecture. Yorke's interest in modern materials and construction overrode the already established European canon. An article about General Houses, probably by Yorke, had been published in the *AJ* in 1933, and explained something about this Chicago-based supplier of pre-fabricated homes.[22] William Lescaze was another American architect to receive considerable coverage. His book *What is Modern Architecture?* was cited by Yorke in 1933.[23] Yorke's originality in selection is one of the most refreshing aspects of the book.

International contacts may subliminally have given Yorke models for a publication on house design. The *Architectural Record* carried frequent surveys of domestic architecture. More specific was 'Die Wohnung Unserer Zeit' (The Dwelling of our Time) by Ludwig Hilberseimer and published in *Die Form* in 1931.[24] Several buildings featured in *The Modern House* were also shown by Hilberseimer, including a house by Adolf Rading, the Berlin Bauaustellung flat by Lilly Reich and both used the same Gropius illustration of Siemenstadt in Berlin.[25]

But the themes of the internationalism of Modern architecture, and the suitability of modern components were not the only constituents of the book. Yorke, in common with many of his MARS contemporaries did believe that architecture had a social role. In the introduction to *The Modern House*, he acknowledged 'the housing problem', and suggests 'the solution ... lies ... in a reformed type of flat dwelling and controlled land development'.[26] Even Yorke's following assertion that, 'There have been many projects for the lay-out of groups of flat blocks ... but there has been little actual development', is a trifle disingenuous. By 1934 there were many examples he could have chosen; the Hofeisensiedlung, Onkel Toms Hutte and Siemenstadt in Berlin; numerous siedlungen from Frankfurt; at a pinch he could have included Le Corbusier's Pavilion Suisse, and he even hints darkly at 'a thorough analysis of the situation followed by extreme experiments' in Russia.[27] Answering why he persisted with a book 'concerning the individual villa type of house' suggests a strategic motive on the part of the publishers, and shows how Yorke's individual qualities fitted into a broader context.

An enormous number of books about English domestic architecture appeared during the first third of the 20th century. Herman Muthesius' seminal *Das Englische Haus* was probably the most authoritative survey of English housing design of its date, but by no means the first.[28] The weekly magazine *Country Life*, founded in 1897, also devoted considerable attention to contemporary house design by architects like Sir Edwin Lutyens. By the end of the 1920s books about English houses had become a familiar genre, from a variety of publishers like the Studio, Country Life and the Architectural Press. The sentiments and examples in each are hard to distinguish. Many of them have titles in any permutation of the words 'Modern', 'house' and 'English'.[29] But what these words implied was often a long way from Yorke's and his fellow modernists' interpretation.

As late as 1929 the Architectural Press published *Recent English Domestic Architecture*, by no less a person than Hubert de Cronin Hastings, son of the company's chairman Sir Percy Hastings.[30] The younger Hastings was in the early stages of establishing himself as the presiding editorial genius, and over the next few years was to introduce more and more modernism into the *Architectural Review*.

The sheer volume of these publications suggests that there was a market for books about domestic architecture.[31] A small number of publications which dealt with European Modernism had already appeared. But with the exception of Bruno Taut's sparse 'Notes concerning England' in his book *Modern Architecture*, there was virtually nothing about modernism in an English context. Books such as *Modern European Buildings* by F. R. Yerbury gave a very Swedish view of modern architecture.[32] A book on Modernism would not have been entirely original, but a book on Modernist houses would make Modernism more palatable by introducing it through an adaptation of a venerable English publishing genre. Yorke's introduction suggests he may have been uneasy about this tactic, but various as-

figure 8
House at Sonnerveld, Rotterdam, 1933.
Brinkman & Van der Vlugt
(photo Kamman, Schiedam).

pects of the Architectural Press's output suggest there was an underlying plan. His opening paragraph states,

This book concerns the individual villa type of house; and though the author does not pretend that the building of villas is a good or even a possible solution to the problem of housing the people, he does believe that for some time to come the majority of people will continue to want to live in detached or semi-detached houses, and it is important for the relation of the villa to modern architecture and the Modern social system to be appreciated.[33]

Starting a book with such an apology for a subject matter is unusual, and it can be read as an implicit justification for using the format of a book about houses. The front cover illustration, of a 'pre-fabricated' home is almost an introduction in graphic form to this apologia.

Yorke has a revealing explanation of the 'relation of the villa to Modern architecture'.

[It] has had, and will continue to have, a great importance as the cheapest complete building unit for examination and experiment, and it is most often in this small structure that modern architecture goes through its complete revolution ... There are many new and untried materials ... and the architect ... is most likely to find in the villa the most easily accessible unit for research.[34]

Yorke's justification for writing a book about villas and their relation to modern architecture played directly to his fabled expertise in materials and construction. A not-so-subtle redefinition of the genre overcame an ideological problem and played to his strengths.

Sir James Richards suggested that the idea for *The Modern House* probably came from H. de C. Hastings himself. Certainly it was conceived at an early stage of Yorke's involvement with the Architectural Press.[35] If Richards was correct, it would explain why Yorke was chosen to write the book; his unique combination of knowledge of modernism and materials allowed him to reconcile the apparent discrepancy between writing a book about villas and modern architecture.

Further evidence of a coordinated strategy is implied by two other AP publications. Only three years before *The Modern House* was published, the company produced Nathaniel Lloyd's seminal *A History of the English House*.[36] Written by a militant Lutyens-dweller, this book does not on the surface seem to have anything in common with *The Modern House*. However, Lloyd explained that the examples were divided into sections on: plans and exteriors; external wall

37. Ibid. p.v.

38. Ibid. p.vi.

39. 'Scenario for a Human Drama' includes
Yorke's preview of *The Modern House in
Architectural Review*, vol.LXXVI, pp.9–16, to
which Shand provided a foreword. The series
continued with 'Immediate Background',
August 1934, pp.39–42, 'Peter Behrens',
September 1934, pp.83–9, 'Van der Velde to
Wagner', October 1934, pp.131–4, 'Glasgow
interlude', vol.LXXVII, January 1935, pp.23–6
and 'Machine-à Habiter to the house of
character', March 1935, pp.61–4

40. F. R. S. Yorke, *The Modern House in England*,
(London: The Architectural Press 1937).

41. Foreword to 'Scenario for a Human
Drama', op. cit.

42. Glasgow interlude in 'Scenario for a
Human Drama', op cit, p.25.

43. *Architectural Review*, vol.LXX, December
1931, pp.171–8.

44. *The Modern House*, p.19.

45. Ibid. p.25.

treatment; entrances; windows; chimneys; interiors; internal wall treatment;
ceilings; fireplaces; staircases; metalwork; and various (including constructional
drawings etc.).[37] It may not fit Yorke's list like a glove, but it certainly shows an
affinity in categorising buildings. Lloyd also credited Hastings, 'The inception
of this history is due to the foresight and imagination of Mr de Cronin Hastings'.[38] There is some evidence, at least, that Hastings was marshalling his publishing forces towards comprehensive coverage of all types of housing.

Explaining the apparent anomaly between Lloyd and Yorke fell to P. Morton
Shand, the Architectural Press's most literate critic at the time. In his occasional
series 'Scenario for a Human Drama', which started in *AR* of July 1934, together
with a preview for Yorke's book, Shand argued that something went wrong with
architecture round about 1830. But through the agency of architects like Peter
Behrens, Henri van de Velde, Otto Wagner, Adolf Loos and C. R. Mackintosh, the
true path was regained.[39] Lloyd's book had conveniently stopped at the Regency.
Shand realised the potential of this concluding point, arguing that until 1830 all
architecture was necessarily nationally specific: hence the inevitability of 'English' in Lloyd's title. However the turbulent 19th century, with its technical, productive and transportational advances, rendered such regionalism obsolete:
hence 'Modern' in Yorke's title, and by implication the futility of books like
Randal Phillips' *The Modern English House* of 1927 – its examples may have been
English, but to Yorke they were certainly not modern. In 1937, when Yorke published his second book, about modern houses in England, it was carefully titled
The Modern House in England.[40]

Shand explained the hiatus between Lloyd and Yorke, implying that there was
no discontinuity between them other than that caused by 'architecture ignoring
structural technique' in the 19th century. *The Modern House* 'is a memorable book',
Shand wrote 'for it is the first in English which liberates architecture from its
narrower self, and shows the Modern house as the technical product it really is.'[41]
Once this is understood, the implication runs, the rest of architecture will follow.

Shand gave Modernism a British lineage combined with a liking for heavy
engineering, covering ground similar to that discussed by Nikolaus Pevsner two
years later in *Pioneers of the Modern Movement*. Writing about C. R. Mackintosh,
Shand said,

*for nearly a hundred years ships and locomotives were almost the only branch of
creative design in which our formal tradition contrived to develop along the lines that the
eliminative elegance of the Regency style had so surely traced.*[42]

figure 9
House Canneel, Brussels, 1931.
L. H. de Koninck.

figure 10
Lovell House, Los Angeles, 1927.
Richard J. Neutra.

figure 11
House to be built from prefabricated
standardised units, 1933. H. T. Fisher.

Here the manifesto is at least partly shaped by the commercial strictures of publishing. 'A Scenario for a Human Drama' put theoretical flesh on what was a common belief among progressive architectural writers at the time, essentially that most architecture in the last two thirds of the 19th century was a terrible mistake. Yorke himself paid lip service to it in *The Modern House*, but had anticipated the argument in a feature in the AR of December 1931, revealingly entitled 'From Order through Disorder to Order'.[43] Its subject was shop fronts, and the theme that Regency shops were rather attractive, the Victorians messed them up, but with Modern design, shops were rediscovering their true destiny.

Here is the source of Yorke's historical determinism. Many of his sentiments closely match Shand. 'There was a gradual evolution [in British architecture]', Yorke wrote, 'but the logical continuity ended with the Regency'.[44] Disaster, Yorke continued: 'For more than a century man has been stumbling along the way of the machine, the way that is leading inevitably towards a new order'. So far, perhaps, so good. But the only way out of this mess was

a period of purification and, largely under the influence of Le Corbusier, the unnecessary was eliminated. A little more than a decade ago there appeared the first buildings of a new architecture, based on a scientific approach to building through an analysis of function.[45]

Modernism had arrived as the true end of historical development. Shand, Yorke, and slightly later Pevsner, may have differed in detail, but the theme they articulated was remarkably consistent.

Other writers and architects were also beginning to recognise the value of Regency architecture and town planning. 1934 saw the publication of Steen Eiler Rasmussen's charming paean to Britain's capital, *London The Unique City*, and the following year John Summerson completed his biography of John Nash.[46] J. M. Richards articulated what seems to have been a common belief when in 1933 he reviewed *The Smaller English House of the Later Renaissance* by A. E. Richardson, first published in 1925.[47] 'It is not', Richards wrote 'that the book has changed, but that our own architectural intentions ... have become clearer'.[48] Richardson's own architecture may have been anathema to the modernists, but his scholarship could be called into service to reinforce their justification of their views. Yorke may not have been the first writer to perceive a link between the Regency and Modernism, but his article 'From order through disorder to order' was in at the beginning of the formation of this popular view. Its popularity, too, shows how close *The Modern House* was to contemporary progressive thought.

The Architectural Press was uniquely placed to promote its books. As well as star billing in *Architectural Review*, its sister magazine *Architects' Journal* also noted its publication with a critique by one of the most prominent European Modernist architects, Eric Mendelsohn. It must have been slightly poignant, as the book included his magnificent house in Berlin's exclusive Wannsee district which he had been forced to abandon after living there for only a few years. Even so, he was largely complimentary, noting the books importance for 'penetrating scientifically to the roots of the matter instead of treating it in a superficial, journalistic fashion', but expressing reservations over some layouts and Yorke's seeming to forget that a house is a small architectural unit.[49] 'A private house', he wrote 'is not an exhibition of architectural and technical devices'. Mendelsohn identified a fair point. But for reasons outlined above Yorke was interested in the house less as a description of an agreeable bourgeois lifestyle or for its own sake than as 'an exhibition of architectural and technical devices'. Mendelsohn, despite his repu-

figure 12
Standard concrete house for one family, 1932. Moise Ginsberg.

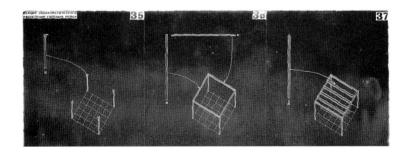

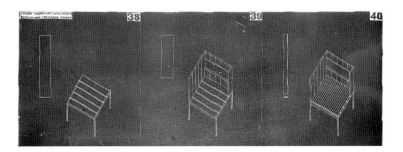

tation as a Modernist, had little to do with the social experiments of his contemporaries like Gropius, Martin Wagner, Bruno Taut or Ernst May. His clients were department stores and cinemas rather than progressive city or regional governments. But Mendelsohn recognised that *The Modern House* gave only a partial view of European Modernism. The demands of publishing and limitations of its author were apparent.

There are other anomalies. As has been noted, *The Modern House* was, for instance, one of few books to recognise the strength of modernism in Czechoslovakia. There are seven houses from that country, including Mies' Tugendhat house in Brno, but also work by Havlicek & Honzik, Ladislav Zak, and Adolf Bens. The choice of format, a book about houses, precluded publication of other important modernist buildings like Havlicek & Honzik's Pensions Institute building in Prague, one of the largest Modernist buildings of the time, and known to Yorke. The Bata shoe company, too, had already commissioned a great deal of modern architecture.[50]

Few of these problems were noted at the time. Most architectural reviewers gave it good notice, although there were several reservations, and the spread of opinion suggests very varied attitudes to architecture. *Country Life* suggested that 'there is something to be said for Herr Hitler's objection to the 'international' [ie modern] style', a comment that became more tasteless with subsequent events.[51] *Design and Construction* (forerunner of *Architectural Design*) accepted that 'the modern movement is here to stay' and that *The Modern House* was the best account of the 'functionalist' house, but regretted the few English examples and the lack of prices.[52] G. M. Boumphrey in the *Spectator* and John Betjeman in the *Evening Standard* liked it, but they should have done because both were contributors to Architectural Press publications, and Betjeman was a colleague of Yorke's at the Architectural Press.[53]

A brief notice in the rival *Architect & Building News* was essentially approving, but the most serious criticisms were penned by E. J. [Bobby] Carter, legendary RIBA librarian and editor of the Institute's journal.[54] He argued that the 'quasi technical' aspects of the book were a side track to the argument although he

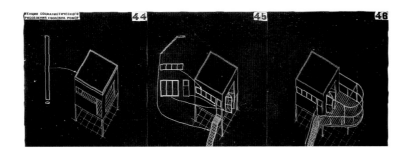

46. Steen Eiler Rasmussen, *London: The Unique City*, (Copenhagen: Gyldendal, 1934; London: Jonathan Cape, 1937), and John Summerson, *John Nash, architect to King George IV*, (London: George Allen & Unwin) 1935.

47. Albert Richardson and H. Donaldson Eberlein, *The Smaller English House of the Later Renaissance 1660–1830*, (London: B. T. Batsford 1925).

48. J. M. Richards, 'The Regency Precedent', in *Architects' Journal*, vol.LXXVIII, 12 October 1933, p.455.

49. Eric Mendelsohn, in *Architects' Journal*, vol.CXXX, 12 July 1934, p.57.

50. See Jane Pavitt, 'The Bata Project: a Social and Industrial Experiment', in *Twentieth Century Architecture*, 1, 1994, pp.31–44.

51. *Country Life*, 18 August 1934, pp.178–9.

52. *Design and Construction*, vol.IV, October 1934, p.422.

53. Betjeman worked as assistant editor of *Architectural Review*, from October 1930 until the end of 1933. See Bevis Hillier, *Young Betjeman*, 1988.

54. *Journal of the Royal Institute of British Architects*, vol.XLI, 1934, pp.929–30.

conceded that they might have been necessary to its appeal – further circumstantial evidence that the marriage of Yorke's skills was seen as essential to the book's success. But Carter did not like Yorke's writing style, taking issue with the 'rather timid, sermonistical unction of his delivery that makes the reader mourn the fire of Corbusier or Ruskin or the incisiveness of Lethaby'.

Carter, a Cambridge history graduate as well as a holder of an AA diploma, was clearly looking for something more literate, with more conventionally presented arguments. Yorke's apparently uncritical stance disappointed him, especially his views of 'functionalism' and economics. 'Neither Mr Yorke nor the architects know if these buildings are "functional" ... he does not know if the buildings are structurally sound', and 'Do economic demands allow the use of

figure 13
Shottery Manor, Warwickshire. Altered and enlarged by F. W. B. Yorke and F. R. S. Yorke for Fordham Flower, 1938.

55. Carter quoted only half of Yorke's sentence. It can be found in its entirety on page 49 of *The Modern House*.

56. Yorke's relationship with Carter can perhaps be assessed by Yorke's absence from the RIBA's refugee's committee, set up at Carter's instigation in 1938 to assist architect-refugees fleeing from the Nazis. Yorke's international contacts would have made him one of the most suitable candidates.

slabs and concrete when brick is the cheaper simply because "brick is not aesthetically a good material for the filling wall?"' But Carter was not being entirely fair, as Yorke's sentence continued 'but economically [brick] remains the most satisfactory surfacing material in general use'.[55] A certain amount of posturing, even rivalry, is evident.[56]

The Modern House's published life coincides almost exactly with the period when orthodox modernism held sway in Britain. Although later editions changed its emphasis, its general character did not alter, at least not until after 1945. It is not surprising that it should reflect the strengths and weaknesses of the Modern movement. Adapting the genre of books about houses, through Yorke's skills, into a book about modern houses was itself as great an Anglicisation of Modernism as the dubious historical ancestry put forward by Shand and Pevsner. Ironically, Yorke's knowledge of materials did give his interpretation of Modernism and English ancestry, for it came straight out of his Arts and Crafts background. In one sense *The Modern House* is an important link between Arts and Crafts and Modernism in Britain. By a few sleights of hand, graphic design and textual argument, it shoe-horned Modernism into an English publishing context, and in this format and with the book's potential for being read in many different ways, it was one of the formative elements of Modernism in Britain. If a definitive study of this subject is to be written, it could do a lot worse than to study the exigencies of publishing as well as more obviously architectural issues.

Yorke's selection of examples is the book's most original feature. But it fitted into the context of an established genre developed for publishing a housing type, which Yorke himself admitted was at best only an intermediate stage in the fulfilment of modernist principles. Current arguments in support of Modernism, which are now rather discredited, were called in to effect the necessary adaptation. Consequently, *The Modern House* can be seen as a crucial component in constructing a British view of Modernism, but now its appeal is as a selection of pictures chosen with some flair.

Patrons of the Modern House

LOUISE CAMPBELL

Patrons of the Modern House

LOUISE CAMPBELL

WRITING in the *Architectural Review* in 1971, Paul Thompson could identify only 33 International Style houses in Britain for the period ending in 1939 and classified the patrons: 'Scholars and educationists account for ten, architects and their relatives for six, other artists, designers and writers for six, and other professionals and businessmen for eleven. There are no other significant groups and the old aristocracy is entirely unrepresented.'[1] By 1977 Jeremy Gould had scanned a broad range of contemporary periodicals and books to produce a gazetteer of several hundred houses, architects and clients, and included some previously unpublished examples.[2] For the architect practising in the inter-war period, private house commissions represented an important area of work. But although the architects who designed modern houses have attracted considerable study, the clients who enabled architects to survive a lean period have received remarkably little. Information on patronage is patchy. It is possible to gather biographical information about a few individuals, well-known in their fields; but in the majority of cases, all that remains is a name on a planning application, with no record of the client's brief, character, taste, or even occupation. Generalising on this basis is a risky business. In 1979 Stephen Bayley characterised clients as 'inspired private individuals with an idea of commitment to the New Architecture'; 'adventurous and independent'; and 'dedicated internationalists'.[3] He presents client as outsiders and non-conformists who made common cause with their architects by defying contemporary aesthetic conventions. We are left with a dramatic but inaccurate impression of a polarised world, with architects and clients allied over the divisive issue of style.[4]

Still more misleading is the inference that the client's outlook and motivation were complementary or identical with those of the architect. The client, like the architect is accorded a heroic, pioneering status and the client's own motivation and taste, are thereby minimised. This notion echoes the writers of the day who claimed that clients were a special breed. F. R. S. Yorke wrote that the patrons of the modern house 'had found a new and more enlightened mode of living'.[5] It probably derives from the way in which modern architecture was promoted. Before the First World War, the leaders of the German Werkbund had urged manufacturers to take the lead in commissioning products and buildings from the best contemporary designers; products and buildings designed by Peter Behrens for the AEG, illustrated in their publications, were accompanied by the suggestion that industrialists had a duty to provide more general cultural leadership. During the 1920s, Le Corbusier, romanticising the industrialist and eager to find new clients, developed the idea that captains of industry were 'natural' patrons of the new architecture. Although working in beautiful, efficient new surroundings, their homes were marred by eclecticism and sham. Why, he asked, did not the businessman, bankers and merchants at the helm of the economy show comparable courage and initiative as clients? 'Our industrial friends seem sheepish and shrivelled like tigers in a cage' he observed.[6] The idea that adventurous architectural patronage accompanied – or should accompany – entrepreneurial activity

1. P. Thompson, *William Butterfield*, (London: Routledge,1971), p.378, n.15.

2. Jeremy Gould, *Modern Houses in Britain, 1919–1939* (London: Society of Architectural Historians of Great Britain, 1977).

3. 'Patrons of the Modern Movement', *Architectural Design* vol. 49, no.10–11, 1979, pp.90–91.

4. See H. Lipstadt,'Polemic and Parody in the Battle for British Modernism', *AA Files* no.3, Jan. 1983, pp.68–76, and A. Powers *Oliver Hill: Architect and lover of life*, (London: Mouton Publications, 1989), for a valuable corrective to this view.

5. F. R. S. Yorke, *The Modern House*, (London: Architectural Press,1934), p.23.

figure 1
Wenman Joseph Bassett-Lowke and Jane Bassett-Lowke outside 78 Derngate, Northampton, converted by C. R. Mackintosh, c.1917. (Mackintosh Coll., Hunterian Museum and Art Gallery, Glasgow)

figure 2
Postcard produced by W. J. Bassett-Lowke
for his own use with views of Peter Behrens'
'New Ways', Northampton, c.1930.

was encouraged by the English critic P. Morton Shand, familiar with developments in both Germany and France, who in 1930 suggested an *Architectural Review* competition to design the interior of a flat for a fictitious client, Lord Benbow – a Clydeside ship-builder of advanced tastes.[7] Echoing him, historians writing about modern architecture in Britain have persistently drawn attention to the industrial background of two early patrons of modern houses, W. J. Bassett-Lowke and F. H. Crittall , despite considerable differences in the character of both the clients and the commissions.[8] Bassett-Lowke was a patron in the Werkbund mould, a knowledgeable and cosmopolitan businessman who participated in the design process of the house remodelled for him by C. R. Mackintosh and the one which Peter Behrens subsequently designed for him by correspondence.[9] F. H. Crittall, who built Silver End village in Essex to house workers at his Braintree factory, is usually spoken of in the same breath; but his patronage appears to have been far less the expression of personal taste, and more a calculated attempt to broaden the market for his firm's products – metal windows – in a 'model housing' development.[10] Moreover, Crittall deliberately commissioned houses and community buildings from a number of different architects, creating not a unified, modern, company style but an eclectic mix – something quite consistent with developments at Port Sunlight, Hampstead and Letchworth. The houses at Silver End demonstrated the compatibility of the firm's windows for a spectrum of the various styles favoured by contemporary speculative house-builders.

Today, with increasingly detailed studies of the architecture of the 1930s and through correspondence which has happily survived between architects and their clients it is possible to look at the issue of patronage from a different perspective. Thompson's occupational categories can be usefully refined and expanded, most obviously with the addition of politicians, people involved in the advertising business, teachers, doctors and lawyers. But occupation, although helping to establish useful links between prospective clients and architects, may not in the final analysis be such a significant indicator. Focussing upon it tempts us to look for some pre-existing set of characteristics (for example, the industrialist's supposed qualities of entrepreneurship and openness to new ideas and forms) which may have disposed clients to favour a particular kind of architecture. The evidence – duller but sobering – suggests that clients chose to commission particular individuals and not a particular kind of architecture, with commissions most commonly determined by ties of family, friendship or personal recommendation. 'Cold' commissions, in which clients were attracted simply by an image or account of the new architecture seen in a magazine or book without having any personal link with the architect are much rarer.[11] Broad, non-occupational, factors like an interest in the outdoors and an informal way of life, or the desire for an easily-run, well-serviced house, are probably more important. But these factors would not in themselves be enough to drive a client into the arms of a Modernist architect, and as we shall see, could be accommodated in a traditional set of elevations. There are striking instances amongst clients of generational revolt (comparable to that which occurred among the patrons of the Queen Anne Movement during the 1870s): a rejection of the attitudes and surroundings of their parents which sometimes manifested itself in an engagement with politics, or aesthetics. Architectural and artistic patronage could accompany this rebellion. This is different from Bayley's picture of the typical patron as an outsider, often foreign, and sometimes Jewish. On the contrary, the patrons of modern houses appear fully integrated into their particular social milieu, and in a way which significantly helped to expand the circle of patronage. Indeed, personal and professional networks emerge as the most significant factor in patronage. The most obvious of these links were the various networks connecting architects, decorators, designers with their potential clients. The MARS Group, one of whose avowed aims was 'propaganda for a contemporary architecture', was one[12]; but architects also benefited from other less easily traceable networks. Individuals involved in advertising, manufacture of building components, and housing associations seem to have played the role of intermediary between architects and prospective client. Maxwell Fry secured a good many commissions in this way.[13] John Gloag, partner in the advertising agency Pritchard, Wood & Partners, helped Fry to procure work with various clients. George Butler, painter and graphic designer with J. Walter Thompson, may have done likewise.[14] Jack Fox-Williams, of the window manufacturers Williams & Williams, undertook to seek commissions for Fry provided that the architect specified their products.[15] Elizabeth Denby, active in the Pioneer Housing Association and in the Kensington Housing Trust, was also helpful in introducing Fry to the Sassoon family, who funded Sassoon House. Other architects probably had similar support systems, which merit investigation. Some of the best-known commissions repay re-thinking from the perspective of the client. A salutary example is a weekend house designed by Frederick MacManus of Burnet, Tait and Lorne for Hugh and Ruth Dalton, a political couple whose working week was spent in gloomy rented London flats. The architect has related the commission

6. Le Corbusier, *Towards a New Architecture*, (London: John Rodker, 1927), p.23.

7. 'Lord Benbow's apartments', *Architectural Review*, LXVIII, November 1930, pp.201–4.

8. 'Both of whom might be expected to have special sympathy for the new architecture from the Continent' H. R. Hitchcock, 'England and the outside world', special issue on Connell, Ward and Lucas, *Architectural Association Journal*, 1956. 'The first houses in England which were Modern as opposed to traditional in form were commissioned – significantly – by industrialists.' Gould, op. cit., p.10.

9. See my 'A modern Patron: Bassett-Lowke, Mackintosh and Behrens', *Journal of the Decorative Arts Society*, no.10, 1987, pp.1–9.

10. See G. Thurgood, 'Silver End Garden Village', *Thirties Society Journal*, no.3, 1983.

11. Mr. Brants (see below) was one; another was Sir Arthur Lowes Dickinson, who commissioned Aldings (now White House), Surrey from Connell.

12. See my 'The MARS Group, 1933–3', *RIBA Transactions*, 8, vol.IV, no.2, 1984–5, pp.68–79.

13. J. S. Allan, *The unknown warriors: architecture in Britain in the inter-war period*, (BA thesis, Sheffield University, 1969) contains much fascinating material on Fry, esp. pp.47 & 115.

14. Butler was Fry's client for the studio-house at Chipperfield.

15. Allan, op. cit., p.54.

figure 3
Ruth Dalton at 'West Leaze', Aldbourne, Wilts, 1935.

to Ruth Dalton's 'keen appreciation of good design' and, specifically, to seeing photographs of the houses he designed at Silver End in architectural magazines.[16] But we gain a different view from other sources. Hugh Dalton's biographer, although stressing that Ruth assumed responsibility for the commission, emphasises the importance for both of the site, high on the Wiltshire Downs. They had honeymooned nearby, and spent walking holidays in the Savernake Forest. Establishing a garden and planting trees gave Dalton great satisfaction, he entertained friends and political allies at the house, and dryly recorded Arthur Henderson's response: 'Asks what is the name of this style house. And which is the front.'[17] A legacy to Ruth Dalton from her mother's wealthy protector enabled them to build the house; significantly, it was a house of a completely different kind from those in which she had helped entertain as a girl. What MacManus regarded as Ruth Dalton's appreciation of good design, and others judged to be an expression of her puritanism may have been part of her reaction against the environment in which she grew up, as was her decision to study at the London School of Economics and not Cambridge, and the Fabian socialism she embraced.[18] Nor did the commission for the house come about quite as MacManus suggests. It is likely that it was on the personal recommendation of Dr Simmonds, whose house at Newbury nearby was designed by MacManus in 1928.[19] And the house was probably not – as the architect implies – the result of an existing interest in architecture, but the beginning of it.[20]

The Wood House at Shipbourne, commissioned from Gropius by Jack and Frances Donaldson in 1937, was to all appearances a perfect match between architect and client: the distinguished refugee from Nazi Germany, and the left-wing intellectual couple. Jack Donaldson was working as secretary of the Pioneer Health Centre in Peckham, and was developing an interest in the scientific methods of farming. He wanted a house within an easy drive of Peckham but also close to the Kent farm which supplied milk and produce for the Centre.[21] Frances Donaldson candidly recalled that their decision to build the house was not the expression of a personal taste in architecture (she admitted that they had little or none), but a feeling that they ought not to build in period style: 'We decided in an almost crusading spirit that the only intelligent thing was to build in the architectural style of our own day. This crusading spirit almost completely prevented me from asking myself whether I actually liked it.'[22] Rather than a particular type of architecture, the Donaldsons wanted a house with a loggia and sleeping porch, open to the sun and air and organised in a way which would allow them and their future family a degree of freedom, even when guests were staying. The reaction of an early visitor, Lady Cunard, reveals how closely she identified her young hosts' new house with what she regarded as their excessively informal way of life. She advised Frances Donaldson to put her husband back on course: 'He is a very intelligent and cultivated man and he cannot spend the rest of his life looking after the poor and camping out,' she warned.[23]

Other, less prominent clients seem to have been attracted not by images of modern houses glimpsed in magazines or exhibitions but by practical advantages. Jean Brants contacted Elizabeth Denby, designer of the 'All-Europe House' shown at Earls Court in 1939, with a view to building 'a really labour-saving house' at Jordans in Buckinghamshire. The widowed Mrs Brants, her sister and Czech brother-in-law compiled a list of their requirements. The emphasis was upon economy and practicality. The facilities were to be modern (a 'Whirldry' washing machine, a shower-room, electric radiators, cooker and refrigerator) and the building materials, local brick.[24] The list also specified 'garage with vegetable and tool-racks'; 'dining-kitchen' and a timetable for the household:

> *Fruit breakfast – tea and toast*
> *Lunch Big meal midday*
> *Tea Home-made cakes and scones*

figure 5
Frances Donaldson (left) with Dr Scott
Williamson and Dr Innes Pearce of the
Pioneer Health Centre.

16. 'Recollections of my early architectural
years', MS at BAL Drawings Coll., p.5.

17. B. Pimlott, *Hugh Dalton*, (London, 1985),
p.197.

18. Perhaps Hugh Dalton too was reacting
against his parents: he had been brought up in
the precincts of Windsor Castle because his
father was a tutor to the future King George V.

19. Dalton's diary notes the name of the
builder used for the Simmonds house, whom
they too resolved to use. Entry for 5 Aug. 1930,
Dalton diaries, vol.13, LSE.

20. The diary records the couple
conscientiously reading up on the subject in
February 1930 – André Lurçat on reinforced
concrete and Creswell's *The Honeywood File* –
and a trip to Paris to look at modern furniture
and interior decoration in September. Ruth's
growing interest in architecture and art later
led her to chair the powerful London County
Council Parks Dept.

21. L. Cormier *Walter Gropius: emigre architect:
works and refugee, England and America in the 30s*
Ph.D. diss, 1986, p.99.

22. *Child of the Twenties*, (London, 1959),
p.179.

23. Ibid, p.181.

24. The house was considerably modified
from Denby's exhibition design – a terraced
house on a restricted site – by Samuel &
Harding who had agreed to draw up detailed
plans and supervise the construction of the
'All Europe House' for Denby's clients and to
split the fees with her.

25. Sa G 68/6, BAL, dated 13 June 1939

26. M. Hall, 'High Cross House, Devon',
Country Life, CLXXXIX, 3 Aug. 1995, p.50.
Leopold Stokowski and his wife paid for the
construction of Oak Lane County Day School,
Philadelphia of which W. B. Curry was
headmaster prior to his appointment to
Dartington. Stokowski believed that when the
children grew up 'most everything would be
modern.' See R. Stern *George Howe Towards an
American architecture*, (1975),p.96, n.24.

27. W. Curry, 'Planning for Education: the
architectural requirements of a modern
school', *Design for Today*, September 1934,
p.322; *Country Life*, 11 Feb. 1933; *Architects
Journal*, 12 Oct. 1933.

28. 'A Planned Seaside Resort', *Country Life*,
17 August 1935, p.182.

*Supper Salad, egg – not much cooking, light meal.
Bottling fruit etc.[25]*

Traditional rural pursuits are combined with modern living arrangements.

Among professional clients it is teachers and doctors who feature prominently. An early example was the headmaster of Dartington Hall School, William Curry, who persuaded his employers to engage the Swiss-American architect William Lescaze in 1931 for the Headmaster's house, High Cross and other school and estate buildings. The brief indicates William and Ena Curry's wish for a range of American domestic appliances installed in the house. However, different factors soon came to the fore. Lescaze had designed a nursery building donated by Leopold Stokowski at the Oak Lane Country Day School in Philadelphia, Curry's previous school. Lescaze believed that architecture had a formative influence on children: 'Whether a building is honest or dishonest, sane or insane, beautiful for contemporary spiritual reasons or beautiful from the defeatist point of view ... affects the pupils' point of view for better or for worse', he wrote.[26] Curry had absorbed these ideas, and Lescaze was commissioned to build three boarding houses, a gymnasium and school offices at Dartington as well as houses for Curry and the dance director Kurt Jooss. The publicity which Lescaze's work at the school received did much to foster an association between modern architecture and progressive education.[27] This association was made explicit in a promotional article in *Country Life* featuring the houses designed by Oliver Hill at Frinton-on-Sea. Readers were told that the Rev Robert Double had established a crammer in one of these: 'It is considered that the advantages of the sea air and sports, combined with the modern surroundings at Frinton, will have a beneficially bracing effect upon the pupils' studies.'[28]

Elsewhere, the developers of speculative housing estates at Churston in South Devon (designed by Lescaze) and at Carlyon Bay, Cornwall (designed by Marshall Sisson) – hoping to sell houses to the professional middle classes – stressed the rational, healthy, efficient and comfortable character of the modern house, as though to remind the public that such houses had already been built to the exacting requirements of experts in the fields of education and medicine. The fact that modern houses were being built by academics, doctors, and lawyers was also emphasised by architects. Connell and Ward, who in 1934 attempted to gain permission to build a pair of semi-detached houses in Ruislip, pointed out in defence of their design that 'we are at present commissioned by two doctors, one an eminent Harley Street physician, to design and supervise the erection of houses of this type because of their efficiency in ordinary living accommodation and healthiness.'[29]

The doctors in question apparently lived in the same block of flats in London as the architects, and knew them well.[30] These commissions, although of course in line with contemporary thinking which associated sunshine and fresh air with health, were prompted by personal friendship. The same appears to be true of many commissions from professional clients.[31] Scholars have also been persistently associated with the modern house. Their commissions bring into sharper focus the central conundrum in the history of patronage: how far were commissions shaped by particular needs and tastes? Or was it more common that, having selected an architect, clients found him themselves, willy-nilly, the owner of a modern house?[32] Bernard Ashmole's commission to Amyas Connell in 1929 for High and Over, Amersham is generally presented as ground-breaking: a spectacular modern house commissioned by the Professor of Classical Archaeology at London University on a conspicuous rural site. '... scholars should dwell in houses of this type, especially archaeologists ...' suggested Howard Robertson.[33] But the importance of Ashmole for the subsequent course of architecture in Britain is probably subtler, and concerns his directorship of the British School at Rome between 1925 and 1928 – a period of unusual creativity and productive harmony between the resident archaeologists, painters, sculptors and architects.

Ashmole had, through his study of classical Greek sculpture, become fascinated by architecture too. He combined a refined aesthetic sensibility with interest in the practical application of technology. His house, to whose planning, siting and landscape gardens he made a significant contribution, seems to have satisfied both aspects of his personality. An accomplished photographer, he pioneered the use of photographs for the study of sculpture, and suggested that film could make a valuable medium for recording its appearance from different angles. Ashmole recorded his delight in the hexagonal motif which appeared in the plan, the central hall, the shape of the day-nursery at the top of the house and the stools designed for it, and the equilateral triangular pattern of the pavement tiles and the hood over the front door.[34] He probably took equal pleasure in the glazed and cellulosed internal doors with riveted steel architraves, and the aeroplane-like strut bracing the door hood against the wall of the house.

Another classical archaeologist, A. W. Lawrence (brother of T. E. Lawrence) on his appointment as Reader at Cambridge commissioned a house from Marshall Sisson, whom he had known at the British School at Rome in 1924–6. Lawrence specified a house with central heating, a garage, and self-contained maid's quarters accessible by a staircase 'perhaps in the style of the "Mason Citron"'[35] Despite his client's reference to Corbusier, Sisson designed a compact brick house. He adopted a basic unit of 5 feet 3 inches in the interests of economy and to give the design visual coherence. Sisson believed that this 'rationalisation' was what made the house modern: a well-serviced, thoughtfully-planned house constructed according to a strict budget. The pragmatism of Sisson's solution suggests sensitivity to building restrictions and cost, but also to his own and the client's shared interest in pre-modern traditions of domestic architecture.[36] Sisson was recommended by Lawrence to A. J. B. Wace, appointed Professor of Classical Archaeology at Cambridge in 1934.[37] 'We want a house simple in construction, but on modern lines and with modern conveniences' wrote Wace. He and his American wife were keen to have 'really efficient' sanitary fittings, baths and plumbing, and suggested 'kitchen, larder and boiler arrangements along the Lawrences' lines.' Ironically, these were the aspects which proved most trouble-

figure 6
Bernard Ashmole and his son Philip outside 'High and Over', Amersham, 1939.

some to achieve, although the clients expressed themselves 'very pleased' with the appearance and plan of the completed house.

Comparable networks of friendship sustain other commissions from academics. For example, Michael Postan, appointed to the Chair of Economic History at Cambridge in 1938, commissioned Hugh Hughes to build him a house there. Postan, born in Bessarabia, and a radical Zionist in politics is treated by Bayley as a prime example of the outsider client. But this commission is far more complex and interesting. Postan moved in a circle which included Wells Coates and Ove Arup; his interests extended to medieval domestic architecture, on which he lectured at the Bartlett School of Architecture whilst teaching at University College in the early 1930s. Postan went so far as to discuss small private houses with Gropius; but when appointed to the Cambridge chair, he decided to commission the local architect Hughes, whose design for a new building at Peterhouse he had helped select.[38] The distinguished economic historian Eileen Power, who married Postan in 1937, herself interested in architecture and a driving force behind his career, no doubt had considerable input in the commissioning of the house, whose large living room was the setting for her collection of objets d'art, and for wonderful parties.[39] The caricature of the foreign radical, keen to break with native traditions of architecture, does injustice to the subtleties and contradictions of such a commission. Rather, professional considerations (the practical and social needs of a Cambridge professor in the 1930s), personal taste, and the pressure – as a newly-apppointed academic from an unconventional academic background – to conform with local practice, all appear to have informed the commission.

The records of a single architectural practice in the 1930s provides an insight into the mechanics of patronage. The Hon. Godfrey Samuel (son of Sir Herbert – later Viscount – Samuel), received many commissions from relatives and family friends.[40] School and university friendships were also significant. Robert Eicholz, a solicitor, and his wife Enid Albu, an interior decorator, were extremely helpful in introducing Samuel and his partner Val Harding to prospective clients, and themselves decided to commission a country house. A fascinating series of letters between client and architect reveals that it was the *architects* who they admired, and not modern architecture, which they regarded as unsuited to the site where they planned to build. 'It is your sense of delicacy and feeling for things that we want ... wrote Enid Albu. Among their requirements were: 'No special shaped rooms ... no new equipment or ideas. But *great* ... care on detail ... Robert Eicholz said 'The house must look as though it were part of the land'. Harding's attempt to convince them to build a flat-roofed house apparently included a visit to see Le Corbusier's Villa Savoye and Villa Stein, in surroundings which were then rural. But the clients' original stipulation of 'a house in a familiar and not an unfamiliar idiom' prevailed: a colour-washed brick house with a slate roof was built, to their great satisfaction, at Withyham in Sussex.[41] Other clients, like the illustrator and engraver Claire Leighton provided a freer brief, asking Harding, then working for Tecton, to design a studio in Bucks 'to be wholly, modern, startling'. The correspondence also reveals the extent of this client network. Harding had been recommended by 'Miss Rathbone of *the Studio*'; and she was sufficiently pleased with her studio to recommend Val Harding to Jennie Lee and her new husband Aneurin Bevan, then planning to build a house nearby.[42]

The evidence invites us to challenge the popular image of the patron: the captain of industry, the radical, even the tweedy art-lover caricatured by Osbert Lancaster in *Homes Sweet Homes* seem equally far from the mark. More typical was the client who may not have looked specifically for a modern house, but for an escape from the formality and restrictions of contemporary middle-class life. Women of independent means – widowed, separated or divorced – also featured, their commissions complementing other aspects of their lives – an involvement

29. *Architects Journal*, 12 July 1934.

30. Information kindly supplied by Barry Russell.

31. Dr. Warren Crowe, rheumatologist, commissioned Kit Nicholson, a fellow member of the Savile Club, to build him a house at Fawley. Dr. John King, who commissioned Basil Spence to build him a house in Edinburgh, was the family doctor of Spence's partner William Kinnimonth. Cecil Walton, headmaster of University College School, commissioned a house in Hampstead from Val Harding, with whom he had been at Rugby School.

32. Paul Thompson argues that it was the enhanced professional status of the architect and the respect shown to a fellow professional by middle class clients which encouraged autonomy and a gap between 20th century architecture and public understanding. Op. cit, pp.370–71.

33. 'An experiment with time', *Architect & Building News*, 3 January 1930, p.13.

34. D. Kurtz, *Bernard Ashmole. an autobiography*, (Oxford, 1994), p.53.

35. Si M/7/2, BAL. Letter of 19 April 1931.

36. In 1926 Lawrence invited Sisson to contribute to a series of books he planned to write on ancient and modern art – and presumably also architecture.

37. Wace had originally planned to use Piet de Jong, an architect with he had worked at the British School at Athens.

38. Bayley, op. cit., p.92, illustrates three interesting alternative designs by Hughes for the Peterhouse building, Fen Court.

39. Maxine Berg's forthcoming biography of Eileen Power will no doubt help to illuminate this issue.

40. See James Bettley's useful catalogue of the papers, 1984, BAL.

41. Sa G/17/4, BAL.

42. Instead they bought and converted a cottage in Berkshire.

with politics, with the making or collecting of art, or with country pursuits.[43] But the most fruitful way in which to explore the issue of patronage in the inter-war period may be to investigate the connections between specific architects and their clients in a small circle, like that at the British School at Rome, or at Cambridge, or between the clients of a specific architect like Maxwell Fry or Leslie Martin. This can reveal some surprising things. 'Class and school ties ... facilitated the progress of the Modern Movement', Hélène Lipstadt has rightly observed.[44] So did the full-time degree courses which had become the normal form of architectural training by the 1930s. For Samuel and many of his contemporaries, it was such networks, and not the existence of clients with a strong interest in modern architecture which generally helped to secure commissions. The web of connections incidentally helps to clarify puzzling events. The sculptress, Dora Gordine planning to build a studio house in London, commissioned a design from Samuel in 1934. From the point of view of style, one might have expected her to commission Goldfinger, pupil of Perret who had designed her Paris studio. Instead, the choice of architect was determined by the connection between Gordine's new husband, the Hon. Richard Hare, and Godfrey Samuel, who had become friends at Balliol.[45] By the end of the 1930s, such networks firmly underpinned the patronage of modern architecture in Britain, something which was not only the prerogative of a special breed of radicals and outsiders, or even of liberal professionals, but even of the upper classes and aristocracy.[46]

figure 7
Osbert Lancaster, 'Functional' from *Homes Sweet Homes*, (London: John Murray, 1939). By kind permission of John Murray Publishers.

43. E.g. Frances Donaldson, whose first, brief marriage ended in divorce; Helen Sutherland the collector and client of Leslie Martin whose marriage was annulled in 1913; Margaret Sewell, miniature painter and Colin Lucas's client at Little Frith, Bucks, widowed in 1917; and Mrs Brants.

44. Lipstadt, op. cit., p.75.

45. It was eventually executed not to Samuel's design, but to one of Gordine's own devising.

46. In 1936, the 11th Earl of Northesk purchased Gull Rock House, one of the speculatively built houses designed by Sisson at Carlyon Bay, Cornwall.

5 Textiles in the Modern House

CHRISTINE BOYDELL

Textiles in the Modern House

CHRISTINE BOYDELL

EXTILES are used in a number of contexts in the interior; they act as screenings for windows and openings; as coverings for upholstered furniture and as floor coverings in the form of rugs and carpets. However, two principal schools of thought regarding the function of textiles in the modern interior existed during the 1930s. On the one hand there were influential voices who promoted the Modernist cause and tolerated textiles only if they were fully integrated within the architect's vision. Fabrics and carpets were expected to operate within the interior as pieces of functional equipment, subordinate to, or in sympathy with, the architecture. While on the other hand there were those who celebrated textiles as the main form of relief from the austerity of the Modernist influenced plain interior and regarded them as the only means of personal expression. Herein lay the Modernist dilemma – the addition of extraneous decoration was invidious yet, with few exceptions, textiles had been used traditionally to add interest in the form of decorative pattern. It was the dominance of the functional ideal during the period (usually within the context of architecture) which led to numerous discussions on the role textiles would take within the home. While a minority felt they should be banished completely, the debate resulted in textiles taking on a renewed significance.

The influence of propaganda from authoritative commentators such as Nikolaus Pevsner, Herbert Read, Dorothy Todd and magazines such as *The Architectural Review* and *The Studio* all had an impact on promoting the use of a Modernist functional aesthetic which was to dominate the avant-garde particularly in the first half of the 1930s. The flow of propaganda had an effect on manufacturers, many of whom responded to lobbying by consciously devoting a percentage of their output to the production of designs which were in sympathy with Modern Movement ideas. Frequently this was achieved by employing the services of the freelance designer or artist. In addition, a torrent of advice flowed in the direction of householders through numerous publications which attempted to guide them through the maze of furnishing possibilities, with much of the advice offered being Modernist in tone. It is the aim of this essay to explain how manufacturers and designers responded to the challenge presented by Modernism, through a discussion of examples of textiles and their use in interiors during the 1930s.

The years immediately preceding the Exposition International des Arts Décoratifs et Industriels Modernes held in Paris in 1925 saw a variety of textile patterns recommended for use in the home. Fabrics and carpets were dominated primarily by abstract designs with some stylised floral motifs, with Art Deco remaining popular into the thirties. However, Modern Movement protagonists such as Pevsner criticised the use of the style, singling out the British carpet industry:

The dominant patterns of the last eight or nine years have been derived from a deplorably misunderstood Continental cubism, the prevailing colours being brown, a blatant orange and in more recent years, a grass-green no less blatant.[1]

1. N. Pevsner, 'The Designer in Industry. 1. Carpets', *Architectural Review*, vol. LXXIX, 1936, p.185.

figure 1
The dining room and sitting room of Serge Chermayeff's house, 52 Abbey Road, London NW8, with rugs of his own design, 1930, p.271. (*Architectural Review*, vol. LXVII, 1930, p.271.)

Noel Carrington in *Design in the Home*, 1933, accused followers of the 'modernistic' of being 'novel at all costs' and recognised it as the antithesis of Modernist ideas. He described the modernistic as:

... a style of sorts, compounded largely of studied unconventionalism, flavoured in this instance with a dash of Cubism. Such interiors are as unrelated to function and construction as the Tudor reproductions of the big shops.[2]

The primacy of function was an issue which occupied Modernists and began to have an impact on textile design at the end of the 1920s. The simplicity in textiles which emerged was largely influenced by developments in architecture from the Continent. These ideas reached Britain through articles in art and design journals and in books like Dorothy Todd and Raymond Mortimer's *The New Interior Decoration* published in 1929; the first of many publications advocating the adoption of Modernism.[3] Through a discussion of primarily Continental developments in art, architecture and design, this influential book pointed towards the possibility of establishing an aesthetic which expressed in new form the sensibility of the age. This early Modernist treatise, relying heavily on the ideas of Le Corbusier, proposed the principles of utility, simplicity and harmony and stated in no uncertain terms the place textiles would take in the contemporary interior. The authors' contention was that the construction of the house should dictate the nature of its furnishings, and functionalism should triumph over all other considerations:

Beauty of function is one of the essential principles on which the furnishing of [such] rooms is based, and every object is designed to explain its purpose clearly, so that the result should be as logical as an equation.

The dominance of architectural form was to be of vital importance in the decade which followed and the place of texture and pattern in relation to buildings was to occupy the thoughts of many involved in the creation of the modern home. Consideration of textiles as 'equipment' rather than mere decoration was felt to be the key to producing interiors which fulfilled Modernist notions of simplicity and function and it was within this context that discussion relating to the suitability of particular textiles took place. Numerous commentators recognised that textiles were beginning to experience a renewed vitality and importance in relation to developments in architecture. M. Dane writing in *The Studio* in 1929 noted that:

In the modern interior, with its predilection for plain floor-coverings and plain wall-surfaces, the patterning of curtains and chair covers takes a very important place.[4]

E. T. Ould in the *Home Owners Handbook* went further, asserting that the success of a room depended on carefully chosen carpets and fabrics:

If sufficient thought is given to "soft furnishing" and accurate choice is made, a room will appear as a complete unit however curiously assorted the furniture itself may be.[5]

The desire for unity in interior decoration was achieved through the careful use of colour, pattern and texture in textiles.

Pattern in an interior was deemed acceptable to Modernists only if it was used sparingly and to provide points of focus in a room. A picture, a specific fabric and increasingly a rug of modern design fulfilled this purpose. The floor in a room acted as a background on which other equipment was placed. As the floor was an integral part of the building it was advisable not to obscure it with wall-to-wall carpeting; it was considered more acceptable to have the floor finished in architectural materials such as wood or terrazzo which harmonised with the rest of the building. If a wall-to wall carpet was to be used it was recommended that it should be plain and of a colour which conformed to other materials used in the room, thus providing a foundation upon which all other components could be placed. Concentrated areas of pattern could be used in the form of rugs to provide defined areas within an interior or fixed points around which furniture could be arranged. The traditional focus of an interior, the fireplace, was often removed completely in favour of a less obtrusive form of heating, thus another focus for a room was required – and a rug was invariably the solution. Edward McKnight Kauffer spoke of the vital relationship of rugs to architecture in an interview in *The Studio* in 1929, referring to the modern tendency towards the horizontal in architecture:

The modern window is definitely wide and horizontal in form ... The modern rug should, therefore, by its pattern, suggest the horizontal (which is also the restful) characteristic of interior decoration.[6]

It was felt that pattern should be conceived in an architectural manner with emphasis on masses and voids. Dorothy Todd recommended self-contained rather than repeating designs which would help to anchor the floor.[7]

At the beginning of the 1930s it was often difficult for architects to find equipment which integrated with their buildings. In order to achieve the desired harmonious unity in a modern home they were usually responsible for devising the interior scheme, and often for designing equipment within it. In Serge Chermayeff's re-design of his London house in 1930, the rugs made to his own design are used to unite dining room and sitting room and their circular patterning is conceived in relation to the plan of the room. The notion that rugs should be designed specifically to suit current ideas relating to architecture could be seen in many linear and abstract rugs produced during the 1930s. Rugs by Terence Prentice for the decorator J. Duncan Miller were patterned simply to suit the modern building for which they were commissioned. In a living room in a country house, Prentice's green rug with narrow white lines was designed to complement Miller's cream room with its waxed pine floor, furniture in ash, sycamore, avodire and pear veneers, and its cream and buff upholstery and cream cotton curtains. The pale and neutral tones of the room are grounded by the green colour of the rug. Marian Pepler's designs for Gordon Russell Limited were similar in conception and were influenced by her architectural training. They were notable for the restrained use of pattern and colour. Simple linear designs were used in combination with Gordon Russell Limited's furniture and Welsh tweeds which the company purchased for upholstery and curtaining from 1936. The firm was one of a small number of retail outlets, along with Heal's, Dunn's of Bromley and Bowman's of Camden where, by the middle of the decade, the consumer could find good modern designs.

Dorothy Todd celebrated the fact that, given its more defined function, the

2. N. Carrington, *Design in the Home*, London, 1933, p.18.

3. D. Todd & R. Mortimer, *The New Interior Decoration*, (London, 1929).

4. M. Dane, 'English Textiles of Modern Design', *Studio*, vol.XCVIII, 1929, p.490.

5. *Home Owner's Handbook: The Complete Guide to Home Making*, (London, 1938), p.45.

6. 'New Rug Designs by E. McKnight Kauffer and Marion Dorn', *Studio*, vol.XCVIII, 1929, p 45.

7. D. Todd, 'The Modern Rug', *Good Furniture*, June 1929, p.305.

8. D. Todd, 'Marion Dorn. Architect of Floors', *Architectural Review*, vol.LXXII, 1932, p.109.

figure 2
The living room in a scheme by J. Duncan Miller with a rug by Terence Prentice, 1935. (*Architectural Review*, vol.LXXVIII, 1935, p.35.)

figure 3
A dining room in a house in Highgate Village by C. H. James with a rug by Marian Pepler available from Gordon Russell Limited, 1936. (*Studio Yearbook of Decorative Art*, 1936, p.76.)

rug had 'attained the pinnacle of its historic significance in the interior scheme'.[8] However, advice on the vogue for restrained interiors given to consumers, be they architects or householders, included warnings about the difficulties of finding appropriately designed floor-coverings. Paul Nash, writing in 1930 encouraged the use of modern simple rugs but accepted that there were few good examples to choose from.[9] In the same year, Frances Mary Punnett recommended designs by Marion Dorn, as well as Donegal rugs of restrained pattern available from the Army & Navy Stores.[10] A number of others recommended the use of Oriental or Persian rugs as suitable for modern interiors if a good contemporary design was unobtainable. But cheap mass produced rugs which suited the modern tendency in interiors remained a rarity. C. Louise Avery accused manufacturers of con-

figure 4
A living room in the Kaufmann house, 55 Victoria Drive, Wimbledon by E. C. Kaufmann and Elisabeth Benjamin with an oriental style rug, 1935. (*Architectural Review*, vol.LXXVIII, 1935, p.129.)

servatism and felt this was the reason for the paucity of suitable rugs, claiming they were unwilling to produce new designs and risk profits.[11] Pevsner in his 1936 investigation of the British carpet industry noted the poor state of design while also blaming the situation on manufacturers' reluctance to invest in new designs. The best designs he identified were hand-tufted examples by Dorn and Pepler. C. G. Tomrley highlighted the importance of the role of the designer and commented that suitable floor-coverings

require an inspired designer with a clear idea of purpose, and that this designer must superintend his design right down to the last stage of its production. Only by this means can notable results be effected.[12]

By 1935 the impact of advice seemed to be making its mark with many more modern rugs available. As well as recommendations for the work of Dorn and Pepler, Ronald Grierson and Evelyn Wylde were commended. Suitable designs for modern interiors were manufactured by the Wilton Royal Carpet Factory who hand-made rugs to the designs of Marion Dorn, McKnight Kauffer, Marion Pepler and others. It is a testimony to the company's commitment to modern design and their recognition of the possibility of commercial advantage that they established a sub-committee in 1933 to consider modern designs that might be put into production.[13] Modern examples were also available from Morton Sundour who had a number of hand-knotted Donegal rugs made on the west coast of Ireland, while Torfyn flat-woven rugs were designed by Ronald Simpson and produced by Scottish Folk Fabrics another off-shoot of Morton Sundour.

As it was difficult to acquire suitable ready-made examples, promoters of Modernism suggested that wherever possible rugs should be specially commissioned for specific interiors in order that they might suit perfectly the architect's scheme. Commentators who were more interested in the placement of decoration in a room advised homeowners to buy their rugs first and conceive their interior decoration around the floor-coverings.[14] However, all agreed that pattern needed to be carefully considered. Several writers recommended designs which emphasised flatness and avoided distracting three-dimensional pattern. It was therefore suggested that natural forms should not be too realistically depicted. Designers also had to be more aware of the fact that their patterns were often partially obscured by furniture and that the design had to be legible from a variety of angles including above; this viewpoint was often chosen by the architectural press when illustrating modern interiors.

Like floor-coverings, fabrics were regarded by Modernists as subordinate to architecture. Anthony Hunt of Edinburgh Weavers emphasised this point when he wrote:

The design of furniture and furnishing fabrics must be compatible with the architectural features it accompanies, unless the furnishing of contemporary buildings is to become a puerile mockery of their exteriors.[15]

Propagandists agreed that the three most important qualities of fabrics were texture, design and colour and the appropriate manifestation of these elements would lead to materials which could be integrated successfully within a modern interior (the importance of durability and colour-fastness were accepted as essential and rarely discussed).[16] Variation in surface texture was regarded as particularly important and Herbert Read felt it should take the place of ornament. In his important book *Art and Industry* (1934), Read asserted that ornament should only be incorporated into any object if it emphasised form, this point was particularly pertinent to a discussion of textiles.[17] He maintained that the construction of cloth should never be disguised and that the visual apprehension of a fibre's inherent tactile qualities was the key to designing successful textiles. Therefore, simple woven cloths were regarded as the most suitable fabrics for curtains and upholstery; Todd and Mortimer recommended tweeds for chair covers, while Smithells and S.John Woods favoured simple stripes, diagonals and checks.[18]

The impact of Modernism resulted in a trend towards patterns which emphasised the horizontality of fenestration, the vertical nature of staircase windows, with the choice of colour considered in relation to the rest of the room. In response to calls for the use of simple weaves, several manufacturers focused on the production of suitable cloths. Edinburgh Weavers, Donald Brothers and Warner and Sons produced many fabrics whose chief interest lay in texture provided by a combination of construction and fibre. They were among a small number of fabric manufacturers who made concerted efforts to respond to calls for textiles which would be in sympathy with Modern Movement buildings. Most did this by devoting a proportion of their output to modern design. James Morton the director of Morton Sundour Fabrics had long established associations with artists, architects and design lobbying organisations such as the Design and In-

9. P. Nash, 'Modern English Furnishing', *Architectural Review*, vol.LXVII, 1930, p.48.
10. F. M. Punnett, 'Some Changes in Modern Rug Design', *Decoration of the House Beautiful*, 1932, p.223.
11. C. L. Avery, *Bulletin of the Metropolitan Museum of Art*, vol.LXIV, November 1929, p.290.
12. C. G. Tomrley, 'Contemporary British Rug Design', *Design for Today*, vol.III, 1935, p.139.
13. Wilton Royal Carpet Factory, Minute Book, 11 Sept 1933.
14. H. G. Hayes Marshall, *Interior Decoration Today*, Leigh-on-Sea, 1938, p.28.
15. A.Hunt, 'Textiles', *Architectural Review*, vol.LXXXII, 1937, p.295.
16. A. Walton, 'Furnishing Textiles', *Journal of the Royal Society of Arts*, no.4285, vol.LXXXIII, 1934, p.168.
17. H. Read, *Art and Industry: the Principles of Industrial Design*, (London, 1934).
18. R. Smithells & S. John Woods, *The Modern Home*, (London, 1936), p.82.

dustries Association (DIA), and in 1928 he set up Edinburgh Weavers as an experimental off-shoot of Morton Sundour with the specific aim of 'creating a laboratory for the best modern textile art'.[19] Initially it was run by Alec Hunter, but was later taken over by Morton's son Alastair, who worked closely with the London-based Anthony Hunt to secure designs from leading artists and designers. Morton Sundour and specifically James Morton, were celebrated by Pevsner as one of the

initiators of the modern movement in the English textile industry, men such as the late Sir Frank Warner, Sir James Morton, the late D. T. and Mr.F. J. Donald, consciously transferred this unconscious tradition of exquisite weaving to the factory and carefully developed it there.[20]

Frank Warner along with Ernest Goodale and Alec Hunter at Warner and Sons

figure 5
A man's bedroom by Derek Patmore with fabric designed by Marion Dorn and produced by Warner and Sons, 1935. (D. Patmore, *Decoration for the Small Home*, London,1948, plate 18.)

figure 6
Rayon curtain fabric designed by H. J.Bull and printed by Allan Walton Fabrics 'produced in bespoke lengths to suit the varying heights of rooms', 1933. (*Architectural Review*, vol.LXXIV, 1933, p.31.)

figure 7
'Elstree' and 'Moidart' by Donald Brothers, 1935. (*Architectural Review*, vol.LXXVIII, 1935, p.285.)

were involved in efforts to improve design in the textile industry. Warner achieved this through his involvement in the DIA, the British Institute of Industrial Art and the Department of Overseas Trade, while Goodale, his successor was responsible for widening the firm's output to include more contemporary designs, employing Alec Hunter in 1932 as head of production. Donald Brothers of Dundee also devoted a certain proportion of their output to modern designs and established their 'Old Glamis Fabrics' in 1927. All of these firms, along with Old Bleach Linen, A. H. Lee, and Turnbull and Stockdale produced fabrics which were conceived in sympathy with the call from lobbyists: 'modern fabrics must suit the modern mind!'[21]

While the desire to satisfy the market for simple woven fabrics existed, many manufacturers relied solely on their own factory studios for designs; the place of the free-lance designer and artist in the production of designs for weaves was negligible. But some free-lance designers were producing simple weaves. Marion Dorn, in order to satisfy demand from a number of clients had fabrics woven initially, by the hand weaver Jean Orage, but by 1931 she was having special orders woven to her designs by Edinburgh Weavers and later Warner's. Dorn's cotton and cotton snarl striped weave, produced for her by Warner and Sons in 1935, was used by Derek Patmore in a scheme for a man's bedroom. The design of vertical stripes which branch at intervals to create short diagonals is used cleverly to emphasise the angular shapes of the furniture. Such a pattern, allowing the structure of the furniture to be expressed, would have met with the approval of commentators such as Herbert Read.

The variety of textures produced by manufacturers was appreciated by architects and interior designers who saw the possibilities provided by the visual and tactile qualities of different yarns. But Read recommended that the end-use of these fabrics be carefully considered:

For some purposes we like a smooth and silky surface; for others a soft and warm surface; for others still, a rough and stimulating surface.[22]

The use of linen, cotton, jute, wool and man-made fibres such as rayon and viscut (a precursor of lurex) provided the textile designer with a range of textural options. The combination of man-made yarns with natural fibres resulted in fab-

19. N. Pevsner, *An Enquiry into Industrial Art in England*, (Cambridge, 1937), p.58.

20. *ibid*, p.55.

21. R. Smithells, 'Modern Fabrics by British Craftsmen', *Decoration*, January 1933, p.16.

22. Read, *op.cit*, p. 123.

rics where the contrast of surface could also provide decorative interest for those who required aesthetic variety. The importance of the play of light on fabrics, emphasising textural and surface effects, was also discussed, particularly as the tendency was towards lighter coloured rooms with larger windows and the greater use of artificial light.

Duncan Miller advised that the choice of particular textures should be carefully made; avoidance of mixing a luxurious cloth with a homespun one was vital and 'chintz, tweed and brocade never look well together'.[23] Rayon was used as a curtaining fabric and printed examples could often be specially manufactured to suit windows of a particular height. But cautionary advice was also proffered regarding the suitability of specific types of fabric for particular func-

tions. In fabrics for upholstery, tactile qualities were especially important; fabric was required to be hard wearing while closely woven construction for furniture was more practical than fabrics which included long and loose threads. Open-structured materials were more suited to curtaining. It was important that all textiles in a room harmonised and this was most often achieved when they were conceived by one person. A few individuals produced designs for both rugs and fabrics. Through her limited company, Marion Dorn provided a complete textile service for her clients. She was commissioned by Brian O'Rorke to design textiles for a house in Devon in 1937. Her rugs with textured patterns of concentric circles were partnered with curtains with a design of horizontal lines, and a simple herringbone fabric was chosen for upholstery. The textiles were coloured in creams and beiges to complement O'Rorke's scheme of white walls, oak floor and bleached elm woodwork. O'Rorke also chose Dorn textiles for other rooms in the house. In 1935 *The Cabinet Maker* reported on textile designs by Ashley Havinden who had produced the 'Milky Way' pattern for both rugs and fabrics for Edinburgh Weavers. It was suggested that this might be one way of overcoming the problems retailers faced of finding fabrics and rugs which would work harmoniously together.[24] If all the textiles could not be conceived together the consumer was advised to achieve continuity through colour and texture.

The precedence given to architecture meant that in many reports on new buildings in the architectural press, textiles were regarded as superfluous, interiors often photographed without curtains at the windows. In reality curtains were seen by most architects as integral components of the interior and appro-

figure 9
Circular staircase in a house at Wentworth by Oliver Hill, 1935. The curtains are a woven fringed fabric 'Lodore' designed by Marion Dorn and first produced by Edinburgh Weavers in 1931. (*Architectural Review*, vol.LXXVII, 1935, p.244.)

priate examples were carefully chosen. Curtains had to function when open and hanging in folds and took on more significance in the evening when closed. Modernists usually favoured textured cloths rather than printed designs. Marion Dorn's 'Lodore' was a particular favourite for Modernist homes. This fringed fabric was woven for her by Edinburgh Weavers in 1931 and a fawn and white version was used by Ian Henderson in his interior scheme for Jean de Casalis' flat, while Oliver Hill chose a pale green and white example for the huge staircase window at the house he designed in Wentworth, Virginia Water, 1935.

The use of texture instead of bold pattern was a characteristic of the early 1930s fashion for muted and unobtrusive tones, which Anthony Hunt christened 'beigery'.[25] During the first half of the 1930s when beige and white rooms were the vogue, texture was also an important consideration in the choice of rugs. Marion Dorn pioneered the design of one-coloured textured rugs which relied for their patterning on the juxtaposition of carved or cut sections of pile. Fret-

23. D. Miller, *Interior Decorating*, (London, 1937), p.26.

24. 'Rug and Fabric Designs to Match', *The Cabinet Maker and Complete House Furnisher*, 14 December 1935, p.380.

25. A. Hunt, *Textile Design*, (London, 1937), p.25.

work patterned rugs were chosen by Syrie Maugham for the decoration of her 'all-white' sitting room in 1933, and versions were also used in schemes by Serge Chermayeff, Wells Coates and Oliver Hill. The subtle use of texture and pattern was used to complement the architect or interior designer's choice of wall colours, veneers, and other decorative finishes. This trend was manifest in buildings where strict adherence to Modern Movement principles was desired. However, in most homes some definite pattern could be detected and became increasingly apparent by the middle of the decade with a number of writers celebrating its return. Eileen Hunter in an article of 1935, 'The Return of Pattern' commented that the vogue for restraint had been overdone and that a possible reason for the reluctance of architects and interior decorators to employ printed patterns was that few designers really understood the possibilities and limitations of pattern design.[26] Committed Modernists would only accept limited pattern, but their concerns influenced the direction of general discussions on the appropriateness of particular types of pattern for specific purposes. The justification for pattern was related to the need for relief from the perceived severity of the Modern Movement home. Most manufacturers recognised the psychological need for pattern and colour and produced fabrics accordingly. Even Alastair Morton, a committed Modernist conceded that:

Most people are not yet sensitive to abstract forms though many are becoming so, and therefore they like fabrics that represent something with associations emphasising the character they want in their rooms.[27]

figure 10
The contemporary treatment of leaves (clockwise from top left): 'Silvan' by Ashley Havinden, a cotton and rayon weave for Edinburgh Weavers; 'Delos' a screen printed linen by Ashley Havinden for Old Bleach Linen; 'Pandora' a linen and rayon woven fabric with printed leaf design by Marion Dorn for Old Bleach Linen; 'Earlswood' cotton and rayon damask by Morton Sundour Fabrics. (*Studio Yearbook of Decorative Art*, 1938, p.42.)

He attempted to classify pattern according to mood, associating restfulness with the design of leaves and plant forms, while dignity could be achieved by using fabrics with patterns of pillars and wreaths. By the middle of the decade it was clear that earlier abstract and linear designs were beginning to be replaced by fabrics with a contemporary treatment of figurative motifs. *The Cabinet Maker* reported the views of several department store buyers in 1935 who all noted the increased popularity of leaf designs. C. W. Mountain of Brewis and Company in Leeds commented that:

As far as designs are concerned, there is a definite demand for all-over patterns; patterns with horizontal lines; herringbone designs; and also natural designs, including leaves and flowers. The latter appeal particularly because they are the very antithesis of the straight lines and angles of the modernist design, and so form a relieving contrast. Spots and checks, we find, do not sell well.[28]

Householders were advised as to the best methods of using pattern. It was generally agreed that large patterns were best used in large rooms as curtain fabrics, whereas smaller repeats should be used on furniture and in smaller rooms. An important consideration needed to be made in relation to whether particular patterns be used for upholstery where it would be seen stretched, used vertically, horizontally and pulled around corners, or whether it was going to be used as curtaining where draping qualities were a priority. The trend towards the contemporary treatment of natural motifs continued in the second half of the 1930s with designs of birds being particularly popular. Modern interpretations of leaves, birds and floral motifs could be seen in designs by Mea Angerer, Alec Hunter, Marion Dorn and Ashley Havinden. Patterns which incorporated classical architectural detail were also popular. Some manufacturers actively sought out modern designs, either because they saw it as a way of gaining commercial advantage over their competitors or because they honestly felt it was their duty to promote Modernism through their products. Many of the more enlightened firms, such as Edinburgh Weavers, believed that the best method of obtaining such designs was to employ the services of fine artists. Printing was felt to be an area where the fine arts would be most useful. Allan Walton commented on this in 1935:

Painting is much nearer to printing, and much of the flexibility of the painter can be used by the designer for print.[29]

This situation was aided by the development of hand-screen printing used commercially in Britain from the early thirties. The process was adopted by firms producing what could be classed as good modern designs. Its development allowed the possibility of the economical production of shorter lengths of fabric. It was cheaper than the two other methods available: machine roller printing and hand-block printing. The technique also provided greater scope for the artist's expression. The facility of hand-screen printing to reproduce fine lines and brush strokes led to designs which often emphasised painterly qualities. While in practice only a small number of artists were employed as free-lance designers by the industry, the attention they received from design journalists and the impact they had on modern design was significant. Allan Walton bought a number of designs from artists for production by his textile printing firm (established in 1931) including Cedric Morris, Vanessa Bell, Duncan Grant and Frank Dobson, while Old Bleach Linen consciously promoted their fabrics using the names of artists and better known free-lance designers.

Simple and appropriately designed fabrics and floor-coverings continued to be the choice of Modernist architects throughout the 1930s. Edinburgh Weavers launched their 'Constructivist' range of fabrics in 1937 as 'a conscious attempt to build a contemporary style in decoration in keeping with modern architecture

26. E. Hunter, 'The Return of Pattern', *Decoration in the English Home*, no.6, October 1935, p.16.
27. A. Morton, *Analysis of Fabric Designs – Character of Present Day Designs*, Personal Notes, Scottish Records Office, GD.326.164.
28. 'Tendencies in Fabric Design by Ten Well Known Buyers', *Cabinet Maker and Complete House Furnisher*, 4 May 1935, p.182.
29. Walton, *op.cit.*

and present-day culture generally'.[30] The designs were by Ben Nicholson, Ashley Havinden, Barbara Hepworth, Eileen Holding, Arthur Jackson and Winifred Dacre. The fabrics, woven and printed were the preferred choice of several architects and interior designers. In spite of the renewed interest in pattern and colour, propaganda from committed Modernists continued to appear. In 1939 Sadie Speight and Leslie Martin's *The Flat Book* was published as 'a useful catalogue of well-designed furniture and equipment'.[31] Their attempt to move away from an emphasis on fashion in furnishing towards 'convenience and efficiency' resulted in a discussion of function and simplicity. They recommended the use of hairtex, haircord or matting for all-over carpets and for fabrics they advised that choice should be based on material rather than solely by pattern or colour. Their emphasis on texture recalls the earlier advice of Todd, Mortimer and Herbert Read.

Textiles made a vital contribution to the modern home during the 1930s and their importance was highlighted in a comment made by James MacGibbon in 1938:

A pair of curtains at 30s. and a set of loose covers can change the character of a room. This cheapness encourages experiment which is ruled out when it comes to buying dining-room furniture and the inexplicable three-piece suite. Good design in the home is still an experiment for the majority. Fabrics are the only means of making it cheaply.[32]

But, the possibility they provided for quick and economical change, along with the opportunity of adding decorative interest presented Modernists with a seemingly intractable problem—how could one successfully incorporate components which had traditionally been regarded as the key method of keeping up with fashionable change, into schemes where the aim was to create a timeless rationality? This dichotomy occupied the minds of many during the 1930s and the resulting discussions meant that textiles enjoyed an unprecedented significance. Modernist commentators agreed that the right choice of textiles, including floor-coverings, could result in rooms which were 'made really convincing rather than vaguely modern'[33] and to some extent manufacturers and designers did provide suitable examples. However, demand for textiles continued to be dominated by a desire for a more traditional treatment of pattern, with many firms subsidising their contemporary production with the more popular conservative styles. Nevertheless, the 1930s will be remembered as a decade in which Modern Movement architecture dictated avant-garde developments in textile design; whether directly, as in fabrics which were subordinate to architecture, or indirectly as a means of providing relief in otherwise austere interiors.

30. A. Morton, Text of Speech Launching Edinburgh Weavers' Constructivist Fabrics, Scottish Records Office, GD.326.164.

31. S. Speight & L. Martin, *The Flat Book*, (London, 1939), p.4.

32. J. MacGibbon, 'Fabrics in Interior Decoration', *Architectural Review*, vol.LXXXVIII, 1939, p.176.

33. J. B. Iles, 'The Beauty of Modern Fabrics', *Studio*, vol.LXXXVI, 1939, p. 182.

figure 11
An illustration of a room in Speight and Martin's *The Flat Book*, the floor-covering is Chinese rush matting and the chairs are upholstered in simple striped woven cloth.

Plastics and the Modern House

ANTHONY WALKER

Plastics and the Modern House

ANTHONY WALKER

T HE 'House of the Future' displayed at the 1928 Ideal Home Exhibition epitomised the increasing role plastics were to play in the building industry in the decade to come.[1] The internal and external walls, floors and some fittings consisted of thin sheets of a horny, tough material made of cellulose paint on plaster which were intended to simulate a material not yet available. Only five years later at the Chicago Exhibition in 1933 the Vinylite House was, apart from the plumbing, an all-plastics house.[2] In the 1938 Frankfurt Building Exhibition the total all-plastics house including the plumbing was on show.[3] In Britain by the beginning of the 1940s, an all-plastics house was planned by the government for a site in Scotland[4] and even such magazines as *Popular Mechanics* wrote of an all-plastic world with plastic houses, cars and aeroplanes.[5]

Thus by 1940, *Fortune* magazine could run a series of articles about the plastics industry and invent an imaginary continent, Synthetica made from all the varieties of plastic then known. Here was a new world that revealed the dichotomy of the role of plastics in the 1930s: at once both a utilitarian material, the means of controlled social stability and at the same time offering the more radical vision of a material capable of proliferating transformations.[6] The reality of the everyday use of plastics was somewhat different and the material had a complex and sometimes contradictory message. Associated with technological innovation in radios, gramophone records, electrical goods and the new film industry, plastics were also used as substitutes for expensive, increasingly rare natural materials such as ivory or jet with associations of luxurious and quality goods as well as plastic jewellery which was highly prized.[7] However the development of efficient moulding machinery in the late 1930s meant that the industry was suddenly open to a wide range of often inexperienced producers and suppliers. By the end of the decade the market was swamped with low cost products (as happened again after the War) largely responsible for the material's low quality image.

The boom of tailor-made plastics had been triggered by Hermann Staudinger unravelling the nature of polymers in the 1920s and work inspired by Carothers in the early 1930s on reactive groups to explain the fundamental differences between thermosetting and thermoplastic plastics. The fact that polymer molecules were different had been understood by the middle of the nineteenth century and in 1861 rubber, cellulose and proteins were classified as 'colloids' as opposed to sugar and salt which were termed 'crystalloids'. It was believed that the colloid molecules were large and the commonly accepted explanation was that they were clusters of molecules held together by an electrical or some other force. Staudinger, in the face of much opposition, developed the theoretical basis for very long macro molecules with molecular weights in hundreds of thousands or even millions. With this knowledge Carothers, as head of the Du Pont research laboratory from 1928 to his death in 1937, expounded the concept of functionality which explained the cross linking between these long chain molecules to produce either mouldable (thermoplastics) or rigid (thermosetting)

1. 'The House of the Future', *Ideal Home*, vol.XVII, March 1928, pp.240–1. For easy chairs inflatable rubber was proposed which could be deflated and rolled up when not in use. The architect was R. A. Duncan of Messrs Percy Tubbs, Son and Duncan.

2. J. G. Davidson and H. B. McClure. 'Applications of Vinyl Resins' Industrial and Engineering Chemistry, vol.XXV No.6, 1933, pp 645–652.

3. Professor Z. S. Makowski. 'Development of Plastics Houses', *The Uses of Plastics for Load Bearing and infill Panels*, September 1974, Symposium University of Surrey.

4. T. Warnett Kennedy 'The First All-Plastics House', *British Plastics and Moulded Products*, October 1941, p.138.

5. J P Leggett 'The Era of Plastics', *Popular Mechanics Magazine*, No.73, May 1940, pp.130A, 658.

6. Jeffery L. Meikle, 'Into the Fourth Kingdom: Representations of Plastic Materials 1920–1950', Journal of Design History, vol.5 No.3, 1992, p.175.

7. Robert Friedel, 'The First Plastic' in Penny Sparke ed., *The Plastics Age*, (London, Victoria and Albert Museum 1990), p.29.

figure 1
E. McKnight Kauffer's mural in the entrance hall, Embassy Court, Brighton (architect Wells Coates 1935).

polymers. With the advent of cheap raw materials as a by-product of the petroleum industry, this new understanding led to many new polymers for the building industry. Among these were: polymethyl methacrylite (acrylics) and polyethylene (polythene) in 1933; polyvinyl chloride (pvc) in 1935; polystyrene (including acronlonitrile, butadiene and styrene ABS) in 1937; polytetrafluorethylene (ptfe) and polymide (nylon) in 1938.

The British Plastics Moulding Trade Association had been established in 1929 and the Plastics Institute in 1931. In this new industry, building was undoubtedly seen as a market with a large potential. Some architects recognised the material's unique qualities. Raymond McGrath declared, after seeing Gropius's use of Trolit in the German Pavilion at the 1930 Paris Exposition de la Société des Artistes Decorateurs that the possibilities were at once obvious.[9] McGrath was

figure 2
A 1930s Bakelite lamp wall fitting
(Sylvia Katz Collection).

instrumental in promoting Beatl, a urea formaldehyde sheet, which was first used for the dado in several of the recording studios at Broadcasting House. It was a substitute for Trolit which was excluded under a ban on the use of any foreign materials. Grey Wornum was certainly an advocate of plastics and on numerous occasions lectured on their virtues.[10] In 1939, Brian O'Rorke, having already used simulated wood laminates, approached Warerite to manufacture the first decorative laminate. It encapsulated a cartoon by Nicholas Bentley, the forerunner of many original works in the post-war era.[11] By 1934 an article had

LIVING ROOM   KITCHEN

BAKELITE TOP

SLIDING HATCH   SHELF

SINK

CUPBOARDS

section.

recess for pulling table from kitchen

8. Sylvia Katz *Classic Plastics*, (London, Thames and Hudson 1985), p.12.

9. *Architects' Journal*, vol.LXXIV, Nov.4 1931, p.598.

10. *Builder*, vol.CXLIX, Nov. 15 1935, p.840. In a lecture to the Society of Chemical Industry Wornum graphically demonstrated the potential of the material although there were still many shortcomings.

11. Warerite had only been established three years earlier and were eager to get into the building market but was experiencing difficulties in interesting architects. O'Rorke first approached Bakelite who turned the job down but recommended Warerite who after considerable experiments with different inks eventually found a means of reproducing the cartoon. (From a taped discussion between St John Brecknell, sales manager of Warerite at the time and Percy Reboul, chairman of the Plastics Historical Society.)

12. *British Plastics and Moulded Products Trader* April 1934 pp.520–1.

13. *Builder*, vol.CXLVIII, 18 January 1935, p.150.

14. *Architect and Building News*, vol.CLIV, 15 April 1938, p.77.

15. Amelia Clough 'Changes in Kitchen and Scullery', *Ideal Home*, vol.XXXI, No.I, January 1935, p.27.

been published illustrating laminate surfaces for kitchen and bathroom worktops, walls and ceilings and claiming that the somewhat high cost was justified by durability, ease of cleaning (due to fewer joints) and increased hygiene.[12]

The next year during the discussion following a lecture by Mr Owen-Griffiths at the Architectural Association in 1935, Wornum took the view that the main opportunities for plastics lay in wall linings.[13] H. V. Potter, managing director of Bakelite, reported that there was resistance from some architects to using Bakelite sheets in bathrooms and kitchens because the thin Bakelite laminate needed a backing sheet usually of plywood which architects were nervous of using in a wet environment. This put the laminates at a disadvantage against Vitrolite and glazed asbestos[14] both of which were self-supporting and strongly advocated by magazines such as *The Ideal Home*.[15]

Bakelite, one of the first synthetic resins, was patented by Leo Baekeland in 1907 when he perfected a method of achieving a moulding powder based on phenol formaldehyde which was to become a household name as Bakelite,

16. 'In and Out of Broadcasting House', *Listener*, 20 July 1932, p.88.

17. Anthony Bertram, *Design*, (Harmondsworth, Penguin Books 1938), p.43.

18. 'Laminated Material at the Ideal Home Exhibition', *British Plastics and Moulded Products Trader*, June 1932, p.14. Report on heat resistant Bakelite finish for furniture. 'Blisterproof veneers', *Architect and Building News*, vol.CLIV, 13 May 1938, p.193.

19. W. Blakey, 'Plastics for Furniture' in V. E. Yarsley ed., *Plastics Applied*, (London, The National Trade Press, 1945), p.147.

20. *Architect and Building News*, vol.CLIV, 15 April 1938, p.77.

21. First used as moulding powders in 1926 and then in the 1930s for the top surface of high pressure laminates.

22. Sylvia Katz, *Plastics*, (London, Studio Vista 1978), pp 62 & 66. Urea is more susceptible to moisture than the Phenol resins and while Bakelite was successfully used for draining boards in dark colours, the light urea formaldehyde resins crazed.

23. F. R. S. Yorke, 'Details', *Architectural Review*, vol.LXXII, August 1932, p.65. Yorke reported '... a laminated sheet made from white paper impregnated with a liquid synthetic resin obtainable in almost any colour but never before manufactured as a wall covering. I understand, however, that since its inception at Broadcasting House it has become a standard product.'

24. Bandalasta catalogue, pp.2 & 4. Bandalasta is described as being made not of celluloid or milk but from a new resin, Beatl, synthetically produced under British Patents and from British materials. When taken from the mould it was polished and claimed to show an almost unlimited range of patterns. It could easily be maintained and, if necessary, re-polished using a metal polish but if broken cannot be repaired. Several other manufacturers were producing similar products including Lanarkite and Catlin both of which are claimed to have properties similar to Bandalasta and used to make various fittings for bathrooms and door furniture.

Warerite or Formica. It had a limited colour range but was widely used in plain blacks and browns, sometimes with rich mottling, as mouldings for light fittings, lavatory seats and a range of other household fittings. First developed in sheet form as a high pressure laminate for industrial and electrical insulation the early blacks and browns with their glossy lustre complemented the chrome streamlined image of the late 1920s and early 1930s[16] and was used both for built-in and free-standing furniture for which it provided exquisite glittering shapes exploiting the conjunction of stainless steel and dark plastic.[17]

A drawback to the Bakelite laminates was their poor heat resistance which meant that a lighted cigarette could leave a burn mark. By the mid-1930s this had been overcome by incorporating an aluminium foil just below the surface of the laminate to dissipate the heat[18] which led to a wide use of the material in cruise liners and for furniture, where it was considered to be a high quality material.[19] Laminate-faced plywoods were sometimes used with intricate inlays of different coloured laminates[20] or metals.

The restricted colours of phenol formaldehyde-based laminates proved an obstacle to their general acceptance for domestic use but one that was overcome with the advent of urea formaldehydes[21] which, while less durable,[22] were clear, colourless and, with the aid of fillers and dyes, produced a wide variety of patterns and colours. By the mid-1930s these transparent resins were used for the top layer of high pressure laminates allowing patterned and light coloured sheets to be incorporated in the surface. Urea formaldehyde was also introduced in sheet form as wall linings in 1932 and F. R. S. Yorke refers to them being widely available.[23] The main use of urea and thioureas in the home however was for mouldings, for example kitchen utensils and the Bandalasta range of bathroom fittings which was described as being available in a variety of beautiful marbled and pastel shades capable of withstanding rougher treatment than china or glass.[24]

Celluloid – cellulose nitrate – one of the earliest of the semi-synthetic polymers, had been in use from the middle of the 19th century and became synonymous with the motion picture where it had justified its reputation for being inflammable with frequent projection room fires. Celluloid collars and cuffs or hair combs had a tendency to ignite if too close to a fire. Fortunately this was not a problem with cellulose paints and it was probably in this form, produced by the new manufacturers such as Nobel Chemical Finishes (later to become ICI), that the greatest use was made of polymers in housing. Plastic paints were promoted for their ability to provide a textured finish by being tooled to any pattern required before hardening.[25]

The growing popularity of synthetic resins for coatings of various types is illustrated by the addition of a chapter on plastic paints in the second edition of *Painting from A–Z*, published in 1938.[26] Resin-based paints were seen as being quick-drying and with increased durability.[27] In 1933 Dulux had announced, under a heading of New Organic Chemicals, a white enamel which it was claimed had novel properties for house decoration.[28] Cellulose resins were particularly recommended for glazing relief decorations where their flexibility removed the risk of cracking[29] and clear formaldehyde resins were used as lacquer coatings for brass and other decorative metals. Sir James Swinburne, beaten by one day by Baekeland in registering a patent for a phenol-formaldehyde moulding material, had greater success in developing a protective resin coating which he named Damard, thereby proclaiming its hard durable nature. He established a factory in Birmingham to be close to the brass industry, his main market.[30]

McKnight Kauffer's mural in the entrance hall of Embassy Court, Brighton by Wells Coates is probably one of the most unusual uses of a polymer in housing. The technique was reported in 1936 as a coating of resin containing a light-sensitive material onto which an image was projected and the surface was then fixed and washed by means of a spray gun.[31] It was marketed as a means of obtaining instant decorative effects at low cost.

Various experiments were made with rubber paints to increase elasticity and paint flow but there were problems with the increased drying time.[32] Nevertheless, they had certain benefits in obviating brush marks and in improving pigment suspension. Rubber had wider uses as a flooring material in tile or sheet form often as a coating to an asbestos core or as an under-surface to mats and loose rugs. It was seen as offering advantages of permanence, economy in use, noise absorption[33] and hygiene[34] and was even used for draining boards.[35]

figure 4
Bathroom fittings from the 1937
Bandalasta catalogue (*Sylvia Katz Collection*).

25. James Lawrence.*Painting from A–Z*, (Manchester, The Sutherland Publishing Co. 1938), p.313.

26. *Painting from A–Z*. First published in 1935.

27. *Ideal Home*, vol.XXXIII, January 1936, p.7.

28. *Architectural Record of Design and Construction*, vol.IV, No.7, May 1934, p.242.

29. *Painting from A–Z*, p.30.

30. Originally founded as the Fireproof Celluloid Company to find a substitute for cellulose nitrates and named as the Damard Lacquer Company in 1910, the company had been started by Sir James Swinburne to find a substitute for celluloid. In the late 1920s it was taken over by Bakelite to form the UK company and the main offices were lined with Bakelite laminates with skirtings, architraves and dado rails all formed with Birds Eye Maple patterns and installed with a complex system of secret fixings.

31. *Architects' Journal*, vol.LXXXIII, 19 March 1936, pp.463 & 464.

32. *Painting from A–Z*, pp.344–354.

33. Joan Wollacombe 'You need not have a Noisy House', *Ideal Home*, vol.XXXII, October 1935, p.249. The Cullum sound-proofing system used rubber pads to isolate the floor battens from the structural concrete slab.

34. *Ideal Home*, vol.XXXI, January 1935, p.27. Tiles had a wide range of colours and were quite rigid with an asbestos core and rubber coating. Rubber sheet was also available but was not as durable. *Architectural Record of Design and Construction*, November, vol.VII, No.I, 1936, p.33. Redfern publicity material suggests that rubber floors offered the advantages of permanence, economy in use, appearance, silence and hygiene.

35. *Architectural Record of Design and Construction*, vol.VII, No.10, August 1937, p.383. The Cellular Steel Residence, Altadena, California by Richard Neutra. A 12 ft long white rubber draining board.

36. *Ideal Home*, vol.XXXIII, February 1936, p.138.

37. *British Plastics and Moulded Products Trader*, December 1932, p.276.

Many of the new plastics provided opportunities to produce transparent and translucent materials. Cellophane was promoted as a material to provide a clear protective film for table tops[36] as well as glazing for green houses.[37] Acrylics were proposed for lay lights and in common with many other plastics (including casein and the formaldehydes) were used for lamp shades and fittings.

Synthetic materials incorporating polymers[38] were used for curtains and upholstery and towards the end of the 1930s Nylon was discovered. Some of these were new fibres woven alone or in combination to make cloth with new properties and others used resins to treat natural materials to improve their performance. Artificial leathercloths now made their appearance and ICI promoted their new Rexine material as a wall covering as well as for upholstery in a booklet entitled *A Collection of Designs for Domestic and Commercial Interiors*, 1938. A series of designs by leading architects of the day were used to illustrate the materials' design qualities and versatility.[39]

Probably the greatest growth in the use of plastics went unnoticed. Towards the end of the decade a means of using synthetic resins for bonding ply veneers had been found: a thin paper impregnated with resin was produced in 1918 but it was not until the 1920s that a phenolic film suitable for plywood manufacture was produced. Initially this was very expensive and only used for special applications such as aircraft and boat building. Widespread use at reasonable prices did not occur until the end of the 1930s when the first waterproof ply sheets were available as a backing to Mr Potter's Bakelite laminates.[40] Other uses of plastics included casein, phenolic and urea formaldehydes for door furniture and similar applications, rubber and gutta percha insulation for electrical and telephonic cables, and rubber and neoprene door seals.

By the end of the 1930s the range of plastics used in housing had expanded dramatically. The plain dark laminates had been developed into a wider range of colours and patterns and with Warerite's first laminated drawing for the Coronation Scot and Bakelite's announcement of a photographic process to implant images on laminates just before World War II,[41] the industry was poised for a major expansion when hostilities broke out. This delayed the development of decorative laminates but stimulated the development of other plastic products such as glass fibre polyesters for radomes, polythene and pvc cable insulation, inflatable structures and silicones.[42] The growing significance of plastics in the home during the 1930s set the scene for the explosion of uses after the War when, accelerated by the shortages of natural materials and the over abundance of plastics in an industry geared up for the war effort, they were seen as the obvious materials for fitted kitchens, vanitory units and an unforeseen variety of new applications.

38. A common example is Rayon, a cellulose acetate, developed as a result of excess production capacity after the First World War.

39. *Architectural Record of Design and Construction*, vol.VIII No 7, July 1938, p.261. Rexine being marketed as a special material for interior decoration. The catalogue shows designs by Raymond McGrath, F. R. S. Yorke, E Maxwell Fry, H. St John Harrison, Julian Leathart and G. Grey Wornum

40. Andrew Dick Wood and Thomas Gray Linn. *Plywoods*, London, W. & A. K. Johnston 1942, pp.83–4.

41. *Architectural Record of Design and Construction*, vol.IX No.3, March 1939, p.91

figure 5
Design by Grey Wornum for a hotel lounge and bar by Grey Wornum from the 1938 Rexine catalogue.

7 Interview with Elisabeth Benjamin

LYNNE WALKER

Interview with Elisabeth Benjamin

LYNNE WALKER

THE entry of women in substantial numbers into the architectural profession is one of the most significant developments in 20th century architecture although often ignored by historians. A growing number of women students attended schools of architecture at universities, polytechnics and art schools, but the opening of the Architectural Association to women during the First World War was a crucial step in providing access to architectural education for many of the most able, and later, most prominent practitioners.

As well as systematic training, the AA provided networks of friends and contacts, a professional ethos, and a sense of being at the centre of contemporary ideas in architecture, in the socially approved surroundings of a private architectural school which was thought appropriate in terms of women students' gender and class.

Like many women of her generation at the AA, Elisabeth Benjamin was an only child from a liberal-minded progressive family which encouraged her architectural interests. Her parents were Jewish: her mother, Elizabeth Abadi, a suffragette, and her father, Alfred Benjamin, an entrepreneurial businessman. collector and designer of pottery. Rose Elisabeth Benjamin was born 7 December 1908 in London and educated at St Paul's School where her childhood desire to be an architect was actively discouraged. After living in Paris for six months (1925) and a stint at art school in St John's Wood (1926), she attended the Architectural Association (1927–32) where her most important encounter was with Godfrey Samuel (1904–82), a fellow student and later a founder-member of Tecton. Her time at the AA was the defining architectural experience for Elisabeth Benjamin who imbibed 'advanced' Continental aesthetics and social concerns along with the standard Beaux-Arts course. Perhaps surprisingly for a budding modernist, she spent her year out in Lutyens' office (1932–3) where she detailed mouldings, with the help of Batty Langley, and was given small jobs, such as a dining room screen for HH the Gaekwar of Baroda's palace, New Delhi, to shield his wives and a column for the Midland Bank in the City, as well as, more substantially, working up a design by Lutyens for the font for the crypt of Liverpool Cathedral.

First working from home in Golders Green (30 Hocroft Road, London, NW2) and then from an office at 42 South Moulton Street in London, Elisabeth Benjamin set up on her own at the height of the Depression. On the left politically, she kept going through this difficult period, joining the MARS Group;[2] sharing an office with Enid Albu, an interior decorator and entering competitions, for instance, the Timber House Competition of 1935, with Godfrey Samuel.[3] Aware of political events in Germany, Elisabeth Benjamin became involved, again with Godfrey Samuel and others (from 1932), in the rescue of a school of German children who were removed to the safety of England. Under Samuel's direction, the buildings for the New Herrlingen School[4] in Otterden, Kent, were sited informally around a country house with huts and other outbuildings (1932; extended 1939), including a sanatorium which Elisabeth Benjamin and Samuel designed.[5] In the mid 1930s, Elisabeth Benjamin designed three modernist

1. I am most grateful to Elisabeth Benjamin for her generous co-operation during our two conversations (March & April 1995) and for the good humour and patience with which she handled all my enquiries. Unfortunately, most of her papers were destroyed by bombing during the war, but some photographs, which she kindly made available for this article, survive in her possession. In addition, there is pertinent material in the Godfrey Samuel Papers in the British Architectural Library Manuscripts & Archives Collection (especially SaG\8\6 and 9\1–4), BAL Photographs Collection (see Samuel & Harding) and in the BAL Drawings Collection.

2. Godfrey Samuel Papers, MSS & Archives, op. cit., SaG\ 91\1.

3. SaG\8\6 MSS & Archives, ibid and, BAL Drawings Collection.

4. Emigré German architects and architectural students participated in this project including Eugen C. Kaufmann (b.1892) EB's collaborator for 55 Victoria Drive Wimbledon: for biographical details of Kaufmann see Thirties: British Art and Design Before the War, (London: Arts Council, 1979), p.294. For further information about the school, see especially SaG\62\1 &3 and 63\1, BAL MSS & Archives, op. cit.

5. Information from Elisabeth Benjamin.

figure 1
Elisabeth Benjamin, 1936.

houses (or more exactly two houses and additions and alterations to an earlier house) of striking coherence and freshness: No.1, Fitzroy Park, Highgate for Dr. Edith Summerskill,[6] 1934; 55 Victoria Drive, Wimbledon (demolished), for her father's partner, Mr Kaufmann, 1934–5, with the experienced and peripatetic, Eugen C. Kaufmann[7] and the 'St. George and Dragon House' (formally known as East Wall) Hedgerley Lane, Gerrards Cross, Buckinghamshire, 1936–7, with Godfrey Samuel.[8]

In 1937, Elisabeth Benjamin married Gunter Nagelschmidt (1906–1981), a mineralogist, and left architectural practice to have a family. Her intention to return to architecture after motherhood was however overtaken by events. The birth of two daughters (Virginia b.1939 and Lucy b.1941), the war and a move en famille to Cornwall (1945–9) and Derbyshire (1949–79) took her far from the centre of architectural culture in London. Like many architects of her generation, including her great friend, Godfrey Samuel, restarting practice in London after the long break of the war was not possible. Her position was compounded of course by her role as a traditional wife and mother, caring for a growing family and committed to following her husband, even to the detriment of her own career. Nevertheless, she continued to work as an architect in the immediate postwar period for the St Austell's Brewery (1946–9), albeit restricted by shortages to design and decoration, rather than building. At this time, she also did a number of domestic jobs for friends, such as a conversion of a barn to cottage in Hathersage, Derbyshire, for Mrs. Singleton. After her husband's death, she returned to London, and although work was occasional and sometimes on a volunteer basis, she came back to the social architecture which had occupied her as a member of the MARS Group in the 1930s. She worked as a consultant for the Catholic Housing Association (a forerunner of Shelter), until she was forced to give up by the RIBA who found her volunteer status unacceptable, and as an adviser on public buildings and disabled access to St Albans Council in 1982.

Now living in Hampstead, Elisabeth Benjamin remains an avid participant in the London cultural scene and still designs when called on (most recently, a granny flat for her daughter in Cobham, 1995).

The period of Elisabeth Benjamin's most active architectural production was intensely creative but brief and truncated by family responsibilities and the war, and her later work, although socially useful, was less central to architectural developments which historians normally value. But clearly architecture, both in theory and practice, is the thread which runs through her life, as the interview which follows confirms.

LW: *You were born in 1908 and by the First World War you had decided to become an architect! What made you take that precocious decision?*

EB: My father was in the army and we moved a lot following the regiment about. We lived in so many furnished houses. I became interested in houses. I can never remember when I wasn't interested in architecture. I was more interested in building bricks than playing with dolls.

LW: *Were either of your parents interested in architecture?*

EB: Both my parents were interested in their own house design. And I remember my mother saying when we were in a particularly inconveniently furnished house, 'I think it would be a good idea if you were an architect. We need women architects because they understand cupboards.' My father was a manufacturer who was interested in design. He did a certain amount of designing pottery himself. He was a collector of porcelain and Persian carpets. He had a very good eye; he was a fine collector who knew what was what.

LW: *What did your parents think of you becoming an architect?*

EB: My parents always supported me, but at St Paul's, I got very little support. The reaction of the High Mistress was horror-utter horror. It is quite different

6. *Architectural Review*, vol.LXXVIII, Nov. 1935, pp.203–204; and vol.LXXXIII, Dec. 1937, pp.250–251.

7. *Architectural Review*, vol.LXXXVIII, Sept. 1935, pp.127–129; vol.LXXX, Dec.1936, pp.259–260; F. R. S. Yorke, *The Modern House in England*, (London: Architectural Press, 1937), pp.40–41; and Jeremy Gould, *Modern Houses in Britain 1919–1939*, (London: Society of Architectural Historians of Great Britain, 1977), p.52 fig.16; pl.25 & 26.

8. Yorke, op.cit. pp.131–133, and Gould, op. cit. p.38; pl.4G. Set of blueprints in BAL Drawings Collection. Exhibited *Women Architects: Their Work*, RIBA, 1984, ex catalogue.

now for children who are interested in this sort of thing but in those days they weren't at all. They had a very mouldy studio where we were taught drawing – autumn leaves in autumn, daffodils in spring – that was just about it. The head-mistress wanted me to go to Oxford or Cambridge, just to be a statistic, and read Modern Languages which I was interested in. She was horrified that I became an architect.

LW: *You then went to Paris.*

EB: I wanted to learn French and I had some cousins who lived in the city. I was intoxicated by Paris. I went for six weeks and after six months my parents had to come and get me back by the scruff of my neck. I was very lucky in that my cousin was engaged to the composer Charles Tournemire who knew about art, and he taught me how to walk about Paris and see a great deal. It was a magnificent trip. I went to a very good series of lectures on the Impressionists at the Caillebotte Collection in the Luxembourg. I was very lucky because the man who gave the lectures also taught one how to look – how to look at pictures it was a revelation to me. I went to the part of the Sorbonne where they taught foreigners, and I did go to a lot of galleries and the different collections. We walked all over the place. I thought Paris was blindingly beautiful.

LW: *You were eighteen when you returned from Paris and went to art school.*

EB: I went to St John's Art School for six months before I went to the AA. This was a useful experience because in those days when you started your architectural education, you started straight away training to be a draftsman. But I started off learning to draw – free-hand drawing which I was lucky enough to do before I went to the AA. I can see that this is a good approach.

LW: *You started at the AA in 1927. Who was in your year?*

EB: All the Tecton people. Godfrey Samuel, Val Harding, Dugdale, Chitty, Skinner. We were all in that year. There were 60 men and four women. I was very close to a woman called Pamela Jackson, who married Raymond Erith, who was a very good architect, not a modernist but extremely competent. Mary Crowley, who became very well-known particularly for her schools later on, worked enormously hard. Whereas we at the beginning of a three week project might spend a lot of time at the cinema and work like mad at the end, she worked like mad all the time. Zoe Maw was also in my year.

LW: *Who were the members of staff who were important to you or whose teaching made an impression on you?*

EB: Louis de Soissons was there when I was there. I don't remember much about the staff really. Grey Wornum I think ...

LW: *Many people who went to the AA would say that they taught each other. Would you agree with that?*

EB: Yes, I was especially influenced by the work of the (later) Tecton group [Godfrey Samuel, Val Harding, Anthony Chitty, Lindsey Drake, Francis Skinner and Michael Dugdale]. We did a lot of talking. When we had a project for three weeks, we would play about for the first week and sketch a little bit and then by the end we would work terrifically hard and work all night with the gramophone and bottles of beer. That was our way of working. We were all very influenced by and excited by Le Corbusier and Gropius. We were very excited by *Vers une Architecture*. We all joined the MARS Group. We did a lot of work on housing. Once a year at the Building Exhibition we used to do a project. We were of course great advocates of high-rise, cordially backed up by sociologists.

LW: *What ideas attracted you to Modernism?*

EB: In an idealistic way, the sweeping away of the unnecessary old rubbish of the past. We were very minimalist in outlook. We thought the world needed a clean sweep and we were going to clean sweep the architectural bit of it.

LW: *Was there a connection there between social conditions and the ideas you had about the Modern Movement in Architecture?*

EB: Yes I know people were very tough on us about the high-rise, but we did consult sociologists. We were not as naive as all that. I suppose our approach comes from our reading of Corbusier and our talking to Corbusier – the idea that this was the way of getting higher density on land that was available. It wasn't really until they were built and inhabited that one could see that they didn't work. And then they didn't work because they were not properly serviced. We were very idealistic. We were very left-wing. It all went together. We thought with any luck communism would be the redemptive feature. Everything seemed to be very clear cut.

LW: *It seemed like you could make this happen as an architect?*

EB: That's right. We could be part of it, providing better housing conditions for people, not necessarily what they wanted but a little bit of persuading them to want what we thought they would ultimately like.

LW: *There was the social programme of modernism, which you have described, but there was also the visual, aesthetic side of the movement. How did those things go together, or not?*

EB: I think very much so. Clearing away unnecessary features, going for good shapes, good proportions, simple lines. We were very minimalist, influenced very much by the Bauhaus of course. We were very left wing. In my year, it would have been unusual not to be left wing. We wanted to clean up the world and architecture was a part of that. We wanted to be very cosmopolitan. This was very much a cosmopolitan movement. Everyone doing the same thing at last. A kind of feeling ... we had a great desire for world unity. We wanted to clean up the universe, a lovely clean sweep.

LW: *Was it this joint programme of the social programme and the aesthetics of modernism that attracted you? Do you remember any specific instance of when you decided this is how I want to design – this is the approach I want to take to architecture?*

EB: No, it grew over how we worked together and how we talked together. And certainly for me, I was very friendly with Godfrey Samuel and I was friendly with the MARS people I was perhaps influenced by them. We all seemed to be having the same ideas at the same time.

LW: *After the AA, you spent a year in Lutyens office.*

EB: That was interesting really. At the end of your course you had to have a year in an office. My uncle had been Mayor of Westminster and had commissioned Lutyens to build those stripy flats. He was friendly with Lutyens and he got me into his office. He was a great architect and I think I learned a lot from being with him because even if I didn't necessarily like all of his designs, he was so meticulous. He was so careful. If two roofs came together, he wouldn't have a valley gutter. There had to be special tiles made to take up the valley. He set a very high standard.

LW: *What did you work on in Lutyens' office?*

EB: What happened was there was a big house just off Eaton Square. Lutyens sat in the top and we all had offices down below. There were 30 of us, something like that, working there. He would send down a little scrap of drawing on a little bit of tracing paper and they turned this into a design. And then we got Batty Langley books of mouldings which were the mouldings he liked, and we could see roughly the kind of shapes he wanted and we would translate it. And I, in fact, did the font in Liverpool Cathedral, which may have been built – I don't know. And I did a column in the Midland Bank in the City. I mean it was a ridiculous way of working in a way but it was good experience. Another thing I did, which shocked my daughters who are rather feminist, was Maharajah Baroda's palace that he was building at the time. I had to design the screen that the harem had to hide behind to look through to see their husbands dining down below. It was just the end of his Delhi period. It was very good experience.

LW: *In our earlier correspondence, you write about what that experience meant and how you didn't find your modernist approach and Lutyens's work incompatible: 'I learnt a lot from*

Lutyens's unswerving insistence on quality and consistency in design. It never interfered with my wish to be a designer of my time and for my time, and I combined it with working with the MARS *Group. I feel strongly that one's taste should be able to embrace any form of excellence.'*

EB: He had a high regard for excellence. I tried to work on simple but good proportions. He was also very, very, meticulous, and in a simplistic way I tried to be meticulous too.

LW: *In your view, what are the connections between Classicism and Modernism?*

EB: A feeling for proportion. We pared down our work when we designed. It was very much a question of proportion and line which are classical concerns.

LW: *You mentioned your daughters' feminism. Was part of your agenda womens' achievement and advancement in the 1930s? Would you have said you were a feminist at that time?*

EB: I don't think specially. My mother was a Suffragette. My daughters are now very feminist. I was interested in politics in general. I was rather left wing at the time [a member of the Liberal Party]. In fact, I don't like a division between the sexes.

LW: *You have called Tecton 'the backbone of the Modern Movement'. What did you particularly admire about them?*

EB: I did some work with the Tecton people, principally with Godfrey [Samuel]. I was very much in sympathy with their ideals and I think the whole concept was a very left wing concept. They wanted it to be a co-operative, a corporate effort as it were. It gradually faded out a bit after a year or two, the name of the architect who had actually brought that job in and who was primarily responsible for it was used. So it would be Val Harding and Tecton or Godfrey Samuel and Tecton or Skinner and Tecton or Chitty and Tecton or whatever it was. But they did work very much together. They had the same ideas. I didn't think at that time that Lubetkin was any more important than any of the others.

LW: *What was your first job after you set up on your own in South Moulton Street?*

EB: My first job was for Dr Edith Summerskill in Fitzroy Park, Highgate. Edith Summerskill was a member of a very left wing group of doctors and one of the other members of the group was a friend of mine who when he heard that she was looking for an architect; he recommended me. She saw herself as about to be a big figure in the left movement. She was a little bit of a Labour Mrs Thatcher. It had to be a great display. Part of this house, when they bought it, was two or three rooms on a lower level – they were more or less outhouses – we made that

figure 2
No.1, Fitzroy Park, Highgate, London, Dining Room, 1933–4 (from *Architectural Review*, November 1935, p.204).

figure 3
Plans, St. George and Dragon House
(East Wall), Hedgerley Lane, Gerrards
Cross, Buckinghamshire, 1935–6 (from
F. R. S. Yorke *The Modern House in
England*, 1937).

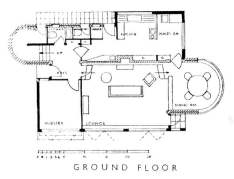

GROUND FLOOR

FIRST FLOOR

into a big sitting room. She wanted a staircase leading down and I had to put a mirror there so that she could look at herself before descending the staircase. She said, 'I am going to sweep down and all these people would be there, George Bernard Shaw etc etc.' Those things had to be rather dramatic, and the dining room had to be rather dramatic. She wanted this glass table and there was a bay window. I put a screen in front of it and white American cloth curtains at the back and lighting so that it had a kind of Japanese effect, when the light fell through. The screen really looked rather good at night when you pulled the yellow oilskins in the frame and with the light behind. She wanted it to look all rather spectacular. But it was so these dinner parties could be dramatic, these great dinner parties the Labour Party were to have. I had a pretty free hand and because she wanted to be so grand it was quite fun. I could do what I wanted.

LW: *Did you design any of the furnishings and fittings yourself?*

EB: Yes, the built-in cupboards and bookcases I designed, and the dining room table.

LW: *In your view, the Gerrards Cross house was 'in every way a better design as architecture; it was a much more imaginative and cohesive design', although you conceded that 'it may have looked less attractive in the photos'. How was it cohesive?*

EB: Godfrey and I thought very much a long the same lines – very much. We worked very closely together. In fact, we sort of sat on either side of the fireplace and tossed ideas at each other. The whole thing came together without any problems. Godfrey had an office in the Haymarket [and he could walk over to South Moulton Street where EB had her office]. The great thing was that we had this wonderful client [Arnold Osorio]. He was a paint manufacturer [Ripolin]. He said that he had seen so many houses fail by clients interfering: 'I am not going to interfere at all and let you have absolute carte blanche. I have seen your other work and I like it and I know it will be a better thing if I don't interfere.' The ideal job! We really had a wonderful time on it. To us, the central underlying theme was of St George and the Dragon. We called it the St George and Dragon House. The dragon being the sinuous brick wall always laid bare and constructed of blue sewer bricks, and St George was the rigid white concrete structure bestriding it. As our client was a Director of Ripolin we were able to be very lavish with the paint. In my view, it held together much better as a concept than the Wimbledon house which ended up a bit of a compromise. Also, it was, I think, one of the earliest examples of reinforced concrete domestic structure and was innovatory in that we used cork to line the inner shuttering and left it in situ as insulation, which proved effective.

LW: *What were the advantages of using reinforced concrete for domestic architecture?*

EB: It enabled one to have so much more elasticity in design – much more. You felt that the world was your oyster and you could do absolutely anything in both plan and elevation. It is very important that the house has got to be an entity. [However] we liked the idea of having two kinds of material, and with brick we could have this fluid [line/structure] moving through this white structure with columns which would only have been possible with reinforced concrete. We tried to be imaginative or perhaps we just were imaginative, we hoped. Wherever there was brick it was left plain, it wasn't painted. It was terribly important not to fudge it. We weren't fudging anything.

LW: *The recent photographs of the Gerrard's Cross house show some changes to its appearance and setting.*

EB: When we built it, it was in the middle of 2 or 3 acres of ground, which was a hazelnut grove. We just cleared the space and left the trees, but now it is surrounded by suburban houses. And they have put up these awful hedges which is quite wrong. You can see by the early photographs. It was very free. There was a lovely big space in front of it. And now the house is all covered in ivy which has rather spoilt St George. The hedges come up in inopportune places which rather spoil the design, especially the column at the end. The clients wanted a balcony. They wanted to be able to get out of their bedroom and sit on a balcony, and down below we had the dining room, where the dragon turned round. The balcony was above this and this was a kind of frame to the balcony.

LW: *Did you plan a garden?*

EB: There was just a big lawn because they had three children. We cut the hazelnut bushes right back at the front of the house. The whole idea was to have a lot of space.

LW: *All of your houses have a definite connection between interior and exterior spaces.*

EB: We worked at that. I think it is very important. The house should be a whole and seen as a whole.

figure 4
Dining room end, St. George and Dragon House (*John Somerset Murray*).

figure 5
First floor corridor, St. George and Dragon House (*John Somerset Murray*).

figure 6
Garden elevation, St. George and Dragon House. (*John Somerset Murray*).

[EB/LW *look at photograph of the kitchen.*]

EB: The all electric kitchen was blue which was thought to be a fly repellent colour by Mr. Osorio.

LW: *Did you design the tiles yourself*

EB: No, everything was off the peg.

LW: *Was this part of your idea about what a modern house should be?*

EB: Yes, especially since money was very tight. I mean the whole thing even in those days was built for £1200/1300, that wasn't a great deal.

LW: *Your second house which was in Wimbledon [now demolished] ,was done with Eugen Kaufmann? You were not as satisfied with it as your other work at this time, I understand?*

EB: The Wimbledon house has its qualities but I'm not very proud of it. The

figure 7
Garden view, 55 Victoria Drive,
Wimbledon, London, 1934–5
(Architectural Press).

Wimbledon house has now been pulled down. It was not reinforced concrete [but brick made to look like that material] it was a fudge altogether. It looked quite nice but I didn't feel any real affection for it.

LW: *Who were the clients for that house?*

EB: The client was my father's partner in the foundry business [Mr Kaufman], and he was a very difficult man. This is partly why it was so awful. He lived in the country and every day he came up to London by train. And every day he would meet someone who would have a different idea. He would ring me up and say 'I've got to have a sunken bath'. We had to lower the ceiling in one of the passages in order to sink the bath. Someone on the train had said that you really must have a sunken bath.

LW: *At Wimbledon did you design built-in furniture?*

EB: Yes, we did. We built-in some bookcases and the walls were lined with wood. We designed that. We designed quite a good through cupboard from the dining room to the kitchen so that you could put the crockery backward and forwards.

LW: *One of the things that is often said about modernist architecture is that it looks wonderful in photographs in the building press, but how do you live in such a perfectly designed everything. What did you have in mind for the use of your buildings? How did you want to see them used. Did you imagine the inhabitants adding the ordinary clutter of everyday life to them or were you hoping that they would keep it in a more pristine state'?*

EB: I was hoping they kept it in a more pristine state. The Osorios did. They consulted us on the furniture that they bought, and on the curtains and so on. Naturally they kept it like that. The Kaufmann house was completely spoilt with pelmets and very fussy furniture, overstuffed chairs.

LW: *What was the division of labour in terms of how you worked between you and your two architectural partners?*

EB: Godfrey and I worked very closely. I can't say who had which idea. Perhaps he had more than I did. We were very good friends all our lives. We had very much the same ideas and there was never any difficulty.[9] With Kaufmann, he was quite an established architect. He had worked in Russia; he had worked in Germany. He was a refugee. It was my first job after Edith Summerskill. For instance, he liked the windows to be fairly regular on the balcony that went round and he said they needed to be lower 'for that shall be the children's room and the children need to look out'. In actual fact they didn't have any children. I didn't like that. I didn't feel that it was my house much really. Some of the ideas of the house were very good. The conservatory running round two sides of the house was, I think, a fine feature.

LW: *What was the connection to your way of thinking between these houses designed for individual clients and social housing? With your social ideals did you see the smaller houses in any way as a model for larger schemes for housing the working classes? Did you see these little houses as a prototype?*

EB: Only in so far as we hoped if we had the chance of working in the social field we would have the same ideals of design: of simplicity, good proportion and a peaceful background to people's lives. For council houses, we were very much concerned that the parlour was hardly ever used, except when grandma came round. We tried to inculcate the idea that extra living space was preferable. We did put forward ideas for designing council houses that would make them more modernistic in feeling – more open and more peaceful.

LW: *Were they put forward through the* MARS *Group exhibition?*

EB: Yes, that was our way of putting them through.

LW: *In the* MARS *New Homes for Old Exhibition, held in the New Burlington Galleries in 1938, which Elizabeth Denby organised, every name in British architecture at that time, Arup, Breuer, Wells Coates, et al, was with you in that enterprise.*

EB: It was very much a co-operative thing. We were there talking all night, having ideas, everybody was working. Everybody pitched in with ideas. Higher density by having high rise, we were all interested in that.

LW: *Did you see the war coming?*

EB: Very much, we were very aware politically and being Jewish, we were very involved in what was going on in Germany. Godfrey and I did a lot of work when we brought this school over. We did that in association with Lady Reading and Victor Gollancz. We felt we wanted to do something to help and it was a good idea to help the children. I was very friendly with Godfrey's sister Nancy. We all talked about it and found an empty house [Bunce Court, Otterden, Kent] and we were thinking about how we could buy it and how we could raise funds for it. I was on a job one day and Nancy rang me up and said come quick I've got a woman with a school and I went up to the Samuel's house, and she had got together the

9. On reading the text of this interview. Elisabeth Benjamin wished to add: 'The Gerrards Cross design was as much Godfrey's invention as mine – but with great generosity he wanted it to be attributed to me the client was my friend.' In Yorke (op. cit.), for instance, the house is credited solely to EB.

10. One of the children was the painter,
Frank Auerbach.

committee. There was this extraordinary woman, Anna Essinger, who was very cross-eyed which she used to enormous advantage because you could never pin her down. She said, 'I've got a school of 30/40 children, either Jewish or half Jewish who were having a terrible time, seeing their parents taken away and so on, and I've got to bring them to England.' In a couple of hours she had persuaded us. We had no way out. We just said all right; we'll do it. I stayed on to dinner at the Samuels. And Gollancz who had sat in the corner and not said anything much, rang up and said he would guarantee it financially. So then Godfrey and I found the house in Kent and brought over the school. We built a sanatorium which was quite good. It was very simple. We had a lot of wood available and we used it. The headmistress was very compassionate, and she said that children at boarding school get so on top of each other that I would like to have separate rooms so that when it's not being used for children who are ill, it could be used by children who want to get away from the hubbub of the boarding school. They could go and have a quiet week-end there by themselves. It was divided into separate rooms. We orientated it so that the rooms all looked out over woodland away from the school itself. It was a very simple little building but sociologically it was very successful. We had a plan whereby the children were allowed to build wooden houses in the grounds of four or five acres so that they would have some place to come during the school holidays.[10]

LW: *You started architectural practice during the Depression and then just when you were getting going with commissions and all these wonderful colleagues around you two things happened – you got married and there was the war. Why did you decide not to practice architecture after you got married?*

EB: I was anxious to have children and our first child was born not so long after we were married. For a bit, I was quite happy to give up working, but the war broke out very soon and the decision didn't arise. I had one child just before the war and one during the war. The war came and everything was so changed. I'm not quite sure that we discussed my stopping work. There was no question of my not looking after them. I was lucky in that I did go on being an architect [after the war] even though I didn't have any designing to do. But I was professionally active for a very long time.

LW: *Motherhood and child care have shaped women's careers differently.*

EB: Professionally also the scales were loaded against us. For example, even though we were doing exactly the same work, Godfrey had much more authority with builders. It was very galling when I tried to get builders to do something and failed but Godfrey was able to get over what was wanted in about two minutes flat.

LW: *What happened after the war?*

EB: After the war, when we were in Cornwall [1945–49], I was very friendly with Ben [Nicholson] and Barbara [Hepworth] and through them I got a job with the St. Austell Brewery Company. They weren't allowed to build anything then because the restrictions were so severe. but I got out plans for development, and I oversaw decoration and commissioned pub signs which was great fun. When we moved to Derbyshire [1949–79], I did conversion work for friends [e.g. a barn made into a cottage]. I felt very much cut off professionally when I was there. Then we moved back to London to Harpenden and then when my husband died, I bought this house [in Hampstead] with my daughter. After my husband died in 1980, I worked with the St Albans Council on disablement projects. Any public building that came into the council they referred to me and I had to oversee them for standards. I also worked for the Catholic Housing Authority on a voluntary basis but the RIBA frowned on that. Shelter arose from our housing association which bought houses and altered them. It was quite interesting. We tended to have families with a lot of children. My job was to go out and look at the houses and see how they might be converted. The last work I did was Sunday before last for my daughter. My elder daughter who lives in Cobham is converting her garage into a granny flat. It was gorgeous getting down to it again. It was very good. I was very glad to do that.

Modern Houses open to the public in Europe and America

EDWARD DIESTELKAMP

Modern Houses open to the public in Europe and America

EDWARD DIESTELKAMP

THE modern house in the 20th century is well documented and extensively described in literature on the history of architecture, but surprisingly few examples are open for visitors to see if one compares them, for instance, with the number of historic houses of earlier centuries open to the public. Photographs published in architectural journals record sparsely furnished interiors, while informal snapshots often show how many of the rooms were actually furnished and used. The image of the modern house does not always conform with the reality, insofar as lived-in interiors invariably contain some element of clutter, no matter how much effort is expended in maintaining control over books, newspapers, journals, and accumulated objects which are the enjoyment of their collectors.

The modern house of this century, like all other average to modest sized homes in the West, has been subject to faster changing lifestyles where families have moved house more frequently, experienced a more mobile existence on a daily basis and have been accustomed to travel more widely than their counterparts of earlier centuries. These factors have greatly affected the modern houses, like all others. The retention of original furnishings and decoration is a rare occurrence, being the exception rather than the rule. Simple every day wear and tear on materials such as wood, glass, linoleum, textiles, early plastics and laminates have taken their toll, not to speak of changing fashion, which in the vast majority of cases has been responsible for wholesale renewal of finishes and furnishings. The fabric of buildings has also fallen prey to the desire for change, to both structural and cosmetic alterations. This factor in particular has resulted in neglect from unsympathetic owners who might not share the same interest in modern architecture and design as the original client and the architect, with serious implications for very important houses. A change of owner will invariably mean the removal of original contents and furnishings. The setting of houses has also been significantly altered in many cases to the great detriment of the original concept. Pre-war modern houses in suburban and rural settings were often built on plots that now have been subdivided for development. Whilst not attempting to examine all the modern houses that are regularly open, this article mentions some of the better known ones and discusses a few of the lesser known examples.

One would expect that in Berlin, where so many important modern houses were built in the 1920s and 30s, there would be examples open to the public, but there are few which open their doors regularly. One, the house designed by Ludwig Mies van der Rohe for Karl Lemke, is open regularly as an exhibition gallery. As with many other houses, none of the furnishings and contents remain in the house, as it did not belong to the original client after the war. This ideal small modern house, begun in 1932, is built on the edge of a small lake called the Obersee which was developed as a suburban residential area between 1908 and 1911. The plot of land was sold in 1930 to Karl Lemke, who owned a graphic art establishment called Von Holten. In February 1932 Lemke and his wife commis-

figure 2
House for Karl Lemke, Berlin, by Mies
van der Rohe,1932, view from the garden.

figure 3
Karl Lemke House, Berlin,
view of the hall.

sioned Mies to design a house, but the first sketches he produced were not to their liking. The second design for a two storey house was also rejected as too expensive. In June 1932 work began on the single storey house and between 1934 and 1938 Lilly Reich designed fixtures and chose furnishings for the interiors.

The single bedroom house, also with a maid's room, is modest in scale and presents brick walls and solid metal garage doors to the street, although there are windows, some placed at high level for privacy. The house is 'L' shaped, with the kitchen and other office spaces facing onto the street, while the living room, hall and bedroom look onto the garden. The garden elevations are characterised by large expanses of glazing from floor to ceiling onto the garden terrace which was paved with stone slabs between the two outreaching arms of the house. The outdoor terrace appears in old photographs with a flourishing fig tree and comfortable outdoor furniture. After the war the windows were walled up, and they remained like this until 1962. In 1963 the house was returned to use as a dwelling but garages for official cars were built in the garden, which remained in place until 1976. As early as 1977 the house was declared a monument. The following year the large windows of the garden elevation were replaced, but not to the original design. In 1983 the elevations were largely rebuilt and openings altered for conversion of the building into a laundry for the East German secret police whose local headquarters were located next door. It remained in this use until 1990, when a major restoration was undertaken and the interiors were returned as far as possible to their original form. However further restoration works remain to be done, and the next programme is scheduled to begin in 1999: this will restore details such as the original design of the internal doors.

The house serves its new purpose as a small gallery well, with white painted walls and reproduction modern seating. A small permanent exhibition of photographs and text, mounted on boards and located in what was the bathroom next to the main bedroom, is very informative about the history of the house and gives an indication of the appearance of the interiors and how these related to the garden terrace.

The Second World War was one factor which resulted in the change of owners and the resultant separation of contents and furnishings from many houses. The air raids on Berlin also caused damage to many modern houses whose owners had to flee for safety. The sculptor, Georg Kolbe, had to leave his studio-house in the West End of Berlin late in December 1943 for Spottow in Silesia, where he remained working until 1945 when he returned home. In 1928 Kolbe had commissioned the Swiss architect Ernst Rentsch (1876–1952) to design a house and studio-house in woodland within sight of the cemetery where his wife was buried.[1] Kolbe was much involved in the design of both buildings, and Rentsch prepared many schemes as the design evolved. The modern flat-roofed buildings, constructed of brick with very large metal framed windows, were

1. The Friends of Villa Müller and the
Friends of Villa Tugendhat may be contacted
as 5 Great College Street, London SW1P 3SJ.

suited to Kolbe's outlook and reflect his interest in modern design. The studio-house and the adjacent house, which Kolbe turned over to his daughter at a very early stage, were to be Rentsch's most significant works and a contrast to other works by him, which include historical references to other architectural styles. Mies van der Rohe was a friend of Kolbe and had introduced his sculpture into buildings that Mies had designed. Most significantly in 1929 the figure of 'Morgen' was placed at one end of the reflecting pool inside the Barcelona Pavilion, and in 1931 the model of the running figure in the Berlin Building Exhibition house. However Kolbe's taste was different to Mies's, as can be seen in the studio-house which contains workrooms as well as rooms for eating and sleeping. There was no living room as such but instead a living studio space which contained his big drawing table, bookcases, seating and his favourite small works of art. Adjacent was the great studio workroom, with a central rooflight and large rectangular glazed openings on two sides, leading directly to the garden.

Following the war, repairs to the studio-house began in 1946 and were completed in 1947, the year that Kolbe died. Since 1950 the studio-house has been open as a museum of Kolbe's work. A proposal to enlarge the studio to enable more works to be displayed was proposed as early as 1970. A design has been chosen by architectural competition and over the past 25 years funds have been secured, so that the work is now nearly completed. Although the studio-house is not arranged exactly as it was when Kolbe worked there, it still retains some original features including pieces of furniture, and most importantly possesses the unique character of the sculptor's studio.

One of the most important modern houses of the 20th century passed into the curatorship of the Director of the Castle Museum in Brno in 1994 and became a public monument on 1 July of that year. The Tugendhat House of 1929–30 by Mies van der Rohe is open to visitors on a regular basis and can be seen in a sparsely furnished form that approximates to the interiors recorded in early photographs. A restoration undertaken some years ago removed later alterations and uncovered original finishes such as the wall of translucent onyx in the living room. Some of the lost fittings and fixtures were restored at that time. Even though the result was not intended to be an exact or careful replication of the original, the effect has been gauged to represent the interiors as they looked in the early 1930s. The future care of both house and garden is the subject of an international appeal by the Friends of Tugendhat which was registered as a charity in this country in 1993. Some of the original furnishings in the Moravian Gallery of Decorative and Applied Arts might be returned to the house in the future and the Institute for the Protection of Monuments in Brno has prepared a report and estimates for necessary repairs and the replacement of furnishings and fittings. As in the case of many modern houses, the technological aspects of the design are of considerable interest. The great plate glass windows of the living and din-

figure 4
Studio House for Georg Kolbe, Berlin, by Ernst Rentsch, 1928, view from the street.

figure 5
Tugendhat House, Brno, by Mies van der Rohe, 1929–30, view from the garden.

figure 6
Tugendhat House, interior view looking toward dining area.

ing rooms can be automatically lowered into the floor so that the living space becomes a belvedere open to the outside. The ingenious air cleaning and cooling chambers in the basement also survive. However, due to the very small area for access, it is difficult to admit more than a few people at one time into these spaces.

The future of the Villa Tugendhat and the international campaign for funds to support it form one of the most exciting initiatives at the moment, along with a related international campaign by the Friends of Villa Muller to seek funding for the Villa Muller in Prague, designed by Adolf Loos and built in 1928–30, and described as a high point in his work. Acquired by the Municipality of Prague last year, the intention is to open the house to the public but much work to the house and to the interiors needs to be done before this will be possible. The furnishings and fixtures which survive are of great interest, even though most of the contents were removed long ago. The campaign to bring the villa within the public domain would enable visitors the chance to experience Loos' concept of the Raumplan which was fully realised here.[2]

The Rietveld Schröder House in Utrecht, designed by Gerrit Rietveld in 1924, is one of the most popular places of architectural pilgrimage for architects, ar-

figure 7
Villa Müller, Prague,
by Adolf Loos, 1928–30.

figure 8
Rietveld Schröder House, Utrecht,
by Gerrit Rietveld, 1924.
(photo Frank den Oudsten).

chitectural students and visitors from all over the world. Revered by many and considered an architectural monument as an embodiment of De Stijl, it is interesting for the way in which the house has been restored to express these theories. In 1923 Mrs Truus Schröder-Schräder was widowed and left to raise three small children, and in 1924 she asked Rietveld to design a new house for her and her children into which they moved in December of that year. Although she had no experience as a designer of buildings and interiors, she possessed a clear concept of the life-style which she wished to lead in the new house and exerted a strong influence on its design. It is particularly important to understand that the restoration was begun while Mrs Schröder was still alive and that she was much involved, and played an important part in discussions with the architect and the Trustees of the Rietveld Schröder House Foundation which had acquired the house from Mrs. Schröder in 1981 for the purpose of preservation.[3] Their main objective was to remove later accretions and additions and to restore the interior to its original concept of an undivided unified space which could by means of

2. Ursel Berger, *Georg Kolbe Leben und Werk*, (Berlin, 1990).

3. P. Overy, L. Buller, F. den Oudsten and B. Mulder, *The Rietveld Schröder House*, (Amsterdam, 1992).

sliding partitions be broken up into individual rooms. Toward the end of Mrs Schröder's life the interior of the house had been made more comfortable and the original partitions could no longer be moved. The restoration which began after Mrs. Schröder's death now enables visitors to experience the character of changing space within the house.

Following the restoration of the house, the Foundation transferred the care of the building to the Central Museum in Utrecht, which opens it regularly to the public five days a week. Given its small intimate scale, visitors are shown the house on guided tours which are limited to groups of twelve. Because of the great interest in the house, it is necessary to arrange visits in advance, either in writing or by telephone. The ground floor of the next door house has been adapted for use as a reception area where groups assemble before the tours commence, and where visitors can see a filmed interview with Mrs Schröder and enlarged historic photographs of the house, including many interior views that show what it looked like with furnishings and contents that are not seen now. These are particularly valuable for the visitor as representations of how the house was lived in. The few smaller contents that were acquired with the house are in the Central Museum and the interiors are arranged with larger pieces of moveable furniture. This facilitates circulation through the small space and enables guides more easily to demonstrate how the moveable partitions and fitted fixtures are arranged to create the varied spatial effects inside. The Rietveld Schröder House is unique as a representation of the theories of De Stijl, and its restoration and interpretation to emphasise this aspect is a valuable and important experience for visitors.

Reconstruction began in 1985 of the De Kiefhoek Housing Estate in Rotterdam which was designed by J. J. P. Oud and built between 1925 and 1927. Significant subsidence and uneven settlement of the foundations had occurred throughout the estate. The original concept of the social housing project contained 294 houses, two shops, two warehouse – workshop spaces and communal hot water to all the houses. The modest two storey houses (3.88 m by 7.5) were compactly planned. A small entrance lobby on the street led directly into the living-eating space and was not separated by a corridor. The stair, with WC tucked beneath the rising treads and landing, and a small tightly planned kitchen looked out to the small garden at the back. Upstairs, two bedrooms looked out to the street and one overlooked the small garden. Parallel terraces of houses faced and backed onto similar terraces.

As part of the reconstruction of the first block on Hendrik Ido Plein, one of the houses was rebuilt in its original form. This block was completed in 1990 and the remainder of the estate is now nearly finished. Whilst fixtures and fittings have been restored to show how the planning of the service areas were organised, there has been no attempt to furnish the rooms other than to arrange beds in the bedrooms upstairs to indicate how many people shared a room. A model and exhibition boards with old photographs and an explanation of the history of the estate and of other examples of Oud's work are displayed in the living-eating room downstairs and in two of the bedrooms. The urban scale of the streets as seen in the old photographs appears more monumental than one experiences now. The scale of the terraces and of the narrow streets was not designed for parking automobiles on both sides. Access is very difficult and the appearance is disorderly rather than planned.

The internal planning of the house and the somewhat tight character of the space are very interesting, even though it is evidently a reconstruction. Visits to the De Kiefhoek museum house are by appointment through the Architecture Centre in Rotterdam and can be made by telephone. To one side of the centre and opposite the Boymans Museum is one of the functionalist villas designed by Van der Vlugt which has recently opened as the Chabot Museum and is open regularly during the week.

figure 9
66 Hendrik Ido Plein,
De Kiefhoek Housing Estate, Rotterdam,
by J. J. P. Oud, 1925–27.

figure 10
De Kiefhoek Housing Estate,
reconstructed 1985–95.

The Villa Savoye at Poissy, one of the icons of the modern movement, was designed in 1928 by Le Corbusier and completed in 1931.[4] Following occupation by the Nazis during the war, Madame Savoye retained ownership of the villa, but over the ensuing twenty years the condition of the house deteriorated badly. As early as 1965 it was listed, restored and opened to the public. Some twenty miles from the centre of Paris, the villa was a weekend retreat in a rural country setting when it was built. However, it was only lived in from 1931 until 1940. Constructed of a concrete frame with block infill walls, the main first floor living rooms are raised above the ground. The interiors have been largely refurnished to appear as they did in the 1930s so that a visit to the house is a rewarding architectural experience.

Le Corbusier's Maisons La Roche-Jeanneret of 1923, are two adjoining houses built in Paris. The one facing the street was for Le Corbusier's brother and his family and since 1971 has been the headquarters of the Le Corbusier Foundation, while the other, Maison La Roche, was designed for an art collector who needed room for his works of art. It is open to the public regularly and like the Villa Savoye, is an interesting and exciting visit.

In 1938 Walter Gropius built a two storey house for himself and his family in Lincoln, Massachusetts, after going to the United States to teach at the Graduate School of Design at Harvard. The modern house is interesting for its use of traditional materials such as clapboard, brick and stone in combination with glass blocks, chrome and steel.[5] The interior is furnished with furniture designed by Marcel Breuer and works of art by artist friends such as Laszlo Moholy-Nagy, Josef Albers and Henry Moore. In 1975 the house was acquired by the Society for the Preservation of New England Antiquities, and it is open on weekends during the months of June through October. Due to the small size of the interiors, visits are by guided tour.

Fallingwater in Bear Run, Pennsylvania by Frank Lloyd Wright, which was designed for Edgar and Lilian Kaufmann in 1935, whilst not perhaps considered 'modern' in an International Modern sense, is one of the most modern designs for houses that Wright produced during his very productive career. This is due to the long horizontal lines of the cantilevered balconies. Actually it is much more closely related to Wright's own individual style and any resemblance to international modernism is peripheral to the context of this brilliant design within Wright's earlier work.[6]

Fallingwater is one of the most visited houses in the United States. As early as 1963 Edgar Kaufmann Jr donated the house and 1,543 acres of surrounding land to the Western Pennsylvania Conservancy, who are responsible now for opening it regularly to the public. Perhaps more than with any other house, the setting of Fallingwater is integral with the concept of the design. The rugged woodland setting with its running stream flowing beneath and over rocks below the house was an important element in Wright's initial sketches. The daring exploitation of the potential of reinforced concrete in the tremendous cantilevers out and over the waterfall, the integral relationship of the form within the landscape and the use of stone as a facing material are the most resonant elements of his design. Inside, long low horizontal living spaces that reach out both visually and physically to the outdoors, the use of stone on floors and walls which relate to and continue the exterior of the house, and the sense of enclosure, shelter and security which are achieved by means of the punctuated exterior are common features to Wright's approach.

R. M. Schindler's own house in Kings Road in Hollywood, California, designed in 1921 and completed in the following year, was an experiment in living. Very much the earliest modern house open to the public, it was intended for two young couples without children and was divided into two parts with a shared kitchen in the centre. The main rooms were directly related to the garden, here integrated as an outdoor living space which could be reached through sliding screens as found in Japanese domestic architecture.[7] There were no bedrooms as such, as Schindler intended the flat roof to be used for sleeping. The reinforced concrete lift-slab walls and concrete floors were integrated with redwood beams, ceilings and fascias. The house contained no finish materials such as plaster or painted surfaces. It was uninsulated and heat was by means of fireplaces. Following the death of Schindler's widow Pauline in 1979, restoration of the house largely to its original form of 1922 by the Friends of the Schindler House began in 1986, and has continued over the past ten years. The structure and the surface materials had deteriorated, alterations had been made, and aspects such as the outdoor garden living-spaces had never been fully realised, all of which the Friends of the Schindler House have undertaken in the phased programme of conservation and restoration. Today the house is stabilised, protected from the weather, partially restored and furnished, and in one very important aspect more fully represents Schindler's concept through the restoration of the intended landscaping.

High Cross House at Dartington in Devon was the first modern house to open to the public in Britain in 1995, following restoration by the Dartington Hall Trust to house the remarkable collection of art and the Trust's archive. The recent restoration is described and illustrated in Michael Hall's article in *Country Life*.[8] The house was built for the headmaster of the progressive Dartington School, William B. Curry, who had been recently headmaster at Oak Lane Country Day School in Philadelphia. Curry was anxious that the new house should be in a modern style and recommended that the founders of the school, Leonard and Dorothy Elmhirst, should commission the Swiss-born architect William Lescaze to design the house. Lescaze had emigrated to the United States in 1920 and more recently had designed the important and much acclaimed extension to the school where Curry had been headmaster. The design was finalised by June 1931 and the house was complete and ready to move into by July of the following year. The International Modern style of the house is constructed of rendered brick walls with ribbon windows, flat roofs and outdoor terraces. Much of the original furniture was suitably modern and ordered from Thonet while the built-in furniture, fixtures and fittings which largely survive, were made locally. The original interiors were described by Christopher Hussey and illustrated in *Country Life* in 1933.[9]

Following the closure of the school in 1987, the Curator of the Dartington archive and of the Elmhirst's collection of art promoted the idea of using the house as a gallery and archive. Repairs have been carried out to the building and the exterior use of vivid sky blue on the guest and servant's wing has been restored. Some of the interiors have been restored and furnished with the surviving pieces of the original furniture and reproductions, whilst the former kitchen is used as gallery space for displaying the collection of paintings, works of art and ceramics purchased for Dartington and commissioned by the Elmhirsts. The two car garage has also been converted into a two-storey exhibition space to show the work of Dartington artists.

No.2 Willow Road, Hampstead, the home of Ernö and Ursula Goldfinger, was built in 1938–9 and completed just before the outbreak of war.[10] Ernö Goldfinger was born in Budapest in 1902, and while still in his teens moved to Paris. He soon decided to study architecture and entered the Ecole des Beaux Arts, joining eventually the breakaway atelier of Auguste Perret, the great French exponent of reinforced concrete construction and structural rationalism during the first decades of this century.

Goldfinger moved in artistic circles and was a friend of many of the Surrealists including Max Ernst, Man Ray, Marcel Duchamp, Stanley William Hayter and Roland Penrose. In 1931 Goldfinger met Ursula Blackwell, an English art student

4. See Alan Powers, 'Villa Savoye, Ile-de-France', *Country Life*, Vol.CLXXXVIII, No.27, 7 July 1994, pp.74–77.

5. Nancy Curtis, *Gropius House*, (Boston: Society for the Preservation of New England Antiquities, 1988).

6. Robert McCarter, *Fallingwater*, (London: Phaidon, 1994).

7. John Pastier, 'Hollywood Classic', *Architects' Journal*, Vol.194, No 20, 13 November 1991, pp.32–39.

8. Michael Hall, 'High Cross House, Devon', *Country Life*, Vol.CLXXXIX, No.31, 3 August 1995, pp.50–53.

9. Christopher Hussey, 'High Cross Hill, Dartington, Devon', *Country Life*, Vol.LXXIII, No.1882, 11 February 1933, pp.144–149.

10. Gervase Jackson-Stops, '2 Willow Road, Hampstead', *Country Life*, Vol.CLXXXV, No.89, 12 September 1991, pp.146–149.

studying in Paris. In 1933 they were married, and in the next year they decided to move to England. In 1936, while they were living in a flat in Highpoint I, the Goldfingers began looking for a site to build a new home. The site which they found on Willow Road contained four two-storey 18th century cottages which were demolished and in their place a terrace of three three-storey (four-storey to the rear elevation) houses was built. No.2 is the centre house in the terrace and larger than Nos.1 and 3. The ground floor was given over to garages and entrances facing Willow Road. Built of reinforced concrete and faced in red brick, the terrace presents a unified facade to the street, organised around a framed continuous window at first floor level that dominates the composition. This window lights the living rooms of the three houses providing generous light from

figure 11
Nos.1–3 Willow Road, Hampstead,
by Erno Goldfinger, 1938.
(photo The National Trust).

figure 12
No.2 Willow Road, interior view of
Dining Room. *(photo The National Trust).*

11. 'Three houses at Willow Road, Hampstead',
Architectural Review, Vol.LXXXVIII, No.89,
April 1940, pp.126–130 and 149–153.
See also National Trust guidebook by Alan
Powers, 1996.

the north. The bedrooms on the second floor have smaller square windows spaced evenly across the front elevation.

The Goldfingers lived at No.2 Willow Road for the rest of their lives and the interiors are a reflection of their modern artistic taste, containing furniture designed by Goldfinger for the house, contents, personal archives, and the collection of works they assembled over five decades. The Trust considered the possible ways in which the house might be presented to the public, and although the spare modern interiors captured in the early photographs of the house taken by Dell and Wainwright for the *Architectural Review* had an appealing freshness and clarity, a return of the house to that period would have involved the removal of many interesting works of art and pieces of furniture designed and acquired later.[11]

A programme of repairs and improvements has just been completed which includes the introduction of fire and security detection systems, the creation of a small film viewing room in one of the garages where a film can be seen about the Goldfingers' life in the house, the impressions of their friends and visitors, events in the history of the house, and a brief account of Ernö Goldfinger's career. The house is open on Thursday, Friday and Saturday afternoons between the middle of April and the end of October and admission to the house will be by guided tours of twelve people.

Dorich House, Kingston

STUART DURANT AND BRENDA MARTIN

Dorich House, Kingston

STUART DURANT AND BRENDA MARTIN

T HE name 'Dorich' is a fusion of Dora and Richard, the builders of the house. Dora Gordine (1906–1991) was a Russian sculptor and her husband, the Hon. Richard Hare (1907–1966), son of the 4th Earl of Listowel, a connoisseur of Russian art who began his career as a diplomat and ended it as the first chair of Slavonic studies at University of London.

The house has a fine position on Kingston Hill with views of Richmond Park on one side and Roehampton Vale on the other. It is an unexpected piece of architecture for South London, and is not a typical product of the British Modern Movement, despite its flat roof. The arched windows recall German Expressionist designs such as Hans Poelzig's chemical factory in Posnan illustrated in the *Deutsche Werkbund Jarhbuch* of 1913, but by the time the house was built in 1936 this kind of architecture, which was never popular in Britain or France, was long out of fashion.

Dora Gordine usually said that she had been born in St. Petersburg on April 13, 1906. She was sent away to school in Paris in the care of her own nurse. The Russian Revolution of 1917 made an emigrée of her. She always proclaimed her Russian origin, for Russian culture was fashionable in Paris due to the popularity of Diaghilev Ballets Russes and such artists as Igor Stravinsky, Leon Bakst, Vaslav Nijinsky and Natalia Goncharova.

Among the artistic influences in Paris in the Twenties, Gordine followed a middle path. She claimed to have worked on a mural for the British pavilion at the Exposition Internationale des Arts Decoratifs et Industriels Modernes in 1925 when she was eighteen. No independent evidence for this has been found. The mural might have been Maurice Greiffenhagen's frieze of colonial subjects *L'Empire Britannique*. In 1926, her head *Chinese Philosopher*, exhibited at the Salon des Tuileries, was greatly admired and sold to a Swiss sanatorium owner Dr Widner. He displayed it there to bring 'an aura of calmness and peace' to his wealthy patients. Gordine's work was seen and admired by the sculptor Aristide Maillol. He advised her to continue working on her own since she had apparently acquired all that she could from a conventional art education. In an interview for the Tate Gallery in 1990 she declared that she still despised art schools which to her seemed shallow and ignorant of real life.

In 1929 Dora Gordine built a studio at 21 rue de Belvedere, Paris to designs by Auguste Perret, who had designed studios in the preceding years for A M Cassandre (1926), Chana Orloff (1926) and Georges Braque (1927).

An exhibition of Dora Gordine's work at the Leicester Galleries, London in 1928 was a sell-out. It included another cast of *Chinese Philosopher* and *Mongolian Head* presented anonymously (by Samuel Courtauld) to the Tate Gallery through the National Art Collections Fund. The oriental cult in which Gordine was immersed reflected the enthusiasm in France for its colonial possessions . These enthusiasms were also found in London, in the work of Orovida Pissaro, daughter of the printmaker Lucien Pissaro who was the subject of a Gordine portrait bust. Many of Gordine's best-known works show a delight in the exotic. Her

figure 1
Dorich House on Kingston Hill. The photograph was taken shortly after Gordine's death on December 29th, 1991. The ugly drainpipes have been removed and the garden re-landscaped to the designs of David Brown and Partners. (*RCHME* © *Crown Copyright*).

figure 2
Dora Gordine's studio 21, Rue de Belvédère, Boulogne-Billancourt, Paris (Hauts-de-Seine), 1929. The studio was designed by Auguste Perret (1874–1954). Gordine had earlier rented her apartment from Perret, which was in the same building as his office, and had become a friend. (from R. Gargiani *Auguste Perret* Edizioni Electa 1991).

husband-to-be Richard Hare presented her *Javanese Head* to the Tate in 1933. *Pagan* was an oriental nude, not unlike *Crowning Glory*, which in numberless painted plaster versions brought an unfamiliar sexual frisson to the windows of suburban hairdressers between the wars as an advertisement for Eugène Permanent Waving. So successful were Gordine's oriental subjects that she was asked to make a a set of bronzes for Singapore Town Hall between 1929 and 1936, depicting the various nationalities who inhabited the city.

Gordine knew British artists including Sir William Orpen (1878–1931) and C. R. W. Nevinson (1889–1946). She made her reputation in Britain in the 1930s with portrait busts including those of the critic D. S. MacColl (1859–1948) and the architect H. S. Goodhart–Rendel (1887–1959) which is on view at the RIBA.

figure 3
Dora Gordine and her husband the Hon. Richard Hare drinking tea from a samovar on the roof of Dorich House, c.1937. Richmond Park can be seen in the background.
(*RCHME* © *Crown Copyright*).

Others were Dame Edith Evans, Emlyn Williams, Kenneth Clark and Dorothy Tutin. She was also known for her heads of children and *Smiling Baby* was commissioned for the maternity Wing of Holloway Prison to bring some comfort to the mothers who were parted from their babies.

Dora Gordine married Richard Hare in November 1936. The couple originally commissioned the architect Godfrey Samuel, a founder member of Tecton, who had been at Balliol College with Hare, to build a house for them in Merton Lane, Highgate with views over Hampstead Heath. The house was unequivocally modernist and the project had to be abandoned as the purchase of the site was entirely conditional upon the acceptance of the scheme by the seller. The exercise must have been a useful one for the Hares. The correspondence with Samuel indicates that they were exacting and pernickety clients. They fussed about rare Malaysian timbers for the floors which had to be tested at the Timber Development Association's laboratory at Princes Risborough.

Godfrey Samuel was not involved with the design of the house at Kingston Hill. Gordine claimed to have designed it herself and if an architect was employed it was merely as an executant of her own and her husband's wishes. The possibility that as amateurs the Hares created an original and structurally sophisticated piece of architecture is not, on balance, believable. The drawings for Dorich House lodged with the Borough of Merton, the local authority, were signed Henry Ivor Cole who was not a registered architect but claimed to have designed a number of important buildings and to have been articled to the Cardiff architect W. Beddoe Rees.

The planning of Dorich House and some of its internal features resemble the Paris studio designed for Gordine by Auguste Perret. Some of the fireplaces are identical. There remains a mystery about the authorship of Dorich House. An

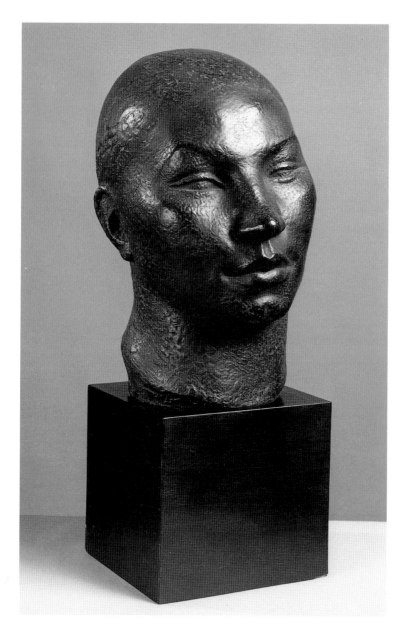

figure 4
Mongolian Head (cast, *c*.1930) by Dora Gordine. The original was commissioned for the City Hall, Singapore. The Tate Gallery owns a cast and another is in the present Dorich House collection. *(Kingston University)*.

article on the house was published in *Country Life* on 5th November 1938 and it was illustrated in Jeremy Gould's *Modern Houses in Britain 1919–1939* (1977) but it has otherwise been neglected by historians.

Dora Gordine lived at Dorich House until her death, and it was bequeathed by her trustees to Kingston University. It was restored 1995–6 by David Brown and Partners with Alan Baxter Associates as consulting engineers. Gordine's sculpture and drawings will soon be exhibited throughout the house and the Russian collection of ceramics, icons, paintings and engravings will recall the Hares' devotion to Imperial Russia. Dorich House was refreshingly unorthodox when first built and remains a delightfully un-English intruder on Kingston Hill.

figure 5
The Hares in the dining room of this apartment on the top floor of Dorich House. The 'moon' doors are an oriental feature and remind one of their enthusiasm for the Far East. The wood for the flooring was specially shipped from Malaysia.
(*RCHME* © Crown Copyright).

10 Long Live modern Architecture. A technical appraisal of conservation work to three 1930s houses.

SUSAN MACDONALD

figure 1
High Cross House, Dartington,
shortly after completion in 1933.

Long Live modern Architecture.
A technical appraisal of conservation work
to three 1930s houses.

SUSAN MACDONALD

MUCH has been written over the last few years on the appropriateness of the listing and conservation of modern buildings and there is now a general recognition that buildings from the 20th century are of cultural value and worthy of care. However, what are the difficulties faced by those involved in the care of the modern house and what new challenges do these exuberant expressions of modern materials and technology bring? How do those involved in their care and conservation approach the problems?

Walter Gropius best summed up the early expressions of modern architecture when he called it 'the inevitable logical product of the intellectual, social and technical conditions of our age.' The pioneers of Modernism in the 1930s not only grappled with new design concepts of planning and aesthetics but used little understood materials in new and innovative ways, experimented with the potential of materials and pushed forward the possibilities afforded in terms of structure, form and services. It is this originality, coupled with the abandonment of traditional weathering details which are the principal causes of modern buildings' deterioration. The misapprehension that modern buildings would require little maintenance compounds many of the material and construction problems such as ungalvanised windows, internal drainage and thin concrete walling. The concept of functionalism is one other difficulty which has meant that a continued or new use for modern buildings is sometimes difficult. This however is of lesser consequence for modern houses remaining in domestic use.

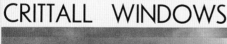

"NEW FARM," GRAYSWOOD, NEAR HASLEMERE, SURREY.
MESSRS. CONNELL & WARD, ARCHITECTS.

The windows are Crittall Standard "N" types, with a few of the same section made to special sizes. The "daylight walls" to the staircase are made of Standard reinforced Sash Sections. The windows are painted dark maroon-red and the walls of the house are tinted pale pink.

II 538.

figure 2
White House, Haslemere, 1932.
(*Book Art Picture Library*).

figure 3
Bungalow 'A', Whipsnade in 1936.
(*Architectural Press*).

Recent and ongoing conservation of three seminal buildings from the early 1930s enables us to examine today's attitudes and approaches to the conservation of modern architecture and scrutinise how technical difficulties are addressed. Lubetkin's Bungalow A (also known as Hillfield, adjoining Whipsnade Zoo but actually off Dunstable Road, Dagnall, Buckinghamshire),1933–36, Amyas Connell's White House, Grayswood, near Haslemere, Surrey, 1932 and High Cross House, Dartington, Devon 1931–33 by William Lescaze are all listed Grade II* by the Department of National Heritage in recognition of their significance in British and international architecture.

All three houses can be described as exemplars of modern architecture in Britain. The architects involved in their conservation have viewed the houses very much as artistic objects – inherently beautiful and significant in terms of planning, architectural form and use of materials. The Lubetkin bungalow and High Cross are further enhanced by their collections of contemporary furniture. The buildings themselves employ different construction methods and materials. While the White House and the Lubetkin bungalow are at the forefront of engineering and modern construction development, in the transatlantic crossing of Lescaze's plans High Cross went from a steel frame and concrete infill structure to a compromise of cement rendered brick cavity walling, thickening the structure and and in essence faking up the the materials with little concession to the original intention in terms of their expression and the way in which they had been exploited to meet their aesthetic. Without the presence of the architect to push the boundaries of construction to achieve sharp silhouettes of thin walls and sleek modern forms, the house lost some of its crispness but it did retain the steel 'Lally' beams in the framing which illustrate the architect's original structural intentions. Although structural innovations in the use of concrete had been seen on a larger scale, the individual house enabled Lubetkin and Connell to experiment with these technological advancements on a domestic scale. Lubetkin explored the use of prefabricated concrete elements alongside thin in-situ concrete walling and the engineer Ove Arup played with the structural expression to produce a building which hovers above its landscape and provides what John Allen has described as a 'stage' from which to observe the view.[1] The bungalow took expression from the machine and the technology of the age and exploited ideas of mass production and prefabrication.[2] Connell at the White House took forward his earlier developments in the use of concrete, achieving a rich expression using a concrete slab and panel technique with huge areas of glazing by Crittalls, a company which played an important role in the development of the steel frame window.

HIGH CROSS

John Winter, the architect for the conservation work at High Cross, has a portfolio of impressive projects involving modern architecture, including Six Pillars, Dulwich by Harding and Tecton and the Augustus John studio at Fryern Court, Hampshire by Christopher Nicholson. High Cross is the largest of the projects examined here, involving the adaptation of the former Headmaster's House of Dartington Hall School to a house museum, a gallery with exhibition spaces, a café and a home for the extensive Dartington archives. The house is exploited as an object, acting as the most important exhibit and this is central to the philosophical approach to its conservation. The alterations to the house include the conversion of the original garage to a gallery for temporary exhibitions and the adaptation of other ground floor rooms to house the Elmhirst collection, with its many paintings and ceramics contemporary with the house. The remaining ground floor rooms provide a backdrop for the collection of period furniture, some of which belongs to the house itself and some of which has been gathered from other buildings on the estate. On the first floor the guest wing which was gutted in the 1950s has undergone some alterations including the removal of a

1. John Allan Berthold Lubetkin, *Architecture and the Tradition of Progress*. (London, RIBA Publications Ltd,1992), p.181.

2. Lubetkin built two bungalows close beside each other to similar designs. Bungalow 'B', also known as Holly Frindle, is within the grounds of Whipsnade Zoo and listed Grade II. It has been empty for some years and its current condition gives cause for concern. The Zoological Society has suggested funding its restoration by an enabling development on part of the same site.

bathroom and walls to provide an airy café opening on to the terrace. Infill was removed from the first floor balcony to reinstate the corner sun terrace.

In addition to the alterations for the house's new use and to meet building control requirements (fire upgrading, the provision of disabled access and security) the house required repairs to the fabric generally. The building had lain empty for many years and suffered from lack of maintenance, ad hoc repairs and previous unsympathetic internal alterations. The significance of the building in terms of its architectural and social value and its potential as a public exhibit was recognised by Dartington's curator, Maggie Giraud who was looking for a suitable home for the collection. Keen to save the house from continued decay, Giraud effectively campaigned and raised money to restore the house and secure its future.

Working with a limited budget, John Winter sought to carry out the minimum repairs required to secure the existing external fabric. Repairs to the drainage and the relocation of rainwater pipes inside the house to accord with the original arrangement added unexpected stress to the already tight budget when asbestos was found encasing the pipes. Areas of roofing which had been a continual problem were repaired and improvements to weathering details such as the addition of drips and overhangs to all openings were made. Although Winter felt such changes were detrimental to the architectural integrity, the upgrading of the weathering details was deemed necessary to avoid the continued problems and subsequent deterioration of the building. The ungalvanised windows had corroded after years of neglect. The originals were carefully repaired where possible, with approximately one third requiring replacement. All the windows were newly glazed in toughened glass. Areas of lost render were patched and the texture and finishes carefully matched to the slightly uneven and rough original.

Internally the work was less conservative and displays more of Winter's personal taste. He argues against the influence of conservation in constraining the design of new buildings and while undoubtedly sensitive to context and old buildings of many periods prefers to respond on his own terms. The services required upgrading and repair to meet modern requirements and and the additional demands of gallery spaces for lighting, heating and security. Although the original flush wall heating panels were retained they continue to heat only the living and dining rooms. In the rest of the house the existing radiators were disconnected, left in place and new radiators introduced. The upgrading of the lighting involved the removal and replacement of earlier fittings and the new scheme reflects its 1990s period and function. Winter's approach to the services is that they have a limited life and are replaceable. The client's requirement to improve the thermal conditions was achieved by the application of additional insulation to the underside of the ceilings, lowering them slightly and providing more insulation within the wall cavities.

The use of colour at High Cross is indicative of the attitude of many owners and architects involved in conservation who consider that it is an ephemeral part of the building fabric and not subject to the same rules as other matters. Colour scrapes were taken and the external colour scheme was reinstated – blue for the former service wing and white for the main house. The internal colour scheme, for example the use of a strong yellow in the hall and stairwell, is a product of John Winter and Maggie Giraud's ideas on the house and its architectural language rather than of evidence discovered during the research. The three houses under discussion exhibit similar approaches to the use of surface colour in conservation.

WHITE HOUSE

Amyas Connell's White House was originally finished in a cement spray coloured 'sugar almond pink' with the steel frames of the windows in black. It was initially known as Aldings, then New Farm but it was repainted in white and subsequently

figure 4
High Cross House following restoration. *(author).*

known as the White House. There is a presumption that modern buildings of the 1930s were normally white, as shown in the photographs of the era. During previous repairs all the windows except those of the stair tower and the study were painted white as well, and the owners did not wish to return the windows or walls to their original colours.

John Allan of Avanti Architects has carried out pioneering work in the conservation and repair of some of England's most important modern architecture, including the Penguin Pool at London Zoo, Highpoint 1 and Finsbury Health Centre (all by Lubetkin and Tecton) and 2 Willow Road by Ernö Goldfinger for the National Trust.

White House received some grant aid from the local authority, Waverley District Council but the limited budget restricted the work to essential concrete repairs and replacement of the main staircase glazing. The building remains occupied as a house and internal works were limited to minor repairs, unlike High Cross where these formed the bulk of the contract. As the work was limited to repairs listed building consent was not required.

White House, because of its radical concrete construction, has suffered more difficult problems with its external fabric than High Cross. Over time, the frequent applications of layers of paint had built up a thick water-retaining barrier to the concrete, keeping it damp and providing an ideal environment for deterioration. The concrete required grit-blasting to remove the layers of paint. The concrete repair specialists Makers Ltd were commissioned to carry out pre-contract investigation works to determine the cause and extent of the problem. Such investigation, long recognised as fundamental to the conservation of traditional buildings has only recently become normal for modern buildings through the efforts of architects such as John Allan. Frequently investigation works are included in the main contract once the repair method has already been established. Thus alternative methods of repair are not adequately explored to ensure that conservation's aim of minimum intervention is met.

In addition to the problems caused by the layers of paint the concrete was not well engineered and its quality was variable. The extreme thinness of the walls, two inches in places, meant that cover to the reinforcement was minimal and far below today's standards. A traditional concrete repair method was adopted to affected areas of deterioration and points where carbonation was putting the reinforcement at risk of corrosion. Reinforcement steel within concrete structures develops its own passivating skin during curing of the highly alkaline concrete. However the alkaline environment of the concrete can be changed by the presence of carbon dioxide and moisture penetrating through the pore structure which forms carbonic acid. This in turn reacts with calcium hydroxide which is present in the concrete and forms calcium carbonate, thereby reducing the alkalinity of the concrete and breaking down the passivating film on the reinforcement steel and corrosion commences. This deterioration is known as carbonation.

Following cutting out of affected areas, the reinforcement was grit-blasted and primed. Patch repairs were made, then a thin 'fairing' layer of mortar was brushed onto the surface to fill the pore holes and to ensure a continuous covering of the anti-carbonation coatings which assist in retaining the alkaline-rich environment necessary to prevent corrosion of the reinforcement. Additional layers of mortar were originally specified to assist in providing this alkaline environment. However, in a cost-cutting exercise this was deleted, leaving a rougher texture which reveals the original shuttering marks and the junctions between different 'lifts' of the concrete construction.

Weathering details were introduced as part of the reconstruction of the parapet, providing drips and falls to eliminate the recurrence of delamination through frost attack. The roof was leaking and required repair. Again, the limited budget meant repair rather than replacement. At the same time Allan took

figure 5
White House at rooflevel prior to repairs. (*John Allan*).

the opportunity to upgrade the roof terrace by the introduction of paving to enable the owners to take full advantage of the views across the site and surrounding landscape.

The glazed stair of the White House plays a pivotal role in the planning of the principal rooms of the house which fan out beyond it. The elegant column rising through the building from which the stairs are cantilevered (and which also contains the chimney flue) is visible through the transparent tower, two sides of which were formed by ungalvanised steel windows originally supplied by Crittall. The windows of the stair tower were suffering extensive corrosion causing cracking of the glass. Previous repairs had dealt with most other areas of glazing with the exception of the stair and study windows. Due to severe corrosion of the existing windows and the large expanse of glazing the decision was taken to replace all the glazing of the stair tower and the study windows, offering the opportunity to upgrade to double glazing and improve the thermal performance. Allan worked with Crittalls to come up with the best possible replacement to match the original sections while incorporating the increased depth required for double glazing and making subtle improvements in the detailing to ensure longevity of the replacement windows. The result has been achieved with the slightest thickening of the extremely slender and delicate fenestration.

BUNGALOW 'A'

The works currently in progress at Lubetkin's bungalow are the most conservative of the three projects examined. The house was bought in 1990 by Mike Davies, a founder partner of Richard Rogers Partnership, for whom it has become a passion. This work could be better described as a personal discovery rather than a defined project, with the minimal budget required to retrieve the house from ruin and nurture its re-emergence as one of England's most important modern houses. Despite its condition the bungalow remains very much the weekend retreat or 'dacha' that Lubetkin intended. Nearly all the original furniture remained in its authentic state when the house was bought from the the owners who followed Lubetkin and this helps us to understand the rationale of the design and the former occupants' living patterns. Davies, his family and friends have been working on the house at weekends and holidays over the last two years and there is thought to be a further year's work before the repairs are complete. The approach is one of minimum intervention and Davies intends to reinstate the house as far as possible to its original condition. As with the White House, the works were limited to repairs and so listed building consent was not required.

The works at Lubetkin's bungalow attempt to embrace the principles of the international conservation charters to achieve the 'conserve as found' idea. They push forward the limits of what can be achieved in terms of material authenticity for modern buildings, still a controversial subject. This is interesting considering that Davies is, of the three architects under discussion, the one least associated with building conservation practice. But as his own client Davies can afford an uncompromised approach. High Cross required adaptation to a new use to secure its adequate care and survival while the White House required minor modifications to meet the modern living requirements of the occupier and to guarantee prolonged performance of the fabric. Lubetkin's bungalow is still a weekend retreat and the owners have adapted to the house in its 1930s state rather than the other way round.

When the house was purchased by Mike Davies it was camouflaged by the undergrowth surrounding it and covered in lichens and mosses. The initial works dealt with the weatherproofing of the house and its general external condition. Despite the ruined appearance of the building there were in fact no structural weaknesses and the concrete problems were also non-structural, the original concrete being of high quality. Many of the slender prefabricated concrete members of the loggia and fenestration has sagged but were not in danger of collapse. The site was first cleared of undergrowth to enable full access to the house and then the concrete surfaces were cleaned down using a high pressure water lance. Davies's approach of minimal repairs did include some work to the concrete. The decision was taken to deal only with the areas visually identified as at risk, and spalling and blown surfaces were cut out and patch repaired, following a series of trials, using the Bellzona system of concrete repair. This is an epoxy resin based system which is high in strength and claims good adhesion to existing material but it is fundamentally different from the original concrete with different strength properties. Davies chose to deal with visible decay only rather than treating all the 'at risk' areas as was done at the White House. During concrete investigations one of the tests normally carried out is to examine how close the carbonation front is to the reinforcement bars. At the White House where carbonation was within 5mm for the steel, repair was carried out to ensure future corrosion did not occur. It will be interesting to see how the concrete repairs to Lubetkin's Bungalow perform over time as certainly any means by which exiting material can be retained are of interest to those involved in conservation and

figure 6
The sun trap, Bungalow 'A', Whipsnade
following cleaning of inner face.
(author).

figure 7
The loggia, Bungalow 'A', Whipsnade
with external fireplace. *(author)*.

figure 8
Bungalow 'A', Whipsnade, general view
of present condition. *(author).*

it is only by examining and monitoring repairs over time that we can help establish the best repair options for the future.

The glazing system with its steel frame windows and 'Thermolux' panels had been replaced some time before with plywood which was now leaking. There is some uncertainty as to whether the backing to the original panels was translucent or not. The mica boards which replaced the plywood as a temporary measure will remain in place until further research reveals more about the original panels and suitable replacements are made.

The services of the bungalow required overhauling to serve the building adequately. The roof was renewed ten years ago but required resurfacing. The rainwater pipes were fortunately in working order and simply needed flushing clear, additional rainwater pipes having been added when the house was re-roofed.

The electrical services of the house posed a particular challenge. The house is believed to be one of the earliest all-electric houses in the British Isles, thus the wiring, switches and fittings were of importance in their own right, The present system therefore required careful adaptation to meet modern standards without compromising architectural integrity. A contractor was found with experience dealing with concrete buildings and early modern services and the success of the work is testament to the contractor's skills. The existing conduits were reused and the new wiring fed through. Original fittings were retained and repaired and switches were found in the United States to match the originals which were mounted on the doors. The flush wall-mounted heating panels were very cleverly reused, the contractor virtually re-threading the wiring into the panels. The service repairs at the bungalow, which were carried out reusing existing services and fittings with minimal disruption to the fabric have achieved what few architects and their consultants ever manage in conservation terms and have some important lessons for those involved in the repair of historic buildings generally.

As with High Cross and the White House, Mike Davies approached the use of colour in the building with some reference to the original scheme; however he feels that surface paint colour, being transient, is one area where the owner can afford some personal expression. Internally the colour scheme was documented exactly before being painted white, while the final decisions regarding colour is deferred until all the repair works are completed. Selected specific surfaces of the interior were originally painted blue and others left white. Davies may choose his own colours but intends in the placement to respect Lubetkin's original colour arrangement philosophy.

The gradual emergence of Lubetkin's bungalow from the landscape through the clearing of vegetation, cleaning and repainting has re-established its relationship with the landscape and revealed the house as a work which embodies the essence of his architecture. The bungalow highlights the importance of the immediate environment and surrounding landscape as part of the experience of the modern house. Heritage bodies and local authorities in particular need to ensure that protective controls to such buildings take this into account if we are not to find that subsequent developments reduce the significance of the building by interfering with this relationship between the house and its setting.

CONCLUSION

The three houses examined required fundamentally similar work – repairs to the external walling systems, repairs to ensure the flat roofs adequately waterproof the buildings and window repairs. The additional works at Dartington to adapt it to its new use as a public gallery introduced building control and client requirements which had to be dealt with and involved some alterations to the internal planning of the house. The approaches, although illustrating some differences, share a common respect for the buildings and empathy for the original architects' ambitions and ideals. In fact the results in conservation terms differ more due to requirements of the clients, their resources and the resulting project structure than any fundamentally divergent philosophical ideas about how to restore the individual buildings concerned.

John Allan's work seeks to achieve a fine balance between the retention of authentic fabric and a return to the authenticity of the original design, and improved technical performance to prolong the life of the house and fulfil the needs of the private owner in terms of current standards. Mike Davies at his own house, free from client requirements and constraints imposed by the very nature of project work and secure in the knowledge that it will remain a weekend house, has reached an uncompromised solution which ensures maximum retention of existing fabric and therefore architectural authenticity. At High Cross, where continued survival of the house has meant adaptation to a new use, greater compromises have had to be made. Integrity has been balanced to achieve the needs of this new use with some loss of original structure and fittings. The operational pressures, both during the project and in the future, for the Dartington estate, are very different from those of Mike Davies as owner/architect.

Despite the fact that modern architecture is now increasingly recognised as an important contributor to our cultural heritage, there is still work to be done in gaining recognition in the wider context. It is still difficult to obtain financial assistance for conservation works to modern buildings and technical research into appropriate methods of retention and conservation of modern materials and methods is only just beginning. However over the last five years much progress has been made as an increasing number of twentieth century buildings are repaired, documentation begins to emerge, training is developed and national and international networks are created for the exchange of information. As more buildings from this century are recognised by the listing process in the UK and by its equivalents in other countries, more information will become available and new repair methods will be developed to achieve conservation aims.

It is encouraging to see what can be achieved with a limited budget in this comparatively new area of work at a time when many modern buildings are under threat due to their supposed irreparable condition. Admittedly none of the three houses was suffering from severe structural problems, but the careful work carried out by the architects has proved that it is possible to repair modern materials, deal with built-in construction faults while retaining architectural integrity and much of the original fabric.

11 Gazetteer of Modern Houses in the United Kingdom and the Republic of Ireland

JEREMY GOULD

Gazetteer of Modern Houses in the United Kingdom and the Republic of Ireland

JEREMY GOULD

The purpose of this gazetteer is to present a fair picture of the variety and extent of Modern house building in the British Isles between the wars. Most items listed are free-standing, specially commissioned houses; speculative housing is nevertheless included, both semi-detached and terraced, but flats are omitted. Unexecuted designs and exhibition houses are omitted, with the single exception of the Gane Show House.

The common characteristic of the Modern house was a flat roof, and although monopitched and double-pitched roofs were introduced by architects committed to Modern design, a flat roof is in general here taken as the criterion for inclusion in the gazetteer. Beyond that, no stylistic bar has been applied, so that good, bad and indifferent are all listed together.

Exhaustiveness is impossible, but virtually all published houses are included, and have been identified by address as far as possible. Unpublished houses take their places in the body of the gazetteer wherever detailed information about them could be obtained. Some additions and external remodellings are included and so marked, but internal remodellings are omitted.

The list was initially compiled in 1977 by Jeremy Gould with John Newman of The Society of Architectural Historians. Further information has come from many different sources. The architects themselves, the clients and their relatives, subsequent owners and the planning departments of local authorities have all contributed richly. This is the place to thank them for their co-operation and for, in many cases, going to considerable trouble to supply correct facts. Others who have kindly allowed the results of their researches to be used here are Ray Barker at Nottingham, Michael Baws at Kingston, M. Cox at Sheffield, Alan Crawford and Eva Ling at Birmingham, John Frew at St. Andrews, Rodney Higgins and Grace McCombie in Northumberland, Edward Hubbard in Cheshire, Terry Hughes at Castleford, Dr. Paul Larmour in Northern Ireland, Jim Lowe at Hull, Prof. Charles McKean in Scotland, Hector MacDonald at Inverness, Derek Mason on Arthur B. Grayson in the Channel Islands, Niall Morrissey at Bristol, Alanah Murphy on 'Sunspan' houses, Alan Powers and David Brady of The Twentieth Century Society, G. Richards at Gerrards Cross, Dr. Sean Rothery in Republic of Ireland, Graham Thurgood at Silver End, Clifford Walters at King's Lynn and Peter Wickham in Devon.

Abbreviations and Explanations

REFERENCES

Reference is generally given to the best-illustrated article on each house, in the following periodicals:

A&BN	The Architect & Building News
AJ	The Architects' Journal
AAJ	The Architectural Association Journal
AR	The Architectural Review
AI	Architecture Illustrated
B	The Builder
	Building
BT	The Building Times
CL	Country Life
D&C	Design & Construction
DfT	Design for Today
F	Focus
GH	Good Housekeeping
IH	The Ideal Home
IB&E	The Irish Builder & Engineer
RIBAJ	Journal of the Royal Institute of British Architects
NB	The National Builder

and the following books:

R. McGrath	Twentieth-century Houses (1934)
F.R.S. Yorke	The Modern House in England (1st edn 1937, 2nd edn 1944)
E. Carter	Seaside Houses and Bungalows (1937)
H-R. Hitchcock	Modern Architecture in England (1937)
H. Casson	New Sights of London (1938)
H.M. Wright	Small Houses (1938)
A. Hastings	Weekend Houses (1939)
R. Phillips	Houses for Moderate Means (1939 edn)
R. Smithells	Country Life Book of Small Houses (1939)
P. Abercrombie	The Book of the Modern House (1939)
N. Pevsner	The Buildings of England, Wales (1951 &c.) (B of E, B of W)
RIBAD	RIBA Drawings Collection

DATING

Dating is, if possible, to the nearest month. The starting month given is that of the final design, or, where [P] occurs after the date, the month in which planning approval was given or the application lodged, provided that there was no significant delay in the granting of building consent. The designer in a partnership is indicated by underlining.

STRUCTURE

Basic information about the structure of houses is given by the following symbols:

C	monolithic concrete
CF	concrete frame
SF	steel frame
TF	timber frame
B	facing brick
PB	colour-washed brick
RB	render on structural block or brick background
BL	facing blockwork
ST	structural stonework.
†	A dagger indicates that a house has been demolished
‡	A double dagger that it has been drastically altered, generally by the addition of a pitched roof, by cladding or by large-scale extension. Minor alterations, such as the replacement of windows or the removal of balustrades, are not noted, although unhappily many houses have suffered from them.

LISTING

I / II* / II   The listing of houses is indicated by grade.

SOURCES

Sources of information are indicated as follows:

[A]	The architects themselves
[C]	The clients
[R]	The clients' relatives
[O]	subsequent owners
[P]	the planning departments of local authorities

England

CITY & COUNTY OF BRISTOL

Bristol

▶ 10 AVON GROVE, SNEYD PARK
F. L. Cottle
July 1935[p]-. RB. [P]

▶ 7 AVON GROVE, SNEYD PARK
Mark Hartland Thomas for Dr & Mrs Skinner
Feb 1934[p]–1935. RB. A&BN, 3 May 1935 pp.124–126

▶ 'SNEED HOUSE' 30 OLD SNEED PARK, STOKE BISHOP
Mark Hartland Thomas for H. J. Hampden Alpass
April 1936[p]–1937. RB. A&BN, 15 Oct 1937, pp.76–78. [P]

▶ 'ORCHARD HOUSE' MARINERS DRIVE, STOKE BISHOP
A. E. Powell for Vernon Hayes
March 1933[p]–1934. RB. A&BN, 7 Sept 1934, pp.264–268. [P]

▶ 'GLENESK', SEA WALLS ROAD, SNEYD PARK
A. E. Powell for the Electrical Association for Women (Mrs A. J. Newman)
1935. RB ‡ A&BN, 1 Nov 1935, pp.134–136

▶ 'CONCRETE HOUSE', 4 RIDGEWAY, WESTBURY-ON TRYM
Connell & Ward for Ronald H. Gunn
May 1934[p]–March 1935. C. [Grade II]. AR, April 1936, pp.170–172. RIBAD

▶ 'CORONATION HOUSE', 46 BRISLINGTON HILL
Bristol Ideal Homes Exhibition (P. Munro Son & Pearce) for H. F. N. Greenhill (builder)
Nov 1936[p]–1937. RB.

▶ 'HILLANDALE HOUSE', 163 WEST TOWN LANE, BRISLINGTON
Unknown architect for A. Miller (builder)
1934–35. RB.

▶ EXHIBITION HOUSE, BRISTOL ROYAL SHOW
F. R. S. Yorke & Marcel Breuer for P. E. Gane Ltd.
April 1936-. ST †. AR, Aug 1936, pp.69–70. RIBAD

▶ 'WITHEY HOUSE', WITHEY ROAD WEST
A. E. Powell for the Electrical Association for Women (Mr & Mrs Moss Garcia)
May 1935[p]–1935. RB.

▶ 2, 4 & 6 DOWNS COTE VIEW
J. L. Chaffe for C. H. Pearce Ltd. (builder)
1935–1936. PB ‡

▶ NOS. 27–35 (ODD), DRUIDS HILL, STOKE BISHOP
Late 1930's. RB.

▶ 24 DOWNS PARK WEST (REMODELLING)
Marcel Breuer for Crofton Gane
1935–36. AR, Decoration Supplement 13, Vol. 79, 1937, pp.139ff

BEDFORDSHIRE

Dunstable

▶ 'HOLLY FRINDLE' (BUNGALOW 'B'), WHIPSNADE PARK
Lubetkin & Tecton for Dr Ida Mann
1933–36. C. [Grade II]. A&BN, 5 Feb 1937, pp.174–179

Kempston

▶ 136 SPRING ROAD
Frank E. Sanders with Edward J. Smith for Frank E. Sanders
July 1934 [P]-. [P]

Leighton Buzzard

▶ 'GARNSGATE', HEATH ROAD
H. Rolls for Mrs A. Downham
May 1946 [P] - 1946. [O]

Luton

▶ 278 OLD BEDFORD ROAD
Evelyn Simmons for Mr. Dillingham
Sept 1934 [P]–1935. RB. [P]

▶ 'GREEN GATES', 324 OLD BEDFORD ROAD
P. B. Dunham for Mr & Mrs T. Corney
Jan 1935[p]-. RB. [P]

▶ 230 STOCKINGSTONE ROAD
P. B. Dunham for P. B. Dunham
April 1935 [P]-. RB. [P]

BERKSHIRE

Ascot

▶ 'GREENACRES', (NOW 'BUTTERSTEEP HOUSE')
Francis Lorne of Burnet, Tait & Lorne for Francis Lorne
c.1938–39. B. CL, 2 Jan 1942, pp.24–27

▶ 'CHILSTON', WINKFIELD (ADDITION)
W. E. Tatton-Brown & Lionel Brett for Hon. Mrs. Maurice Brett (Zena Dare)
B ‡. AR, May 1940, pp.169–170. [A]

Bourne End

▶ 'NOAH'S HOUSE' & BOATHOUSE, SPADE OAK REACH
Colin Lucas of Lucas Lloyd & Co. for R. Lucas
1930. C. House ‡. A&BN, 19 Aug 1932, pp.223–227. [P]

Eton

▶ AINGER HOUSE & BENSON HOUSE, WILLOWBROOK
F. R. S. Yorke & Marcel Breuer for Eton College
1937–38. B. AR, Jan 1939, pp.32–33. RIBAD

Inkpen

▶ UNKNOWN ADDRESS
Raglan Squire for Victor Bonham-Carter
1937–38. B. Squire, Portrait of an Architect (1984). pp.64, 67

Maidenhead

▶ 133–135 BRIDGE ROAD
G. Alan Fortescue for Marchant Hirst & Co. (builders)
–Nov 1932. B. Building, May 1932, pp.223–225; Nov 1932, pp.494–495

Newbury

▶ 'CROWSTEPS' (NOW 'THE HAVEN'), TYDHAMS
T. S. Tait of Sir John Burnet & Partners for Dr Alan Simmons
Aug 1928–29. ‡ RB. A&BN, 13 Sept 1929, pp.311–315

▶ 'SHEPHERDS', TYDHAMS
Pakington & Enthoven for Dr Alan Simmons
1934. RB. Wright (1938), p.64

Reading

▶ 191 WOODCOTE ROAD, CAVERSHAM
RB. ‡

Slough

▶ 'COOMBE WARREN', ALBERT STREET
E. C. Kaufmann for J. H. Ockeufels
1936. † [A]

▶ BATH ROAD
W. David Hartley
1935. RB† ? Phillips (1939), p.88

Sonning

▶ 'CHARWOOD COTTAGE' (ADDITION)
C.K. Capon of The Architects' Co-operative Partnership for Mrs Capon
1939–40. B, T, AJ, 21 Oct 1948, pp.381–382

Sunninghill

▶ 'BROADLANDS'
Minoprio & Spenceley for F. C. Minoprio
c.1931. PB. CL, Nov 1934, pp.496–500

▶ 'CHARTERS'
Adie, Button & Partners for Frank Parkinson
1936–1938. B faced ST. CL, 24 Nov 1944, pp.904–907

Theale

▶ 51 HOUSES IN BLOSSOM LANE, BLOSSOM AVENUE & THE CRESCENT
Messrs McAlpine for Imperial Tobacco Co.
1938–after 1940. B ‡ [P]

Twyford

▶ 'LAND'S END HOUSE', CHARVIL
Guy Morgan for F. G. Miles
March 1934[p]–1935. RB. [Grade II]. AR, July 1935, pp.33–36, [P]

BUCKINGHAMSHIRE

Amersham

▶ 'HIGH & OVER' AND LODGE, HIGHOVER PARK
Amyas Connell of A. Connell & S. Lloyd Thomson for Professor Bernard Ashmole
1929. CF, RB. [Grade II]. CL, 19 Sept 1931, pp.302–307. RIBAD

▶ SUN HOUSES, 4, 6 & 8 HIGHOVER PARK
Connell & Ward for Charles de Peyer
June 1934[p]-. C. [Grade II]. AI, Aug 1942, pp.99–100. [P]

Beaconsfield

▶ 'CASABLANCA' (NOW 'CAMBRIDGE HOUSE'), CAMBRIDGE ROAD
Stanley Hamp of Colcutt & Hamp
1931. RB. BofE (1994), p.177

▶ 'WHITELANDS', CAMBRIDGE ROAD
Stanley Hamp of Collcutt & Hamp for Mr & Mrs A. H. Brooks
Jan 1933[p]-. AR, Aug 1934, pp.57–58

▶ 'WHITEWALLS', CAMBRIDGE ROAD
Stanley Hamp of Collcutt & Hamp
1933. RB. BofE (1994), pp.176–177

Chalfont St. Giles

▶ 'SHRUBS WOOD', NEWLAND PARK
Mendelsohn & Chermayeff for R. L. Nimmo
Dec. 1933–34. C. [Grade II]. AR, Nov 1935, pp.174–178. RIBAD

Dagnall

▶ 'HILLFIELD' (BUNGALOW 'A'), DUNSTABLE ROAD
Lubetkin & Tecton for B. Lubetkin
1933–36. C. [Grade II*]. A&BN, 5 Feb 1937, pp.174–179

Farnham Common

▶ 'EGYPT END' (NOW 'GORDONBUSH HOUSE') & GARDEN HOUSE
Harding & Tecton for Valentine Harding
1934–35. C ‡. Garden house TF. AR, Oct 1935, pp.123–126. RIBAD

Fawley

▶ 'KITS CLOSE', FAWLEY GREEN
Christopher Nicholson for Dr Warren Crowe
1936–37. PB. [Grade II]. AR, June 1938, pp.305–309. RIBAD

Gerrards Cross

▶ 'WESTWOOD', WINDSOR ROAD
James Burford for Miss Burford
‡. A&BN, 15 Nov 1935, p.201

▶ WINDSOR ROAD
Mary Crowley and Mauger & May for -. Crowley
1936. Casson (1938), p.2

▶ 'CASA BLANCA', WINDSOR ROAD
Stanley Hamp of Collcutt & Hamp for B. Pope
1934. RB. Smithells (1939), pp.22–23 [P]

▶ 'LINDEN LEA' (NOW 'KINGS LEA'), WINDSOR ROAD
Stanley Hamp of Collcutt & Hamp
Feb 1934 [P]-. RB. ‡.

▶ 'THE WELL HOUSE', WINDSOR ROAD
Stanley Hamp of Collcutt & Hamp for Miss Floretta Collings
Jan 1935[p]-. RB.

▶ 'TAEDA', WINDSOR ROAD
Stanley Hamp of Collcutt & Hamp for Mr Mittell
1934. RB. †. AI, Sept 1934, pp.84–88

►'WHITEWOOD',
WINDSOR ROAD
Stanley Hamp of Collcutt & Hamp
1934–35. RB. ‡

►'GOSMORE', WINDSOR ROAD
Stanley Hamp of Collcutt & Hamp
1934–35. RB. ‡

►'TIMBERCOMBE',
WINDSOR ROAD
C. Mervyn White, Prentice &
Partners
1936. RB.

►'EAST WALL',
HEDGERLEY LANE
Elisabeth Benjamin with Godfrey
Samuel for Arnold Osorio
Feb 1936[p]-. C, B. [Grade II]. Yorke (1937
edn.), pp.131–133 [A] [P]. RIBAD

► UNKNOWN ADDRESS
E. R. Bill
RB. AJ, 15 April 1937, p.667

Great Missenden
► POTTERS ROW
Stanley Hamp of Collcutt & Hamp
RB. IH, Jan 1939, pp.20–22

Hambledon
► THE FLAT ROOF HOUSE',
LITTLE FRIETH
Colin Lucas for Mrs Margaret Sewell
1933. C. [Grade II]. AR, Dec 1979 pp.336–
337 [O]

Iver
► 99 HIGH STREET
F. R. S. Yorke for R. V. Palin
1936. C † AJ, 31 Dec 1936 pp.906–907
RIBAD

Jordans
►'TWITCHELL'S END',
TWITCHELL'S LANE
C. R. Crickmay for Mr & Mrs J. G.
Jenkins
1934. PB. AR, Aug 1935, pp.53–54 [cr]

►'JORDAN'S END',
TWITCHELL'S LANE
J. Edmund Farrell for Clifton Reynolds
May 1935[p]-. B. [P]

►'THE SHIELING', PUERS LANE
Samuel & Harding for Mrs Brants
July 1939[p]- Jan 1940. B. [A] [P]

Little Chalfont
►'PER ARDUA', VACHE LANE
P. J. Doran for P. J. Doran
RB. †? Smithells (1939) pp.42–43

►'FIVEWAYS'
Roger Smithells for Roger Smithells
RB. DFT, March 1934, pp.96–97

CAMBRIDGESHIRE

Babraham
►'WORSTED BURROWS'
Leopold Edmund Cole for Sir Arthur
Lowes Dickinson (Mrs C. C. Brownlow)
1928. B.

Cambridge
►'THE WHITE HOUSE',
1 CONDUIT HEAD ROAD
George Checkley for George Checkley
1930–31. CF, RB. [Grade II]. A&BN, 6 Nov
1931, pp.167–169. [P]

►'THURSO'
(NOW 'WILLOW HOUSE'),
CONDUIT HEAD ROAD
George Checkley for Hamilton
McCombie
1932. CF, RB. [Grade II*]. A&BN, 17 Feb
1933 pp.226–229. [P]

►'BRANDON HILL', (NOW
'SALIX') CONDUIT HEAD ROAD
H. C. Hughes for Sir Mark Oliphant
1934. CF, RB. [Grade II]. AJ, 30 Aug 1934,
pp.298–299

►'SHAWMS',
CONDUIT HEAD ROAD
Justin Blanco White for Dr W. A. W.
Rushton
1938. TF. [P] [A]

► 16 LATHAM ROAD
R. C. Tuely & Anthony Cooper for
Miss M. Stephenson
1934. B. [P]

► 31 MADINGLEY ROAD
Marshall Sisson for A. W. Lawrence
1932. B. AR, Dec 1932, pp.266–268. RIBAD

► 26 MILLINGTON ROAD
Marshall Sisson for Professor A. J. B.
Wace
Nov 1934-. RB. RIBAD

►'FINELLA', QUEENS ROAD
(REMODELLING)
Raymond McGrath for Mansfield
Forbes
1927–29. AR, December 1929, p.265 ff

►'THE SUN HOUSE',
23 QUEEN EDITH'S WAY
Mullet & Denton-Smith for William
Cairns
1938–39. [P]

►'POSTAN', 2 SYLVESTER ROAD
H. C. Hughes for Professor M. Postan
1939. B.

► 9 WILBERFORCE ROAD
D. Cosens for Dr W. Thorpe
1937. RB. AJ, 16 March 1939, pp.448–449.
[P]

► 19 WILBERFORCE ROAD
H. C. Hughes for Dr. Zachary N.
Brooke
1933–34. [P]

► UNKNOWN ADDRESS
G. Alan Fortescue
B. IH, May 1934, pp.339–342

Ely
► OFF CAMBRIDGE ROAD
c.1940. B.

Great Shelford
►'WHITEWAY'
H. Redhouse for H. Redhouse
RB †. A&BN, 23 Oct 1931, p.95

Hilton
►'KING'S WILLOW',
ST. IVES ROAD
Dyson & Hebeler for J. H. Leycester
Aug 1936[p]-37. RB. AR, Oct 1938, pp.159–
160. [P]

Linton
► WARDEN'S HOUSE,
LINTON VILLAGE COLLEGE,
CAMBRIDGE ROAD
S. E. Urwin for Cambridgeshire County
Council
– Oct 1937. B. [Grade II]

CHESHIRE

Handforth
► 20 WOODLANDS ROAD
RB.

►'CINTRA',
21 WOODLANDS ROAD
RB.

Mickle Trafford
►'BLUE TILES',
WARRINGTON ROAD
Raglan Squire for Reginald Ward
1937-c. May 1938. RB. AR, July 1939 p.12.
[A]

Prestbury
►'PENSYLVANIA',
SUMMERHILL ROAD
H. S. Jaretski for Charles Needham
B. ‡ IH, Oct 1936, pp.266–274

Willaston
►'WHITE GATES',
WHITEGATES CRESCENT
Hubert A. Thomas for Mr Burns
1935. B of E, p.383

Wilmslow
► 29 CARRWOOD ROAD
RB/B.

►'AILSA CRAIG'
(NOW 'THE WHITE HOUSE'),
CARRWOOD ROAD
Unknown architect for Mr Crosby
(builder)
c.1930. RB. [O]

► 9–19 (ODD) & 21/23 KINGS
ROAD
RB/B. 15,17 & 19 ‡

CORNWALL

Carbis Bay
► BEACH BUNGALOW
Cowell, Drewitt & Wheatly for F. A.
Secrett
Jan 1936-. RB. Carter (1937), p.90 [A]

Carlyon Bay
►'GULL ROCK HOUSE'
Marshall Sisson for Staverton (Builders) Ltd.
1933. C. [Grade II]. AR, Dec 1936, pp.306–
307. RIBAD

► TWO HOUSES
Marshall Sisson for Staverton (Builders) Ltd.
1934. RB. Wright (1938), p.99. RIBAD

Fowey
►'TOYNE HOUSE', CASTLE DOR
RB.

Looe
► COASTAL ROAD, EAST LOOE
RB.

Manaccan
►'MACHAN', GILLAN
Unknown architect for Bernard Crossley
Meats (?)
c.1930. RB.

Par
►'WHEAL FORTUNE',
LANESCOT, TYWARDREATH
1936. RB. [O]

Penzance
► 4 CAPTAIN'S ROW,
SOUTH TERRACE

Perranporth
►'WHITE WALLS',
PERRANCOOMBE
A. J. Cornelius for Mrs Lee-Booker
RB. [O]

Trevose Head
►'POLVENTON'
Crowe & Careless for R. H. Stein
1936. SF, RB. [Grade II]. Yorke (1944 edn),
p.75. [O]

CUMBRIA

Brampton
►'BRACKENFELL'
J. L. Martin & Sadie Speight for
Alastair Morton
Dec. 1937[p]–38. B, ST. [Grade II]. AR, July
1939 pp.13–15. [P]

Crofton
► THREE FARM COTTAGES
Pakington & Enthoven for Land
Settlement Association
CL, II Dec 1937, p.596

Dockray
► COCKLEY MOOR (ADDITION)
J. L. Martin & Sadie Speight for
Helen Sutherland
1939. ST, TF. AR, May 1941, pp.103–105 [A]

Kirkby Stephen
►'CUSHAG', NATEBY ROAD
Bernard le Mare for Mr & Mrs A. S. le
Mare
1937. TF. AJ, 12 Jan 1939, pp.63–64. [A]

Wasdale
►'GHYLL DALE', (NOW
'GRINDLEBECK'), GREENDALE
Unknown architect for The Misses M. J.
& F. A. Wilson (for Calder School for
Girls, Seascale)
1938. [O]

DEVON

Bigbury On Sea
►'FIRLE', (NOW 'THE CEDAR
HOUSE'), CLEVELAND DRIVE
Felix Goldsmith for Mr Stephenson
TF. A&BN, 24 June 1938, pp.374–376

▸'KILDRUMMY', FOLLY HILL
RB.

Brixham

▸'SUNPARK', 1 PARK AVENUE
Melville H. Aubin for G. B. Jordain
Mar 1935[p]. RB. [Grade II]. [cr]

Churston Ferrers

▸ 1,2,4,6 ROCK CLOSE, 1,3,4,5,6
& 8 BROADSANDS ROAD
William Lescaze for Staverton (Builders) Ltd. for Dartington Trust
1935. RB. BT, Nov 1935, pp.8–10

Dartington

▸'HIGH CROSS HOUSE',
DARTINGTON HALL
Howe & Lescaze for Dartington School
(W. B. Curry Headmaster)
Aug 1931-June 1932. RB. [Grade II*]. AJ, 12
Oct 1933, pp.443-445

▸ PAIR OF HOUSES,
3 & 4 WARREN LANE,
DARTINGTON HALL
Howe & Lescaze with Robert
Hening for Dartington Hall
1934. RB. [Grade II]. AR, Dec 1936,
pp.263-264

▸ TERRACE OF HOUSES,
5, 6 & 7 WARREN LANE,
DARTINGTON HALL
Howe & Lescaze with Robert
Hening for Dartington Hall
1935. RB. [Grade II]. AR, Dec 1936,
pp.263-264

▸ PAIR OF HOUSES,
8 & 9 WARREN LANE,
DARTINGTON HALL
Robert Hening for Dartington Hall
1938. PB. [Grade II].

▸'THE WARREN' (NOW 'WARREN
HOUSE'), 10 WARREN LANE,
DARTINGTON HALL
Howe & Lescaze with Robert
Hening for Dartington Hall (Kurt
Jooss)
1935-36. RB, SF. [Grade II]. Yorke (1937
edn), p.44

Dartmouth

▸'HIGH & OVER',
140 ABOVE TOWN
Bill Tozer for Eric Edward Hannaford
1934-1935. PB. [cr]

▸ 21 TOWNSTAL PATHFIELDS
RB.

Down Thomas

▸'OVERSOUND HOUSE',
HEYBROOK BAY.
William Walter Wood for William
Walter Wood
1930. C. . AJ, 15 April 1931, pp.554-556. [A]

▸'SEATHWAITE', OVERSOUND,
HEYBROOK BAY
William Walter Wood for -. Mornes
1931. C ‡ A&BN, 3 June 1932, p.333. [A]

Exeter

▸'VITACOP', OLD RYDON LANE
R. M. Challice & Son for Claud Pratt
c.1935. RB. [O]

▸ 15 & 16 SYLVAN AVENUE,
PENNSYLVANIA
Archibald Lucas of Lucas Roberts &
Brown
1935. RB. ‡ [O]

▸ SWEETBRIAR LANE, WHIPTON
RB.

Plymouth

▸ 6 TORLAND ROAD, HARTLEY
Unknown architect for Torr Venn Garden
Estates Ltd. (Alfred W. Marks)
July 1936 -. RB. [O]

▸ 55/57 TORLAND ROAD,
HARTLEY
RB.

Putsborough

▸ HOUSE AT BAGGY POINT
John Stafford & Terence Snailum
for Miss Aileen Langton-May
c.1936-37. PB ‡. A&BN, 11 Feb 1938,
pp.200-201. [A]

Stokenham

▸'HOLBROOK FARM'
Bill Tozer for Roland Arthur Reeve
1936-1937. RB. ‡. [cr]

Teignmouth

▸'FORT INVERTEIGN',
INVERTEIGN DRIVE

▸'LINDISFARNE',
INVERTEIGN DRIVE

▸ 79, 81 TEIGNMOUTH ROAD,
HOLCOMBE
J. G. Best (builder) for Mr Lake
RB. [O]

Tiverton

▸'SHRINKHILLS',
DEYMAN'S HILL
G. G. G. Saunders of Dixon &
Saunders for Gregory Eastmond
1934. RB. Thesis in RIBA.

Torquay

▸ 29, 31, 33, 16, 24 & 26
BROADPARK ROAD,
LIVERMEAD
Unknown architect for Sherwell Builders
Ltd.
1936. 29, 24‡. RB. [O]

▸ 43, 45, 54 & 56 MEAD ROAD,
LIVERMEAD
Unknown architect for Sherwell Builders
Ltd.
RB. 43, 45‡

▸ 2, 4, 3 & 5 ROUNDHILL ROAD,
LIVERMEAD
Unknown architect for Sherwell Builders
Ltd.
c.1938. RB. 2,5‡. [O]

▸'BLUHAZE', 16 BROADPARK,
LIVERMEAD
Cyril Buswell with architect for Cyril
Buswell
1937. RB. [O]

▸'COMPASS SOUTH',
ILSHAM MARINE DRIVE

▸'GORSE HILL',
ILSHAM MARINE DRIVE
†

▸'VILLA PALMA', 42 MEADFOOT
LANE AND 'INVERMEAD',
44 MEADFOOT LANE

▸'WESTLEIGH', 46 MEADFOOT
LANE AND 'INGLEWOOD',
48 MEADFOOT LANE

▸'BEGGAR'S ROOST',
PARKHILL ROAD
RB †. [O]

▸'WHITE WALLS',
PARKHILL ROAD.
William Walter Wood
1931. C † AR, Nov 1932, p.210

▸'MOONGATES',
PARKHILL ROAD
Gerald Bridgeman for Mrs K. W.
Torry
RB ‡ [O]

▸'ROMILEY', PARKHILL ROAD
Unknown architect for Emily Ethel
Walker & Jane Heaton (?)
Post 1934. RB. [O]

▸'BLUE HAYES', PARKHILL ROAD
Rebuilt 1940s. RB.

DORSET

Dorchester

▸'HYDE CROOK HOUSE' &
GATEHOUSE, FRAMPTON
John C. Procter
1936. B. ‡ [O]

▸ 8, 10 GARFIELD AVENUE
R. Thorne for R. Thorne
1938. [P]

▸ 18 MAIDEN CASTLE ROAD,
C. W. Pike
1937. [Grade II]. [P]

▸ 42 MAIDEN CASTLE ROAD
George Norman for Mr Pritchard
1936. [P]

Poole

▸'LANDFALL', 19 CRICHEL
MOUNT ROAD, PARKSTONE
Oliver Hill for Dudley Shaw Ashton
April 1936-38. RB. [Grade II] AR, May
1939, pp.224-225 RIBAD

▸'SHOWBOAT',
BANKS ROAD, SANDBANKS
A. J. Seal of Seal & Hardy for A. J. Seal
RB. A&BN, 12 Feb 1932, pp.227-228

▸'DUNE CREST',
BANKS ROAD, SANDBANKS
A. J. Seal
RB. † BofE, p.332

▸'CONNINGTOWER', HARBOUR
HEIGHTS ESTATE, CANFORD
CLIFFS
Jasper Selwey of A. J. Seal & Partners
for Sam Goodman
1935-36. SF, RB. A&BN, 21 Aug 1936,
pp.216-218

▸ TERRACED HOUSES,
HAVEN CLOSE
A. J. Seal & Partners of Bournemouth
1935-36. RB. BofE, p.332

▸ 32, BURY ROAD,
BRANKSOME PARK
A. J. Seal
RB. BofE, p.331

▸'BEL ESGUARD', 23 BURY
ROAD, BRANKSOME PARK
A. J. Seal
1939. RB. BofE, p.331

▸'THE BOAT HOUSE',
HAMWORTHY
Unknown architect using interiors from
'Mauritania'.
1936.

Poole Harbour

▸ ROUND ISLAND
Edward Maufe for Leslie Laurence
1934-35. RB. RIBAD, Maufe Collection [P]

Portland

▸ 9, CASTLE ROAD

Shaftesbury

▸'LONG COPSE',
SALISBURY ROAD
A. E. Powell
RB. [A]

Weymouth

▸ 31 DORCHESTER ROAD

▸ 12A LITTLEMOOR ROAD
Sidney Tewson for S. J. Herbert
Aug 1933[p]-. RB. [P]

EAST SUSSEX

Bexhill

▸ 10 SOUTHCOURT AVENUE
Reginald A. Kirby for Howard
Wadman
1936. B. AJ, 20 Oct 1938, pp.644-646 [P]

▸ 107 COODEN DRIVE,
58 SOUTH CLIFF
J. E. Maynard for R. A. Larkin (builder)
& C. Baker
1935. RB. [A]

▸'THE WHITE HOUSE',
37 SOUTH CLIFF
H. A. Hambling for G. Ravenshear
May 1938[p]-. RB. [P]

Forest Row

▸'SUN HOUSE', CHELWOOD
GATE
Colin Lucas of Lucas Lloyd & Co. for F.
R. Lucas
1931. C. AAJ, 1956, pp.102, 114-115

Groombridge

▸'MOTTS DOWN', MOTTS MILL
Samuel & Harding for Robert Eicholz
1937. PB. [A]

Halland

▸'BENTLEY WOOD'
S. Chermayeff for S. Chermayeff
1935-38. TF. [Grade II]. AR, Feb 1939,
pp.61-78

Hastings

▸ FAIRLIGHT AVENUE
Jeffrey & Wyatt
1934. RB.

Hove

▸ UNKNOWN ADDRESS
Building, May 1936, p.207

Pevensey Bay

▶ 50 HOUSES, BEACHLANDS, MARINE AVENUE
Unknown architect for Anderida Ltd.
c.1938

Rye

▶‘STARLOCK’, MILITARY ROAD
Frank Scarlett of *Scarlett & Ashworth* for Col. & Mrs Templar
1930. RB. AR, Oct 1932, pp.124–125 [A]

Saltdean

▶ 30, 32, & 36 CHICHESTER DRIVE EAST
RB.

▶ 56, 62 & ONE OTHER, WICKLANDS AVENUE
<u>Connell</u>, Ward & Lucas for Mr. Snow
1934. C. ‡‡† AJ, 7 Feb 1935, pp.226–227

▶‘BELFORD’, 33 ARUNDEL DRIVE WEST
Duke & Simpson for Cyril Shrubsall
May 1934[p]-. RB. BT, March 1935, pp.5–7 [P]

▶‘WHITEWALLS’, 13 FOUNTHILL AVENUE
Claude H. Cowney for Mrs A. M. Matthew
May 1934[p]-. RB. [P]

Seaford

▶‘SPINDRIFT’, MARINE DRIVE
Horace W. Parnacott for A. C. Parnacott
RB ‡ Building, Jan 1932, pp.30–31

ESSEX

Braintree

▶ 1–41 CLOCKHOUSE WAY, 152–194 (EVEN) CRESSING ROAD
C. H. B. Quennell & W. F. Crittall for Crittall Manufacturing Co. Ltd.
1918-. BL. [21, 22 Clockhouse Way & 156, 158 Cressing Road, Grade II] AR, Jan 1919, pp.64–66

Brentwood

▶‘BROOME PLACE’, NEAR STATION
William Walter Wood
RB. AR&BN, 27 Dec 1935, p.383

Broxted

▶‘HILL PASTURE’
Ernö Goldfinger & Gerald Flower for D. H. W. Waterfield
1938. B ‡ Yorke (1944 edn), p.56. RIBAD

East Tilbury

▶ 32 HOUSES, BATA AVENUE
Vladimir Karfik & Frantizek Gahura for Bata Shoe Company
1930–33. C/B. [Grade II]. 12 houses † [P]

▶ QUEEN ELIZABETH AVENUE

▶ KING GEORGE VI AVENUE

▶ THOMAS BATA AVENUE

▶ PRINCESS MARGARET ROAD

▶ QUEEN MARY AVENUE

▶ PRINCESS AVENUE

▶ GLOUCESTER AVENUE
Bata Architects of Zlin for Bata Shoe Company
1939–60. B/RB. [P]

Frinton On Sea

▶ UNKNOWN ADDRESS
Gilbert C. Roberts
RB. † Carter (1937) p.66

Frinton on Sea, Frinton Park Estate

▶ LAYOUT BY OLIVER HILL FOR FRINTON PARK ESTATE LTD. (F. ARNATT)
July 1934/May 1935-c. 1938. RIBAD, Building, Dec 1934, pp.482–487

▶‘THE LEAS’
Oliver Hill
c.Yorke (1937 edn), pp.104–105

▶ 4,6, 7 CLIFF WAY
Oliver Hill
RB. [7 Cliff Way, Grade II]

▶ 1,3,4 AUDLEY WAY
Oliver Hill
RB. Yorke (1937 edn), p.38

▶‘DAWN’ & ‘SUNNYHOLME’, QUENDON WAY
Oliver Hill

▶ 16 WARLEY WAY
Oliver Hill
RB. Yorke (1937 edn), p.38

▶ 1,2,4 EASTON WAY
Oliver Hill
[P]

▶ 10 EASTON WAY
Percy Tubbs, Son & Duncan
[P]

▶ 12 EASTON WAY
Stanley Hall, Easton & Robertson
[P]

▶ 14 EASTON WAY
E. Wamsley Lewis
Carter (1937) p.33

▶ 19 EASTON WAY
Frederick Etchells
[P]

▶ 21 EASTON WAY
Marshall Sisson
RIBAD. [P]

▶ 23 EASTON WAY
Frederick Etchells
[P] ‡

▶ 5–17 (ODD) GRACES WALK
AI, Oct 1941, p.138

▶ 8–18(EVEN) GRACES WALK

▶ 8, 14, 16, 20, 22, 24 / 26, 40 WALTHAM WAY

Great Easton

▶‘NEW FARM’
W. F. Crittall with Messrs Joseph & Owen Williams for W. F. Crittall
1934. PB. [Grade II]. AJ, 14 May 1936, pp.727–729 [cr]

Hadleigh

▶‘SHIPWRIGHTS’, 241 BENFLEET ROAD
Wells Coates for John Wyborn
1936. CF, RB. [Grade II*]. Hastings (1939), pp.30–31

Hockley

▶‘FORSYTE’
F. E. Towndrow
1930. RB. McGrath (1934). Ex. 14, p.91

Holland On Sea

▶‘BIANA’, 25 HAVEN AVENUE
Ronald H. Franks for G. Sherwood
1934. RB. ‡ Wright (1938), p.98 [A]

Loughton

▶ 38 TYCEHURST HILL
P. Wynne Williams for B. G. Hyatt
Nov 1935[p]-. RB. [P]

▶ 50 TYCEHURST HILL
C.J. Manning (Builders) Ltd. for C. J. Manning (Builders) Ltd.
Oct 1934[p]–35. RB. ‡ NB, Oct 1936, Suppl. p.1 [P]

▶‘PEMBERLEY’, 82 TYCEHURST HILL
P. D. Hepworth for W. D. Reynolds
Sept 1935[p]–36. RB. A&BN, 4 Sept 1936, pp.278–279 [P]

Pitsea

▶ UNKNOWN ADDRESS
E. David Hoffmann
1937–38. AJ, 3 June 1937, p.978

Silver End

▶‘LE CHÂTEAU’, BOARS TYE ROAD
T. S. Tait of Sir John Burnet & Partners for D. Crittall
April 1927–28. RB. [Grade II] AR, July-Dec 1928, pp.330–331

▶ 67,77 BOARS TYE ROAD
T. S. Tait of Sir John Burnet & Partners (F. MacManus) for Crittall Manufacturing Co. Ltd.
Sept 1927-. PB. [Grade II] AR, July-Dec 1928 pp.332–336

▶ 1–32 SILVER STREET
T. S. Tait of Sir John Burnet & Partners (F. MacManus) for Crittall Manufacturing Co. Ltd.
1927–28. PB. [Grade II] Thirties Society Journal No. 3 (1982), pp.36–42

▶ 33–60 SILVER STREET, 5 FRANCIS WAY
Crittall Development Co. for Crittall Manufacturing Co. Ltd.
1928. RB. Thirties Society Journal No. 3 (1982), pp.36–42

▶ BROADWAY, FRANCIS WAY, 69–75 SILVER STREET
James Miller for Crittall Manufacturing Co. Ltd.
1929–30. RB. Thirties Society Journal No. 3 (1982), pp.36–42

Westcliff-on-sea

▶ 62 CLATTERFIELD GARDENS
N. Martin-Kaye for N. T. Thurston
Dec 1932[p]–33. RB. [Grade II]. AI, Oct 1935, p.132, [P]

▶ UNKNOWN ADDRESS
N. Martin-Kaye
AI, Jan 1936, p.30

GLOUCESTERSHIRE
(including South Gloucestershire)

Cotswolds

▶ UNKNOWN ADDRESS
C. J. E. Marshall of Praxis for Artist
1934. CL, 20 Feb 1937, pp.208–209

Downend (Bristol)

▶ 139 BADMINTON ROAD
RB.

GREATER MANCHESTER

East Didsbury

▶ 878 & 880, KINGSWAY, CRANDON DRIVE

Sale

▶ 265–277(ODD) WASHWAY ROAD
R. A. Cordingley & D. McIntyre
RB. AJ, 18 June 1936, pp.940–944

▶ 295 WASHWAY ROAD
J. P. Nunn for architectural lecturer
RB. Building, July 1938, pp.280–281

HAMPSHIRE

Burghclere

▶‘SILVER BIRCHES’
Colin Lucas of Lucas Lloyd & Co. for Miss Madge-Porter
1927. C. ‡ AAJ, 1956, p.94

Fordingbridge

▶ STUDIO AT FRYERN COURT, UPPER BURGATE
Christopher Nicholson for Augustus John
Dec 1933–34. CF, PB. [Grade II]. AR, Feb 1935, pp.65–68. RIBAD

Havant

▶ 47 PORTSDOWN HILL ROAD
Wells Coates & D. Pleydell-Bouverie (‘Sunspan’ house)
RB.

Hayling Island

▶ SANDY BEACH ESTATE, OFF SOUTHWOOD ROAD
Kemp & Tasker (?) for Dr Wright
1934-.

▶‘SALTINGS’, 42 SINAH LANE
<u>Connell</u> & Ward for Dr R. D. Lawrence
Late 1933-Oct 1934. C. [Grade II]. AJ, 30 March 1977, pp.582–583 [A], [O]

▶‘THE WHITE HOUSE’, 44 SINAH LANE
<u>Connell</u> & Ward for Dr L. Haydon
–July 1934. C. [Grade II].

Lee-on-the-Solent

▶‘SHANGRI-LA’, MILVIL ROAD
F. R. S. Yorke & Marcel Breuer for Hugh Rose
July 1936–37. C. ‡ AR, Jan 1939, pp.33–34. RIBAD

▶ UNKNOWN ADDRESS
R. Myerscough-Walker
Myerscough-Walker, Choosing a Modern House. (1939), Ex 5

Portsmouth

▶ HOUSES IN ALLAWAY AVENUE, PAULSGROVE
*c.*1935. A. Balfour, *Portsmouth* (1970), p.77

Romsey

▶ 'BRACKEN WOOD', JERMYNS LANE
Raglan Squire for *Harold Wrohan*
Oct 1937[p]-. PB. AR, July 1939, pp.10–11
[A] [P]

HEREFORD & WORCESTER

Bewdley

▶ 'LOBDEN', UPPER COLWALL
Pritchard, Godwin & Clist
B. A&BN, 2 Sept 1932, p.285

Bredon

▶ 'HEATHERDALE', DOCK LANE
Geoffrey Boumphrey with F. R. S. Yorke for *Geoffrey Boumphrey*
1937. PB. AJ, 28 Oct 1937, pp.651–652

Colwall

▶ 'LOBDEN', UPPER COLWALL
R. D. Russell & Marian Pepler
1932. RB. AR, Oct 1933, pp.140–141

Hereford

▶ 'WARHAM ASH', BREINTON
E. Maxwell Fry for *A. M. Hudson-Davies*
1938. B. J. & M. Fry, *Architecture for Children* (1946), pp.41–43

Kidderminster

▶ 'BLAKEDOWN ROUGH', BLAKEDOWN
S. N. Cooke
1934. RB ‡.

HERTFORDSHIRE

Bishop's Stortford

▶ 4 THORNFIELD ROAD
S. Rowland Pierce for *Miss E. M. Barnett*
Sept 1933-. PB. A&BN, 19 April 1935, pp.68–69. RIBAD

Bovingdon

▶ 'GREEN FALLOW', BURY RISE
J. W. M. Dudding for *B. R. Blofield*
July 1936-. PB. [A]

▶ 'JOURNEYS END', SHOTHANGER WAY
Towndrow & Ransom for *Mrs J. Hodgson*
1937–38. PB. D&C, Aug 1939, p.306 [cr]

Bushey

▶ 'WHITE END' (NOW 'PAPER MOON'), 2 GRANGE ROAD
Broad & Patey
1933. C. GH, Sept. 1934, pp.54–55; Nov 1934, p.55 [O]

Chipperfield

▶ 'LITTLE WINCH', CHIPPERFIELD COMMON
E. Maxwell Fry
1934. B, TF. [Grade II]. AR, Jan 1936, pp.25–26

Chorleywood

▶ 'PHEASANTS RIDGE', BERRY LANE
Horace A. Ward for *A. D. N. Cooper*
July 1937-. B. [rc]

Hatfield

▶ 'TORILLA', WILKINS GREEN LANE, NAST HYDE
F. R. S. Yorke, *extended by* Yorke & Breuer for *Mrs Barbara MacDonald*
Sept 1934–35 & Sept 1936-. C. [Grade II*]. AR, Sept 1935, pp.97–100

Letchworth

▶ 'HILL HOUSE', KEYSHEATH, CAMBRIDGE ROAD
R. B. Hall for *F. C. Tollafield*
Nov 1937-. RB ‡ [P]

Moor Park

▶ 6 TEMPLE GARDENS
Connell, <u>Ward</u> & Lucas for *H. Tanburn*
March 1936[p]–37. C. [Grade II] RIBAJ, 17 July 1937, pp.901–909 [P]

Radlett

▶ 'KIMMERIDGE', 14 THE RIDGEWAY
C. J. E. Marshall of Praxis for *Mr & Mrs B. H. Frost*
1938. B. AR, Feb 1944, pp.44–46 [O]

▶ GOODYERS AVENUE/ WATLING STREET
RB.

Tewin

▶ SEWELLS ORCHARD, 102, 104, 106 ORCHARD ROAD
Mary B. Crowley & Cecil G. Kemp for *Miall family* (102), *Crowley family* (104) & *C. G. Kemp* (106)
Feb 1935–36. B. [Grade II]. A&BN, 26 June 1936, pp.388–391. RIBAD [A]

Welwyn

▶ 2 LANERCOST CLOSE, MARDLEY HILL
Wells Coates for *Mrs. H. M. Hill* ('Sunspan' bungalow)
1935. SF ‡. Yorke (1944 edn), pp.76–77

Welwyn Garden City

▶ 34 CONEY DALE
J. W. M. Dudding for *Hugo Leakey*
1937–38. B. [A]

▶ 24 PENTLEY PARK
E. C. Kaufmann for *E. C. Kaufmann*
1937–38. B. AR, Oct 1939, pp.205–207

▶ 26 PENTLEY PARK
Paul V. Mauger of Mauger & May for *Paul V. Mauger*
1937–38. B. [A]

Wheathampstead

▶ 'LINDENS', BLACKMORE END
C.W. Hutton
1936. Casson (1938), p.5

HUMBERSIDE

Hull

▶ 14 HOUSES IN ELLERBURN AVENUE
Claud H. Benwell & J. R. Ausdell for *R. G. Tarrans of Tarrans Industries Ltd.*
April 1935[p]-*c.* 1940. RB. AJ, 14 July 1976, pp.79–80 [P]

▶ SWANLAND ROAD, FERRIBY
J. L. Martin & Sadie Speight for *Max Zzerny*
1935–36. B. AR, May 1941, pp.106–108

▶ 'FOUR ACRES', WOODGATES LANE, FERRIBY
J. L. Martin & Sadie Speight for *Godfrey Robinson*
May 1938[p]-. [P]

▶ ANLABY ROAD
J. H. Napper for *J. H. Robinson*
1937–38 [A]

KENT

Birchington

▶ 'THE WHITE HOUSE', 102 MINNIS ROAD
C. J. Hawkes(?) for *Mrs Kathleen Hawkes*
RB. IH, May 1935, p.380

▶ 'FORT GRENHAM', CLIFF ROAD
Harry V. Ward for *Harry V. Ward*
1936. RB. [C]

▶ 'GUESEND', CLIFF ROAD
Robert Messenger & Son with Roger Caplat for *G. McCausland Hoey*
1937–38 RB, B. [A]

Broadstairs

▶ 'LERRYN', CONVENT ROAD (ADDITION)
Oliver Hill for *W. J. Martin-Tomson*
1931. RB. † AR, Feb 1932, p.58 [C]

Canterbury

▶ 211 THANINGTON ROAD
C. J. Hawkes (builder?)
Feb 1935-. RB. [O]

Cliftonville

▶ 2 GLOUCESTER AVENUE
Jane B. Drew of Alliston & Drew for *Dr T. S. Stone*
1936–37. PB. A&BN, 28 May 1937, pp.258–259

▶ NOS. 20, 24, 25, 37 & 38 PALM BAY AVENUE

Crockham Hill

▶ 'SPENCELEYS', GOODLEY STOCK
H. G. C. Spenceley of Minoprio & Spenceley for *H. G. C. Spenceley*
B. CL, Nov 1936, pp.xliv–xlviii

Dymchurch

▶ 'MANHATTAN', HIGH KNOCKE
Stracey A. Edwards for *Bertram R. Marks (developer)*
1938. C. [P]

Herne Bay

▶ 'NEWHAVEN', HILLTOP ROAD
1936. RB. [O]

▶ 'THE WHITE HOUSE', 5 ALMA ROAD
Robert Messenger & Son with Roger Caplat for *Mrs R. Hall*
1936–37. RB. [A]

▶ 21 ALMA ROAD
Roger Caplat for *Roger Caplat*
RB.

▶ 'GILDORO', 150 BELTINGE ROAD
Roger Messenger & Son with Roger Caplat for *Gilbert L. Kaye*
1936. RB. ‡. [A]

Kingsgate

▶ 20 FITZROY AVENUE (Daily Mail House)
1938. RB. [O]

▶ 'SEA BREEZES', 22 FITZROY AVENUE
Brian O'Rorke
1939. B, timber-clad. AJ, 4 April 1940. pp.349–352

Luddesdowne

▶ 'LUXON FIELD', GREAT BUCKLAND
Frederick Etchells for *Miss H. Drysdale*
Feb 1933[p]-. PB ‡. AJ, 5 Oct 1933, p.419 [P]

Maidstone

▶ 1 TERRACE ROAD
Gordon E. Bowden for *A. E. Verrall*
1933–34. RB. [cr]

Meopham

▶ 'THE HAVEN', HOOK GREEN
Marjorie Tall for *C. G. Brown*
1936. PB. AR, Dec 1936, pp.261–262 [P]

St. Margaret's Bay

▶ 'THE WHITE HOUSE', ST. MARGARET'S ROAD
Mr. Dukes for *Mrs Toye*
1930. RB. [O]

St. Mary's Platt

▶ 'THE HOPFIELD'
Colin Lucas of Lucas Lloyd & Co. for *Colin Lucas*
1933. C. [Grade II]. McGrath (1934), Ex. 27

Shipbourne

▶ 'THE WOOD HOUSE', SHIPBOURNE GREEN
Gropius & Fry for *Jack Donaldson (Lord Donaldson)*
1937. TF. [Grade II]. AR, Feb 1938, pp.61–63

Tonbridge

▶ 1 CORNWALLIS AVENUE
Frank Scarlett of Scarlett & Ashworth for *J. C. V. Brooks*
1931–32. RB. AR, Dec 1936, p.258 [A]

Westerham

▶ 'RYSTED', WESTERHAM HILL
Percy Rothwell with A. H. Jones for *Percy Rothwell*
1931. RB. [cr]

Westgate-on-Sea

▶ 'RAY HOUSE', SEA DRIVE
Unknown architect for Sir Richard
Fairey for Mrs. F. Hulme
1933 RB †. [O]

Unknown Location

▶ 'RED WALLS'
Mary Crowley
c.1935 B. RIBA, Women Architects (1984)
Catalogue.

LANCASHIRE

Hoghton

▶ 'WHITE WALLS', BELLS LANE
Frank Waddington
PB. AJ, 30 Sept 1937, p.505

Morecambe

▶ 2 BROADWAY
Richard Dobson for Miss Gibson
June 1934[p]-. RB. [P]

▶ 27 BROADWAY
Frank Atkinson for J. Wild
Aug 1936[p]-. RB. [P]

▶ 448 MARINE ROAD
Richard Dobson for J. B. Miller
July 1934[p]-. RB. [P]

Whalley

▶ 'STAPLEHURST',
PORTFIELD BAR
A. R. Gradwell for T. S. Porter
RB. A&BN, 25 Oct 1935, p.108

LEICESTERSHIRE

Castle Donnington

▶ 75 PARK LANE

Dadlington

▶ CNR. STAPLETON LANE/
STOKE ROAD
RB. †

Galby

▶ 'LAND'S END',
(NOW 'CARRYGATE')
Raymond McGrath for C. R. Keene
(Sir Charles Keene)
1937-39. B,T. [Grade II] AR, Nov 1941,
pp.132-134. [A]. RIBAD

LONDON

Barnet

▶ 7 WEST HEATH CLOSE,
HAMPSTEAD, NW3
R. A. Duncan of Percy Tubbs, Son &
Duncan for M. A. Alder
Nov 1932[p]-34. C. AJ, 11 April 1935,
pp.563-565 [P]

▶ 28 SPENCER DRIVE,
HAMPSTEAD GARDEN
SUBURB, N2
Welch, Cachemaille-Day & Lander
for G. L. Schwartz
March 1934[p]-. RB. A&BN, 16 Nov 1934,
pp.210-211 [P]

▶ 26-30 (EVEN) VIVIAN WAY,
HAMPSTEAD GARDEN
SUBURB, N2
G. Brian Herbert for G. B. Herbert &
C. F. Partridge
March 1934[p]-. RB. AJ, 9 Jan 1936, pp.60-
62 [P]

▶ 1-18 LYTTON CLOSE,
HAMPSTEAD GARDEN
SUBURB, N2
G. G. Winbourne for W. L. M. Estates
Nov 1934[p]-. RB. BT, Sept 1936, p.96 [P]

▶ 11 TALBOT CRESCENT,
HENDON, NW4
Harold Alexander for C. H. Barclay
July 1934[p]-. B. AJ, 6 April 1936, pp.553-
555 [P]

▶ 29-37 (ODD), 42-46 (EVEN)
ASHLEY LANE, AND
47 SHERWOOD ROAD,
HENDON, NW4
Welch, Cachemaille-Day & Lander
for Haymills Ltd.
1932-33. B. AI, June 1934, pp.200-201,
204-206

▶ 'EVEREST', 54 ASHLEY LANE,
HENDON, NW2
Welch, Cachemaille-Day & Lander
for Mr & Mrs Leslie MacMichael
March 1935[p]-. RB. IH, Jan 1937, pp.18-26
[P]

▶ 72 DOWNAGE, HENDON
Evelyn Simmons of Simmons &
Grellier for Haymills Ltd.
RB. NB, Jan 1936, Suppl. p.1

▶ WEST GROVE, HAMMERS LANE,
(REMODELLING)
Tecton for Mr Cohen
1936-37. RB. [Grade II]. Allan, Lubetkin
p.593

Bexley

▶ 67-71, 75-81 (ODD) DANSON
ROAD, BEXLEYHEATH
D. C. Wadhwa for Messrs Martin & Co
Dec 1934[p]-. RB. [P]

Brent

▶ KENTON
Walker & Westendarp
RB. Wright (1938), p.84

▶ 54-60 (EVEN) BARN RISE,
WEMBLEY
Welch, Cachemaille-Day & Lander
for Haymills Ltd.
June 1932[p]-. B. Building, Sept 1933, p.379.
[P]

▶ 13/15, 75, 83 THE AVENUE,
AND 2, 10/12, 14/16 32
MAYFIELDS, WEMBLEY
Welch & Lander for Haymills Ltd.
Sept 1933/Oct 1934[p]-. B/RB. [P]

Bromley

▶ 119 FOXGROVE ROAD,
BECKENHAM
Norman Keep for F. P. Watts
Apr-Nov 1933. [P]

▶ 82-90 (EVEN) BUSHEY WAY,
BECKENHAM
Roger Brothers (surveyors) for Health
Ray Development Co.
May 1934-35. RB. Adverts in H&G, Nov
1934, p.xix; Sept 1935, p.xiii [P]

▶ 'CASTANEA', 4 WOODLANDS
ROAD, BICKLEY
P. D. Hepworth for Ellis J. Collins
March 1930[p]-31. RB ‡. A&BN, 22 May
1931, pp.247-249 [P]

▶ 'BY-THE-LINKS'
(NOW 'SQUIRREL CHASE'),
LODGE ROAD, BROMLEY
Samuel & Harding for R. M. Thomas
Oct 1934[p]-35. C. [Grade II]. AR, Dec
1936, pp.287-290. [P]. RIBAD

▶ 'STILLNESS',
LODGE ROAD, BROMLEY
Gilbert Booth for J. B. Parnall
Oct 1934[p]-. RB. BofE: West Kent, p.182. [P]

▶ 'LUCAN', ORPINGTON ROAD,
CHISLEHURST
W. Whiteley Kenworthy for E.
O'Sullivan (Kenley) Ltd.
-1932. RB ‡. Building, Nov 1933, pp.452-
453

▶ 4 PARK AVENUE,
FARNBOROUGH
Oswald P. Milne for G. H. R. Fawcett
Feb 1935[p]-35. RB. BT, July 1936, pp.5-6.
[P]

▶ 2/4 MEAD WAY, HAYES
H. Boot (Garden Estates) Ltd. for H.
Boot (Garden Estates) Ltd.
May 1934[p]-. RB. [P]

▶ 311 COURT ROAD,
ORPINGTON
Unknown architect for Lee & Moy
Oct 1934[p]-July 1937. RB. [P]

▶ 77 ADDINGTON ROAD,
WEST WICKHAM
Kemp & Tasker for Morrell (Builders)
Ltd.
1934. RB. H&G, May 1934, p.557.

▶ 64/66, 68/70, 72/74 GATES,
GREEN ROAD, WEST WICKHAM
T. Spencer Bright for Morrell (Build-
ers) Ltd.
Feb 1935[p]-. RB. [P]

▶ 'THE LIGHTHOUSE',
41 HARTFIELD CRESCENT,
WEST WICKHAM
H. L. Allston for L. R. Allston
March 1936[p]-. RB. [P]

▶ 'RODINGS', 105 HARVEST
BANK ROAD, WEST WICKHAM
G. M. Boyes for S. T. Boyes
July 1934[p]-. RB [P]

Camden

▶ 'SUN HOUSE', 9 FROGNAL WAY,
HAMPSTEAD, NW3
E. Maxwell Fry for P. H. Goodbrook
Jan 1935-36. C. [Grade II] AR, Aug 1936,
pp.55-60. [P]

▶ 13 DOWNSHIRE HILL,
HAMPSTEAD, NW3
M. J. H. & Charlotte Bunney for M.
J. H. Bunney
1936. RB. Yorke (1937 edn.), pp.49-52

▶ 1-6 FROGNAL CLOSE,
HAMPSTEAD, NW3
Ernst L. Freud for Ralph Davis(?)
Nov 1936[p]-. B. AR, Aug 1938, pp.54-56.
[P]

▶ 66 FROGNAL,
HAMPSTEAD, NW3
Connell, Ward & Lucas for Geoffrey
Walford
1936-38. C. [Grade II] AR, Oct 1938, pp.155-
158. RIBAD

▶ 13B ARKWRIGHT ROAD,
HAMPSTEAD, NW3
Samuel & Harding for Cecil Walton
May 1937-38. CF, B. AR, Oct 1939, pp.149-
150. [P]

▶ 1-3 WILLOW ROAD,
HAMPSTEAD, NW3
Ernö Goldfinger of Goldfinger & Flower
for Contemporary Construction Ltd. for E.
Goldfinger (No. 2), Stephen Wilson (No.
3)
Nov 1937-39. CF, B. [Grade II] AR, April,
1940, pp.126-130. [P]. RIBAD

▶ 'THE HILL HOUSE',
REDINGTON ROAD,
HAMPSTEAD, NW3
Oliver Hill for Gerald L. Schlesinger
Dec 1936-38. CF, B. AR, April 1939, pp.187-
189. RIBAD

▶ 48 MARESFIELD GARDENS,
HAMPSTEAD, NW3
H. Herrey-Zweigenthal for Paul
Jolowicz
Aug 1938-Sept 1939. B. [P]

City Of Westminster

▶ 33 MAUNSEL STREET, SW1
Harry Barnes & Partners
May 1938[p]-. RB. [P]

▶ 32 NEWTON ROAD,
PADDINGTON, W2
Denys Lasdun of Wells Coates &
Partners for F. J. Conway
Sept 1937[p]-38. CF, B. [Grade II]. AR,
March 1939, pp.119-132. [P]

▶ 3 ALBION CLOSE,
PADDINGTON, W2
Peter Smith
1934. RB. A&BN, 15 March 1935, Suppl. at
p.338.

▶ 52 ABBEY ROAD, NW8
(REMODELLING)
Serge Chermayeff for Serge Chermayeff
1930

▶ 12 CAVENDISH ROAD, NW8
(REMODELLING)
P. G. Freeman
1937. Casson (1938) p.5

▶ 3-5 COCHRANE STREET, NW8
David Stokes
1937. A&BN, 24 Sept 1937

▶ 58 HAMILTON TERRACE,
ST. JOHN'S WOOD, NW8
Francis Lorne of Burnet, Tait & Lorne
(Gordon Farquhar) for Mrs Dudley Ward
(Marquesa de Casa Maury).
May 1936[p]-. B. IH, Sept 1938, pp.164-170.
[A], [P]

▶ 1, 3, 4-10 (EVEN) WELLS RISE,
ST. JOHN'S WOOD, NW8
Francis Lorne of Burnet, Tait & Lorne
(Gordon Farquhar) for Mrs Dudley Ward
(Marquesa de Casa Maury).
March 1934[p]-. RB. [A], [P]

Croydon

▶ 75 FAIRDENE ROAD
G. Nemes
1937. [Grade II]

▶ 25 GROVE WOOD HILL,
COULSDON
Edward Banks for Edward Banks
Nov 1936- Sept 1937. B. AJ, 18 Feb 1943,
pp.123–128

Ealing

▶ 2 SOUTH PARADE,
BEDFORD PARK, W4
F. A. Ruhemann of Dugdale &
Ruhemann for Mr & Mrs L. M.
Neumann
Oct 1937[p]–38. B. [Grade II] AR, Feb 1939,
pp.88–89 [A] [P]

▶ 1 THE RIDINGS, EALING, W5
Welch, Cachemaille-Day & Lander
for Haymills Houses Ltd for Mrs M. B.
Blackwell
June 1933[p]-. RB. AI, Aug 1934, pp.52–54
[P]

▶ 99 HANGAR LANE, EALING, W5
Welch, Cachemaille-Day & Lander
for Haymills Houses Ltd
Feb 1934[p]-. B. AI, June 1935, p.181

▶ 2, 4, CHATSWORTH ROAD

▶ 7, 9, 11A, 17, 21, 29, 33 THE
RIDINGS

▶ 1, 14, 19, HEATHCROFT

▶ 93, 150, 158 CORINGWAY
Welch & Lander for Haymills Houses
Ltd
1934-c. 1937. B/RB. Phillips (1939), p.76

Enfield

▶'WINDRUSH', THE RIDGEWAY,
POTTERS BAR
P. D. Hepworth for W. G. Battersby
c.1934. RB. CL, 30 May 1936, pp.lxii, lxiv

▶ 24 CLAY HILL, PATTENS-WARE
Bayes & Bishop
RB. AJ, 22 Aug 1935, p.275

▶ 1–17 (ODD) ABBOTSHALL
AVENUE, ARNOS GROVE, N14
RB. DFT, Aug 1935, pp.324–325

▶ 23 LANGSIDE CRESCENT,
SOUTHGATE, N14
Alan Green for architect's neice
1934. B. [O]

▶'TREETOPS', 19 WAGGON
ROAD, HADLEY WOOD
Joseph Emberton
1935. ‡

Greenwich

▶ 10 ELTHAM HILL,
ELTHAM, SE9
T. Scott for Dr. Donald Buchanan
1930. RB. Crown Estate Office records

▶ 75–81, 89–101 (ODD) MAZE
HILL, GREENWICH, SE10
J. T. Walford (builder) for Walford
Houses
Jan 1934/April 1935 [P]-c. 1936. RB. [O],
[P]

▶ 85–91 (ODD) GENESTA ROAD,
PLUMSTEAD, SE18
B. Lubetkin & A. V. Pilichowski for
L. Abrahams
1933–34. C. [Grade II] Yorke (1944 edn),
p.125, [P]. RIBAD

▶ 57A WESTCOMBE PARK ROAD
RB. 1937

Hammersmith & Fulham

▶ CARETAKER'S HOUSE,
BURLINGTON SCHOOL FOR
GIRLS (NOW BURLINGTON
DANES SCHOOL), WOOD LANE
Burnet, Tait & Lorne for Burlington
School for Girls Trustees (Mrs H. Dalton)
1936. B. [Grade II]. AR, Jan 1937

Haringey

▶ 6 DUKE'S HEAD YARD,
HIGH STREET, HIGHGATE, N6
Tayler & Green for Roger Pettiward
July 1938[p]- May 1939. RB. [Grade II] AR,
Sept 1940, pp.71–80

▶ 9D THE GROVE,
FITZROY PARK, HIGHGATE, N6
Elisabeth Benjamin
1935. Casson (1938), p.5

▶ SOUTHWOOD LANE,
HIGHGATE, N6
M. Furniss
Sept 1939-Dec 1940. B. AR, Oct 1945,
pp.108–110

▶ 44–48 & 50–54 (EVEN)
SHEPHERDS HILL AND 1–4 &
6–9 BROUGHTON GARDENS
N6
RB.

Harrow

▶'WHITEOAKS',
2 ROSE GARDEN CLOSE,
CANNONS DRIVE, EDGWARE
P. G. Freeman for A. Limburg
1934. RB. A&BN, 31 May 1935, p.235. [P]

▶'SUNMORE', 173 UXBRIDGE
ROAD, HARROW WEALD
Frederick MacManus for J. M. Milner
1939-Oct 1939. B, TF. AR, March 1941,
pp.47–48; RIBAD [A]

▶ 14 KERRY AVENUE, STANMORE
R. H. Uren for Mrs R. H. Uren
1937. B. [P]

▶ 1–6 KERRY AVENUE,
STANMORE
Gerald Lacoste for Warren Estate (Sir
John Fitzgerald)
1935. RB, B, 8 Oct 1937, pp.639–640

▶'ALTHAM HOUSE',
ALTHAM ROAD, HATCH END
Unknown architect for W. J. Flower
1934. [P]

▶ 2–10 (EVEN) VALENCIA ROAD,
STANMORE
Douglas & J. Wood for Warren Estate
(R. & E. Davis)
1933–34. RB. NB, Jan 1935, pp.252–254 [P]

▶ 1, 2 HALSBURY CLOSE,
STANMORE
Rudolf Frankel for M. Rachwalski
(No. 1) & R. Frankel (No. 2)
1938. No. 2 ‡. AR, Nov 1940, pp.136–137
[P]

▶'THE CEDAR HOUSE',
COMMON ROAD, STANMORE
Max Lock for Miss M. Welsford
1938. TF ‡. F, summer 1938, pp.41–49;
winter 1938, pp.39–42

Havering

▶'ST RAPHAEL', 64 NELMES WAY,
HORNCHURCH
Stewart Lloyd Thomson for W. E.
Hill
Dec 1932[p]–33. CF, RB ‡. AR, Dec 1933,
pp.213–214 [P]

▶'ORONSAY',
FAIRWAY, UPMINSTER
Unknown Architect for the Engineer
of P & O SS 'Oronsay'
–Sept 1934

Gidea Park Estate
Competition for building houses at
various fixed prices for Gidea Park
Ltd, 1933–34. The following can be
identified [P]:

▶ 60 HEATH DRIVE
Scott, Chesterton & Shepherd
1933–34. B. Fry, The Changing World (1934),
pp.58–59

▶ 64 HEATH DRIVE
Skinner & Tecton
1933–34. C. AJ, 19 July 1934, p.79

▶ 1 BROOK ROAD
H. S. & F. R. Pite
1933–34. B. Fry, The Changing World (1934),
pp.68–69

▶ 3 BROOK ROAD
L. W. Thornton White
1933–34. B, AJ, 19 July 1934. p.81

▶ 5 BROOK ROAD
H. Spence-Sales for Gidea Park Ltd.
1933–34. C. AJ 9 Aug 1934, p.189

▶ 7 BROOK ROAD
Scott, Chesterton & Shepherd
1933–34. B. DFT, Sept 1934 p.344

▶ 9 BROOK ROAD
H. S. & F. R. Pite
1933–34. B. Fry, The Changing World (1934),
pp.76–77

▶ 13 BROOK ROAD
Geoffrey E. Ransom
1933–34. PB. AJ, 9 Aug 1934, p.188

▶ 15 BROOK ROAD
J. R. Moore Simpson
1933–34. B, AJ, 19 July 1934, p.81

▶ 18 BROOK ROAD
Minoprio & Spenceley
1933–34. RB. AJ, 9 Aug 1934, p.188

▶ 20 BROOK ROAD
L. W. Thornton White
1933–34. B. AAJ, Aug 1934, p.77

▶ 312/314 EASTERN AVENUE
EAST
J. R. Moore Simpson
1933–34. B. AJ, 19 July 1934. p.80

▶ 316/318 EASTERN AVENUE
EAST
Scott, Chesterton & Shepherd
1933–34. B. AJ, 9 Aug 1934, p.188

▶ 320/322 EASTERN AVENUE
EAST
Holford, Stephenson & Yorke
1933–34. RB. Yorke (1937 edn), p.39

▶ 332/334 EASTERN AVENUE
EAST
I. Schultz & T. A. L. Concannon
1933–34. B. Fry, The Changing World (1934),
pp.98–99

▶ 336/338 EASTERN AVENUE
EAST
J. R. Moore Simpson
1933–34. B. Fry, The Changing World (1934),
pp.96–97

▶ 340/342 EASTERN AVENUE
EAST
Scott, Chesterton & Shepherd
1933–34. B. Fry, The Changing World (1934),
pp.94–96

▶ 344/346 EASTERN AVENUE
EAST
A. Maxwell Allen
1933–34. B. AAJ, Aug 1934, p.78

▶ 348/350 EASTERN AVENUE
EAST
Andrews & Duke
1933–34. B. Fry, The Changing World (1934),
pp.90–91

Hillingdon

▶ 97/101 PARK AVENUE, RUISLIP
Connell & Ward for Walter Taylor
(Builders) Ltd.
June 1933-35. C. [Grade II]. AR, Dec 1936,
p.311

▶ 156–186 (EVEN) JOEL STREET
AND 1–39 (ODD) NORWICH
ROAD, NORTHWOOD
Robert De Burgh for Modern Houses
Ltd.
1934. RB. DFT, Aug 1935, p.328. [P]

▶ 153–163 (ODD) NORTHWOOD
WAY, NORTHWOOD
Unknown architect for Morgan &
Edwards Ltd.
1934. RB. [P]

Hounslow

▶'LONG MEADOW', CHISWICK
MALL, W4 (REMODELLING)
Scarlett & Ashworth for Dr Chipnall
1932. SF. AJ, 26 Oct 1932, pp.521–522 [A]

Kensington & Chelsea

▶ 33 COLLEGE PLACE,
CHELSEA, SW3
P. Evans Palmer for P. Evans Palmer
Sept 1933[p]-. RB. A&BN, 25 May 1934,
pp.228–229 [P]

▶ 64 OLD CHURCH STREET,
CHELSEA, SW3
Mendelsohn & Chermayeff for Denis
Cohen
June 1935[p]–36. SF, RB. ‡. [Grade II*]. AJ,
24 Dec 1936, pp.869–874 [P]

▶ 66 OLD CHURCH STREET,
CHELSEA, SW3
Gropius & Fry for Benn Levy
Sept. 1935[p]–36. SF, RB ‡. [Grade II] AJ,
24 Dec 1936, pp.869–874 [P]

Kingston Upon Thames

▶'MIRAMONTE' AND LODGE,
WARREN RISE, COOMBE
E. Maxwell Fry for Gerry Green (North
West London Estates)
May 1936–37. C. [Grade II] AR, Nov 1937,
pp.187–192. RIBAD

▶'TURRET HOUSE', FITZGEORGE
AVENUE, COOMBE
A. B. Llewelyn Roberts for F. L. Hird
Aug 1934[p]-. B. [P]

▶'NEWSOMES',
(NOW 'BIRCHGLADES'),
COOMBE PARK
A. B. Llewelyn Roberts for F. L. Hird
Sept 1937[p]-. RB. D&C, Aug 1939, p.304
[P]

▶'STUDIO HOUSE',
7 NEVILLE AVENUE, COOMBE
H. A. Townsend for F. E. MacWilliam
July 1936[p]-. RB. [P]

▶ 8 THE DRIVE,
GEORGE ROAD, COOMBE
T. Bates & Sons (builders) for Madam
D. Kacinek
May 1936[p]-. RB ‡. [P]

▶'DORICH HOUSE',
KINGSTON VALE
Dora G. Hare (Dora Gordine) with
Henry Cole for The Hon & Mrs R.
Hare
1935–36. B. [Grade II]. CL, 5 Nov 1938,
pp.456–457 [A]

▶ 4–7, 9, 11 BARNFIELD AND
7–10, 20–23, 32–33 MEADOW
HILL, MALDEN
Wates & Wates with R. A. Duncan
for Wates & Wates
1934–35. RB. Building, 9 March 1934,
pp.403, 408

▶ 57, 65, 69 WOODLANDS
AVENUE, NEW MALDEN
Wells Coates & D. Pleydell-
Bouverie for E. & L. Berg Ltd.
('Sunspan' houses)
RB.

▶ 16, 39 WOODLANDS AVENUE
AND 25,70 HIGH DRIVE,
NEW MALDEN
Unknown architect for E. & L. Berg Ltd.
RB. IH, May 1934, p.334

Lambeth

▶'DORCHESTER HOUSE',
DORCHESTER DRIVE,
HERNE HILL, SE24
Kemp & Tasker for Morrell (Builders)
Ltd.
1935. B. B, 10 April 1936, pp.736–737

▶ 32 HERNE HILL, SE24
Keller & Kompfner
1936. B. Wright (1937), pp.34–35

Redbridge

▶'CEDAR LODGE', THE WHITE
HOUSE, WOODFORD GREEN
B. le Mare & A. E. Proskauer for Lt-
Col. S. Mallinson
1936. TF. AR, Dec 1936, pp.285–286 [A]

Southwark

▶ 9 COLLEGE ROAD,
DULWICH, SE21
D. Goddard of Praxis for D. Goddard
1937. B. F, spring 1939, pp.53–58

▶'SIX PILLARS', CRESCENT
WOOD ROAD, DULWICH, SE26
Harding & Tecton for Rev. J. H.
Leakey
1934–35. C. [Grade II*]. AR, Feb 1935,
pp.51–56. RIBAD

Wandsworth

▶ 26 BESSBOROUGH ROAD,
ROEHAMPTON, SW15
Connell, Ward & Lucas for Philip
Proudman
March 1938[p]-. CF. [Grade II]. AAJ, 1956,
p.109 [P]. RIBAD

▶'ILEX', 21 QUEENSMERE ROAD,
WIMBLEDON, SW19
E. Maxwell Fry for Dr Fry (no relation)
1935. B †. AR, Jan 1936, p.26

▶ 15 KINGSMERE ROAD,
WIMBLEDON, SW19
M. Halliburton Smith for Edward
Hale
Feb 1934[p]–35. B †. AR, March 1935, p.III.
[P]

▶ 90 PRINCES WAY,
WIMBLEDON SW19
RB.

▶ 55 VICTORIA DRIVE,
WIMBLEDON, SW19
E. C. Kaufmann of Towndrow &
Kaufmann with Elisabeth Benjamin for
Mr. Kaufmann (no relation)
1934–35. RB †. AR, Oct 1935, pp.127–129

MERSEYSIDE

Birkdale

▶'THE WHITE HOUSE',
54 WATERLOO ROAD
RB.

▶ 61 WATERLOO ROAD
RB.

Crosby

▶ 116 MOORE LANE
G. Stephenson & D. W. Aldred
1936. RB. Yorke (1944 edn), pp.38–39

NORFOLK

Beeston Regis

▶ UNKNOWN ADDRESS
W. F. Tuthill
1933. RB. AJ, 29 March 1934, p.474

▶ 1–9 SEACLIFF, VINCENT ROAD
P. L. Martindale for East Anglian
Estates Agency
Feb 1936[p]-. [P]

Hunstanton

▶ 1/2 HAMILTON ROAD,
OLD HUNSTANTON
1921. BL.

▶'SEAFIELD',
8 HAMILTON ROAD WEST,
OLD HUNSTANTON
Gerald Lacoste for H. G. Ferguson
April 1935[p]-. RB, B. AJ, 8 Oct 1936,
pp.498–502 [P]

King's Lynn

▶'REDRAILS', 90 NURSERY
LANE, SOUTH WOOTTON
Keeble Allflatt of Allflatt & Courtney
for S. R. Beaumont
1932. B. †. IH, Oct 1933, pp.243–245

West Runton

▶'SILVER FIRS', 3 CAMP LANE
W. F. Tuthill for G. N. Scarfe
Feb 1933[p]-. RB. AJ, 4 Jan 1934, pp.24–25
[P]

NORTHAMPTONSHIRE

Northampton

▶'NEW WAYS',
508 WELLINGBOROUGH ROAD
Peter Behrens for W. J. Bassett-Lowke
1925–26. RB. [Grade II*] AR, Nov 1926,
pp.175–179. RIBAD

▶'GUILSBURGH HOUSE',
22 ABINGTON PARK CRESCENT
W. W. Webster for Stephen Patrick
RB ‡. IH, Jan 1935, pp.19–22

NORTHUMBERLAND
(including Newcastle-upon-Tyne
and North Tyneside)

Alnwick

▶ 3 FOXTON ROAD
–. Bradbury for Mr Jackson
1938. RB. [O]

Hexham

▶'RIDGEWAY-ON-YARRIDGE',
YARRIDGE ROAD
J. Walter Hanson & Son for R. W.
Gregory
1934. RB. [O]

▶'CONTIMBRET', SHAW'S LANE,
ALLENDALE ROAD
RB. ‡

Killingworth

▶'GATE HOUSE' AND 'THE
TOWER', WEST LANE
Unknown architect for Mr Eagle
c.1926. C.

Newcastle Upon Tyne

▶'ASHBOURNE',
JESMOND DENE ROAD
Pascal J. Stienlet
1934. RB

▶'THE WEDGE',
MOORSIDE NORTH, FENHAM
Cackett, Burns Dick & Mackellar for
G. W. Dick
Nov 1934-. B †. Wright (1938), p.76. [P]

▶'THE SHILLING HOUSE',
342 WEST ROAD, FENHAM
Michael F. W. Bunney & Clifford
Makins
1925. C. [O]

Rock

▶ THE VICARAGE
(NOW 'OLD ROCK VICARAGE')
J. L. Martin & Sadie Speight for
Helen Sutherland
1938–40. B. ‡. BofE (1957), p.287

Whitley Bay

▶'THORNLEIGH HOUSE',
2 THE BROADWAY
B. ‡

▶ 2 PAIRS OF HOUSES,
31–37 CRANESWATER AVENUE
RB.

▶ 4 PAIRS OF HOUSES,
103–110 THE LINKS
RB.

▶ 11A SHAFTESBURY AVENUE
Leonard Greenwell (builder) for John
Harold Greenwell
1939. RB. [O]

NORTH YORKSHIRE

Filey

▶'WHITE HOUSE',
PRIMROSE VALLEY
D. C. Carmichael
RB. B, 20 Nov 1936, pp.997, 1004

Harrogate

▶'WHITE LODGE'
R. B. Armistead
RB. A&BN, 28 June 1935, pp.394–398

▶'GROSVENOR COURT',
76 LEEDS ROAD

▶'THE RABBITS NEST',
90 LEEDS ROAD
1935

Kirkby Overblow

▶'KIRKBY HOUSE'
John C. Procter for Mr McLaren
1931. RB. AJ, 14 Oct 1931, pp.500–501

Richmond

▶ CARETAKER'S HOUSE,
GIRLS' HIGH SCHOOL,
DARLINGTON ROAD
Denis Clarke Hall for North Riding
Education Committee
1937–39. ST. [Grade II]. Yorke (1944 edn),
p.40

NOTTINGHAMSHIRE

Daybrook

▶'FARR HOUSE',
MANSFIELD ROAD

Mapperley

▶ 125 BRICKHILL ROAD

▶ 47 CORONATION ROAD

Nottingham

▶ 27, 29 WOLLATON VALE
Hedley B. Marshall for Mrs. G. M.
Keall (29)
Apr/Oct 1933[p]–34. RB. [P]

▶ 57 WOLLATON VALE
H. S. Wood for Mrs E. M. Wood
July 1934[p]-. RB. [P]

▶ 608 DERBY ROAD
Reginald W. Cqoper for J. Levin
Jan 1935[p]-. [P]

▶'CHERRY HOLT', RED HILL
William Walter Wood for T.
Hammond
Apr 1933[p]-. B. A&BN, 12 Oct 1934, pp.50–
51 [P]

35 HALLAMS LANE, CHILWELL
R. Myerscough-Walker for R. J. T. Granger
1936–37. RB. [Grade II]. A&BN, 25 June 1937, pp.398–401 [P]

Ruddington

▶'SUN-TRAP' HOUSE
F. A. Broadhead
RB. Advert in IB&E, 23 March 1935, p.225. Advert AR, Feb 1936 p.xxxv.

Woodthorpe

▶ 36 WENSLEY ROAD

OXFORDSHIRE

Mongewell

▶'GRIMSDYKE COTTAGE', SHEEPCOTE FARM
Nuttall-Smith & David Booth for Miss Townsend & Miss Rathbone
TF. AR, Feb 1938, pp 65–66 [cr]

▶'CROWSNEST' (NOW 'LALIQUE'), SHEEPCOTE FARM
John Hilton for Mrs Bircher
1938. B.

Oxford

▶'MANOR HOUSE CORNER', 59 OSLER ROAD, OLD HEADINGTON
Stanley Hamp of Collcutt & Hamp for The President & Governors of the Radcliffe Infirmary, Oxford for A. G. E. Sanctuary
c.Oct 1931–June 1932. RB. AR, June 1934, p.210. [C]

▶'OVERSHOT', BADGER LANE, HINKSEY HILL
Samuel & Harding for (Sir) Ellis Waterhouse
1937. B, TF. Yorke (1944 edn), pp.62–63. [C]

SHROPSHIRE

Oswestry

▶'SYCHTYN HOUSE', SYCHTYN
Sidney Fox-Davies for Richard Metcalf
1936. B.

Shrewsbury

▶ 11 LONGDEN ROAD
A. E. Williams for F. A. Herbert
Summer 1932–33. RB. [P]

▶ 31 SHELTON ROAD
Shayler & Drake for A. H. Jones
July 1934–35. RB. [P]

▶ 33 SHELTON ROAD
G. Ward Deakin for Mrs W. A. Deakin
July 1934–35. RB. [P]

▶ 21 RIDGEBOURNE ROAD
Shayler & Dilks for Mrs Fred Adams
April 1935–36. RB. [P]

▶ 33 OAKFIELD ROAD
G. Ward Deakin for C. Hudson
Aug 1935–36. RB. [P]

SOMERSET
(including North West Somerset, Bath & North East Somerset)

Bath

▶'KILOWATT HOUSE', NORTH ROAD
Molly Taylor of Alfred J. Taylor & Partners for Antony Greenhill
Sept 1935[p]-. C. B, 27 Oct 1939, p.618. [P]

Bawdrip

▶'SHANNON', BAWDRIP LANE
W. M. T. Parsons for W. M. T. Parsons
1937. RB ‡. [A] [O]

Bishopsworth

▶'FLAT HOLME', BRIDGWATER ROAD
Hayes (Builders) Ltd.
1933. RB.

Brockley

▶'THE WHITE HOUSE'
A. E. Powell for W. S. Dening
1936. RB ‡ [A]

Clevedon

▶'SUNWAY', 33 DIAL HILL ROAD
N. H. N. Darby of Leete & Darby
1934–35. RB.

▶'LITTLEMEAD', SWISS VALLEY
Doris Hatt for Doris Hatt (artist)
1932. RB.

Dulverton

▶'WESTERFIELD HOUSE', BRUSHFORD
Horace Ashton Jewell (Surveyor) for H. A. Jewell
1938. RB. ‡. [O]

Failand

▶'LINDSEY HOUSE', CLEVEDON ROAD
RB ‡

Glastonbury

▶ 57 HILL HEAD (REMODELLING)
Mr Hawkins (builder) for Mr MacCauley
1937. RB. ‡ [O]

▶ 'WHITEHOLM', 46 ROMAN WAY
Unknown architect for Donald James Weight
Post Sept 1935. RB.

Keynsham

▶ 189 WELLSWAY
RB.

Penselwood

▶'PEN PITS' AND MUSIC ROOM
P. J. B. Harland for (Sir) Arthur Bliss
1935. RB, TF. [Grade II]. A&BN, 16 Aug 1935, pp.194–197

Portishead

▶ 54 NORE ROAD
c.1939. RB ‡

Priston

▶ PRISTON NEW FARM (ADDITION)
Mark Hartland Thomas
CF. Thomas, Building is Your Business (1947)

Radstock

▶'EDGEHILL', 35 FROME ROAD
Unknown architect for Mr. C. H. Perry (registrar)
July 1935–May 1937. RB. ‡. [O]

Redhill

▶'FIELD HOUSE', LYE HOLE LANE
c.1935. RB.

Stoke Sub Hamdon

▶'BEVERLEY', MONTACUTE ROAD
Reg Fish for Mr & Mrs P. Dike
1935. RB. [C]

Street

▶ 1–27 (EVEN), GRANGE AVENUE
G. H. Samuel for C. & J. Clark Ltd.
March 1935[p]-Feb 1936. RB. [O]

Taunton

▶'FAIRMILE', 1 HIGHLANDS, OFF SHERFORD ROAD
Stone & Francis for Mr Farmer (?)
1934–35. RB.

▶'STONEGALLOWS HOUSE', JEFFREYS WAY, STONEGALLOWS
H. S. W. Stone for J. T. Bent
July 1935[p]-. RB. [O]

Wells

▶'THE WHITE HOUSE', 71 PORTWAY
1936. RB.

West Camel

▶ 1–8 HOWELL HILL
Petter & Warren, Lt. Col P. N. Nissen
1925. RC. [P]

Weston-super-Mare

▶ 17–27 (ODD), 22–26 (EVEN) 33, 35 NEVA ROAD AND 39–48 STATION ROAD
N. H. N. Darby of Leete & Darby
c.1936. RB.

Yeovil

▶'NOBLES NAP HOUSE', COOMBE NAP LANE
W. R. Roydon Cooper for W. R. Roydon Cooper
1932. RB ‡. [A]

▶ 78, 80, 82 & ONE OTHER COOMBE NAP LANE
W. R. Roydon Cooper of Petter, Warren & Roydon Cooper
1933–34. RB ‡. [A]

▶ 172 & 174 GOLDCROFT ROAD
Petter & Warren, Lt Col P. N. Nissen for Yeovil Town Council
1925. RC. [Grade II]. [P]

▶ 175 ILCHESTER ROAD
Unknown architect for Mrs L. E. Davis
Oct 1936[p]-. RB. [P]

▶ 28 SWALLOWCLIFFE GARDENS, THE PARK
W. R. Roydon Cooper
RB. [A]

STAFFORDSHIRE

Audley

▶'EARDLEY HOUSE', ALSAGER ROAD
Joseph Emberton for Dorothy Emberton
1939. B, T. Ind, Emberton (1983), p.92.

Blythe Bridge

▶'THE UPLANDS', STALLINGTON LANE
A. Glyn Sherwin for F. W. R. Wildblood
Dec 1937–38. B. AI, Oct 1938, pp.108–112

Shenstone

▶'VIEWPOINT', ST. JOHN'S HILL
A. J. Seal & Partners for Mr & Mrs W. Harper
1938–39. B. IH, Jan 1942, pp.21–24. [C]

Stafford

▶ 73 CASTLE BANK
G. M. Boon for G. M. Boon
1936. PB. [A]

SUFFOLK

Aldeburgh

▶ 26 FAWCETT ROAD
C.H. Huke with W. C. Reade for C. H. Huke
1935. RB. [C]

Ipswich

▶ UNKNOWN ADDRESS
James E. Noller
B. Building, April 1934, pp.141–144

Southwold

▶ 33 HALESWORTH ROAD, REYDON
F. J. Meen for G. F. Williams
Nov 1936[p]-. RB. [P]

Woodbridge

▶'KINGS KNOLL', BROOM HEATH
Hilda Mason for Hilda Mason & sister
RB ‡.

SURREY

Ashtead

▶'HANGING LANDS', GRAYS LANE
Walker & Westendarp
1933. RB. AJ, 11 Jan 1934, p.79

Bagshot

▶'WHITE LODGE', GUILDFORD ROAD
E. Maxwell Fry for a Doctor
1935. RB †. AR, Jan 1936, p.27

Banstead

▶ 82 WINKWORTH ROAD
Laurence Wright for Dr W. W. Gerrard
1934. RB. [C]

Betchworth

▶'THE WEALD', PEBBLE HILL
Ernst L. Freud for Mrs Marsh
1939. RB. [O]

Chertsey

▶'ST. ANN'S' (NOW ST. ANN'S COURT), ST. ANN'S HILL
Raymond McGrath for Christopher Tunnard & G. L. Schlesinger
1936–37. C. [Grade II]. AR, Oct 1937, pp.117–122. RIBAD

Chobham

▶'LONGACRES', STATION ROAD
Forbes & Tate & Enid Caldicott
PB. A&BN, 6 July 1934, pp.20–21

Churt

▶'AVALON', 'BRON-Y-DE'
Anthony Chitty for Frances Stephenson (Lady Lloyd George)
1935. TF. Yorke (1944 edn), p.80

▶ GARDENER'S COTTAGE, 'BRON-Y-DE'
Anthony Chitty for Frances Stephenson (Lady Lloyd George)
1935. TF. A&BN, 14 June 1935, pp.315–317

Dormans Park

▶'THE BRIDGE HOUSE'
P. D. Hepworth for J. W. Drawbell
1934. RB. IH, June 1937, pp.524–528

Esher

▶'THE HOMEWOOD', PORTSMOUTH ROAD
Patrick Gwynne with Wells Coates for Cdr & Mrs Gwynne
Sept 1937[p]–39. CF, B. [Grade II]. AR, Sept 1939, pp.103–116. [P]. RIBAD

▶'KINRARA', 9 WAYNEFLETE TOWER AVENUE
Christian Barman for Hugh Quigley
April 1934[p]-. B ‡. AR, April 1935, pp.153–157. [P]

▶'BLUE HILLS', ESHER CLOSE
Imrie & Angell & Scott-Willey for H. B. Dixon
Dec 1933[p]-. RB. AI, March 1935, pp.90–91. [P]

▶'SENTOSA', ESHER CLOSE
Stanley Hall & Easton & Robertson for C. A. Erhardt
June 1934[p]-. RB. [Grade II]. AJ, 7 May 1936, pp.699–701. [P]

Ewell

▶'STANTON', 3 THORNDEN GARDENS
John Izod & A. V. Pilichowski
April[p]–Sept 1936. PB. Yorke (1937 edn), pp.62–63. [P]

Grayswood

▶'ALDING' ('NEW FARM'), (NOW 'WHITE HOUSE')
Amyas Connell of Connell & Ward for Sir Arthur Lowes Dickinson
1931–32. C. [Grade II*]. AR, March 1933, pp.118–119. [A]

Guildford

▶'SOLARIA', 12 CHANTRY VIEW ROAD
Robert De Burgh of East Horsley for Arthur Frederick Mason
1935–Feb 1936. RB. [O]

Hinchley Wood

▶ 1, 19 AVONDALE AVENUE AND 23 SOUTHWOOD GARDENS
Wells Coates & D. Pleydell-Bouverie for E. & L. Berg Ltd.
('Sunspan' houses)
Feb 1934[p]–35. RB. Daily Mail Ideal Home Exhibition catalogue, 1934. [P]

Holmbury St Mary

▶'JOLDWYNDS', HOLMBURY HILL
Oliver Hill for Wilfred Greene
May 1932–34. RB. [Grade II]. AR, Oct 1934, pp.115–119. RIBAD

▶'THE WILDERNESS', BY 'JOLDWYNDS'
Margaret Church of Tecton for Sir Wilfred Greene
1938–39. RB. Allan, Lubetkin (1992), p.593

▶'EDGMONT', WOODHOUSE LANE
Cole-Adams, Phillips & Cheriton with W. Dalton Ironside
RB ‡. AJ, 20 Dec 1934, pp.920–921

▶'HIGH LAWNS', WOODHOUSE LANE
W. Dalton Ironside for a Musician
RB ‡. AJ, 10 Sept 1936, pp.335–358

▶'CONEYBARROW' (NOW 'HILLTOP'), WOODHOUSE LANE
R. M. Butler of Butler & Muncaster for Francis Williams (Lord Francis-Williams)
1935. B. [cr] [ar]

Horley

▶ 10, 12 ('BOX HOUSE') AND 14 ('LONGLINTOLS'), HAROLDS LEA DRIVE
F. E. Towndrow
B/PB. Adverts in H&G Sept 1937, p.xliv; Dec 1934, p.xxxiv; IH, Feb 1938, p.101

Kingswood

▶ UNKNOWN ADDRESS
G. Warren Peachey
B, RB. H&G, June 1936, p.20

Leatherhead

▶'THE YEWS', ROOKERY CLOSE, FETCHAM PARK
Frederick Etchells for Mrs. A. Kirk
B. AR, June 1933, pp.235–236. [O]

Leigh

▶'PEVEREL', SHELLWOOD ROAD
F. F. Curtis
1936. PB. Casson (1938), p.3

Long Ditton

▶ 1, 2, 3 WENTWORTH CLOSE
Wells Coates & D. Pleydell-Bouverie for E. & L. Berg ('Sunspan' houses)
April 1934[p]-. RB. Nos 2, 3 ‡. Daily Mail Ideal Home Exhibition catalogue 1934. [P]

Peaslake

▶'LITTLE ACRE'
A. S. Knott & Edna Moseley
1932. Casson (1938), p.3

Redhill

▶'FIRKIN', 4 MILL STREET
Connell, Ward & Lucas for Miss Unwin
1936. C ‡. Yorke (1944 edn), p.139

Virginia Water

▶'WHITE WINGS', (NOW 'DOWN HILL')
Thomas Shepard with Godman & Kay for Ivor Campbell
Oct 1935[p]-. RB. AJ, 22 April 1937, pp.686–687. [P]

Wentworth

▶'HOLTHANGER' (NOW 'CHERRY HILL'), PORTNALL DRIVE
Oliver Hill for Miss Newton
Aug 1933–35. RB. AR, June 1935, pp.241–244; RIBAD. [P]

▶'BRACKEN' (NOW 'GREENSIDE'), PORTNALL DRIVE
Connell, Ward & Lucas for Williamson Noble
1937. C. [Grade II]. RIBAJ, 17 July 1937, pp.901–909

▶'STRAIDARRAN'
Imrie & Angell for J. H. Hunter
Feb 1935[p]-. B. [P]

West Molesey

▶ UPPER FARM ROAD
Unknown architect for Howard Houses
1934. RB. A. Jackson Semi-detached London (1973), p.139 & pl. 13.

Woldingham

▶'SHALLOES', BUTLERS DENE ROAD
E. J. Baigent & Sons for G. F. Thomas
Aug 1930[p]-. RB. [P]

▶'COTSWOLD', SOUTHFIELDS ROAD
Elie Mayorcas for H. F. Morris
Aug 1936[p]-. RB. AJ, 19 Aug 1937, pp.304–306. [P]

▶'HIGH SPINDLE', GARDEN VILLAGE
J. W. M. Dudding for Miss H. E. Coates
1938–39. TF. [A]

▶'HIGH TIMBERS', GARDEN VILLAGE
J. W. M. Dudding for Miss M. Haines & Miss A. Mills
1938–39. TF. [A]

Worcester Park

▶ 95 SALISBURY ROAD
Connell, Ward & Lucas
1937. C. [Grade II]. AAJ, 1956, pp.114–115

WARWICKSHIRE

Leamington Spa

▶'BROXTON', 72 NORTHUMBERLAND ROAD
R. A. C. Churchward for The Coalectric Estate Development Co. Ltd.
1934. RB. [O]

Nuneaton

▶ 110 BULKINGTON LANE, WHITESTONE
H. N. Jepson
1937. RB.

Rugby

▶ 116 DUNCHURCH ROAD
Serge Chermayeff for Mrs E. W. Shann
May 1933[p]–34. C. [Grade II]. AR, March 1935, p.106

Stratford-upon-avon

▶ 60–72 (EVEN) BIRMINGHAM ROAD
F. W. B. & F. R. S. Yorke for Flowers Brewery
Aug 1938[p]–39. B,ST. [Grade II]. Yorke (1944 edn), pp.60–61. [P]

WEST MIDLANDS

Birmingham

▶ 79 WESTFIELD ROAD, EDGBASTON
Douglas Tanner of Tanner & Horsburgh for Lewis Espir
Dec 1928[p]-. RB. Building, Jan 1929, p.35 [P]

▶ 11 CHURCH ROAD, EDGBASTON
W. Haywood (?)
c.1936. B. [Grade II]. [P]

▶ 26-34 (EVEN) GIBSON ROAD, HANDSWORTH
C. K. Shepherd for C. K. Shepherd
1930-. RB/B. [P]

▶'THE WHITE HOUSE', 43 GIBSON ROAD, HANDSWORTH
W. B. & F. T. Archer (builders) for Mr. Nash
1937. RB. [P]

▶ 64 GIBSON ROAD, HANDSWORTH
W. B. & F. T. Archer (builders) for W. B. & F. T. Archer
1938. RB. [P]

▶ 53 BEAKS HILL ROAD, KINGS NORTON
T. Dunkley for H. Thornton
Nov 1935. RB. [P]

▶ 237 MOOR GREEN LANE, MOSELEY
RB.

▶ 36–44 KENSINGTON ROAD, SELLY PARK
C. K. Shepherd for C. K. Shepherd
1930. RB/B. IH, May 1931, p.416

Smethwick

▶ DOCTOR'S SURGERY, HIGH STREET,
T. M. Ashford for Dr McKenzie
July 1933[p]-. B. AJ, 14 July 1938, pp.88–89 [P]

Sutton Coldfield

▶ 9 HILLWOOD COMMON ROAD
C. Edmund Wilford
1936. B.

► 126 LICHFIELD ROAD,
FOUR OAKS
T. M. Ashford for A. Andrews
Feb 1934[p]-. B. [P]

Tettenhall

► 78 WROTTESLEY ROAD
Lavender & Twentyman for Percy Jones
1936. RB. AJ, 1 Oct 1936, pp.446–448 [A]

WEST SUSSEX

Angmering On Sea

►'SEA LANE HOUSE',
COASTAL ROAD
F. R. S. Yorke & Marcel Breuer for J. MacNabb
Sept. 1936–37. CF, PB. [Grade II]. AR, Jan 1939, pp.29–31. RIBAD

►'RUNNYMEDE', COASTAL ROAD
Wells Coates & D. Pleydell-Bouverie ('Sunspan' house)
1936. SF.
'The White House', Coastal Road, Angmering Estate

►'LITTLE MARTINS', COASTAL ROAD, ANGMERING ESTATE
Gordon(?) for Crisp(?)
B.

►'WHITE LODGE',
WESTFIELD AVENUE
Messrs Joseph for C. S. Joseph
PB. A&BN, 12 Jan 1934, pp.58–59

► 14–20 (EVEN) WILLOWHAYNE AVENUE
E. C. Kaufmann for S. & S. Freeman Ltd. (agents)
1936. PB. AR, Dec 1936, pp.271–272

► 'VILLA VILLINA', GOLDEN ACRE, ANGMERING ESTATE

► 'SHALIMAR', GOLDEN ACRE, ANGMERING ESTATE

►'THE WHITE HOUSE', 8 UPPER DRIVE, ANGMERING ESTATE
PB.

►'FAIR WINDS', 6 UPPER DRIVE, ANGMERING ESTATE
PB.

Birdham

►'HARBOUR MEADOW'
Peter Moro & Richard Llewelyn Davies
B, ST. AR, April 1941, pp.63–70

Bognor Regis

►'BEACH HOUSE',
BAY WALK, ALDWICK
Chitty & Tecton for Tecton
Dec 1933[p]–34. C ‡. [Grade II]. AR, March 1935, p.109. [P]

►'SUNWAYS',
BAY WALK, ALDWICK
Evelyn Simmons & Cecil Grellier for G. T. Crouch
Feb 1934[p]-. RB. IH, Dec 1934, [p]
'Bell Lodge', Fish Lane
RB.

Haywards Heath

► UNKNOWN ADDRESS
A. L. Osborne
1931. RB. Phillips (1939), p.32.

► 59,61, 63, 65, 66, 68, 70, 72 SUNNYWOOD DRIVE
Lubetkin & Tecton for Montague Barnett
1934–36. B. No. 72 ‡. AJ, 6 Aug 1936, pp.175–178. [P]

Middleton On Sea

►'MERRI PEBBLE',
SOUTHDENE DRIVE

►'MON REPOS',
SOUTHDENE DRIVE

►'SUNDENE',
18 SOUTHDENE DRIVE

►'WHITEWALLS',
SOUTHDENE DRIVE

►'SEAGULLS',
46 SOUTHDENE DRIVE

►'TOWER HOUSE',
SOUTHDENE DRIVE

► RUSTINGTON
Gerald Lacoste
RB. IH May 1937, pp.395–398

Shoreham-by-sea

► UNKNOWN ADDRESS
O. D. Pearce
Decoration, Jan-March 1938

Sutton

►'FORGE HOUSE', HIGH STREET (ADDITION)
F. R. S. Yorke for (Sir) Gerald Barry
1939. TF. AR, April 1940, pp.122–125

►'POTCROFT'
Connell, Ward & Lucas for Dr. Thomas
1938. TF. F, winter 1938, pp.28–34, 38–44

Woodmancote

►'DRAGONS'
Connell, Ward & Lucas for Dr D. A. Crow
1935–36. C. AJ, 30 April 1936, pp.659–663.

Worthing

► SHAFTESBURY AVENUE ETC.
M. Rainsford Fletcher for Maddison & Brookes
c.1935–39. [A], [P]

WEST YORKSHIRE

Ben Rhydding

►'FIVE OAKS'
John C. Procter for E. W. Chary
April 1929[p]–30. RB. AJ, 5 Nov 1930, pp.684–689. [P]

Castleford

►'CHATELAINE', 234 LOWER OXFORD STREET
Blenkinsopp & Scatchard for Dr M. Innes Pragnell
1934. RB. [O]

Leeds

►'WHITE LODGE', NR ADEL
John C. Procter
RB. H&G, March 1935, pp.495–496

►'VAL D'OR', 28 THE RING ROAD, SHADWELL
– Chappell for Mica Sidi
1935. RB. [O]

Sheffield

► 200–202 NORTON LANE & HOUSES IN CLOONMORE DRIVE & HENLEY AVENUE
Garry Mainwaring for M. J. Gleeson
Dec 1934[p]–39.

Wetherby

►'HELFORD HOUSE',
30 SPOFFORTH HILL
W. A. Jones of Jones & Stocks for Edward Davies
March 1935-. RB. [P]

WILTSHIRE

Aldbourne

►'WEST LEAZE'
T. S. Tait of Sir John Burnet & Partners for Mrs Hugh Dalton
Aug 1930–31. PB. A&BN, 11 Dec 1931, pp.316–319. RIBAD

Marlborough

►'WEST RIDGE',
MANTON DOWN ROAD
Unknown architect for Mr. Surridge
1938. RB. [O]

Scotland

BORDERS REGION

Bowden

►'BACKETT'S FIELD'

Melrose

►'THE KEEP', GATTONSIDE

Kelso

►'BROOMLAW'

Selkirk

►'STABSTANE'

CENTRAL REGION

Kippen

►'GRIBLOCH'
Basil Spence of Rowand Anderson Paul & Partners with Perry M. Duncan of New York for John & Helen Colville
1937–39. RB. MacGregor, Arch. Heritage V (1995), pp.73–96. NMRS Spence Collection

Stirling

► BUNGALOWS,
OCHIL ROAD, CAUSEWAYSIDE

DUMFRIES AND GALLOWAY REGION

Dumfries

► 2 HOUSES, NEW ABBEY ROAD/ PLEASANCE AVENUE
W. N. Thompson & Co.

Portpatrick

►'DRUMMUIE', HEUGH ROAD
A. MacLean Goudie
c.1936. RB.

Stranraer

►'HAWKESWORTH',
BROADSTONE ROAD
A. MacLean Goudie
c.1946.

►'THE MOORINGS',
BROADSTONE ROAD
A. MacLean Goudie
1937.

FIFE REGION

Cupar

►'GUYSEL HOUSE' OR 'GYSELS HOUSE', BRIGHTON ROAD
William Guild
1937. ‡.

► BOWLING GREEN LANE

Dunfermline

►'BELLA VISTA', LINBURN ROAD
A. B. Allan

Kirkcaldy

► 8 BENNOCHY DRIVE
Williamson & Hubbard
1934.

► 5 PAIRS HOUSES,
LADY NAIRN AVENUE
Balfour Bros.
1934. RB.

►'KINCRAIG' OR 'NORIDLO', PEATMAN'S BRAE, THORNTON
1937. RB.

Leven

► 3 PAIRS HOUSES
Lawrence Rolland for Andrew Cook
1936.

►'OBERTAL', LARGO ROAD
c.1935. RB.

►'WESTFIELD'/'SILVERSIDE' & 'SUNNYLEA'/'KALINGA', LARGO ROAD
RB.

St. Andrews

► 44–46 BUCHANAN GARDENS
Thomas Rodger
1945–47. RB.

► 2 MELBURN GARDENS

► 11–29 STRATHKINNESS HIGH ROAD
Thomas Rodger
1945–47. RB, B.

GRAMPIAN REGION

Aberdeen

►'AUCHINLECH', LUMSDEN
Roy Meldrum (?)
c.1937.

► GARTHDEE ROAD
Roy Meldrum
1937

► 2 PAIRS HOUSES, ANNFIELD AND 10 PAIRS HOUSES, BROOMHILL AVENUE
T. Scott Sutherland

Ballater

► GOLF ROAD

Elgin

▶ 13 WITTET DRIVE
J. & W. Wittet
RB. [Listed]

HIGHLAND REGION

Alness

▶‣'ARDMHOR', 43 OBSDALE ROAD

Inverness

▶‣'LAMBURN',
41 OLD EDINBURGH ROAD
R. Carruthers-Ballantyne
1935. RB. [O]

▶‣'CLUNY HOUSE',
87 CULDUTHEL ROAD
William Allan of Carruthers-
Ballantyne, Cox & Taylor
c.1937. RB.

▶‣'BALNABRUACH',
89 CULDUTHEL ROAD
R. Carruthers-Ballantyne
1935. RB.

▶‣'GARTMORE',
135 CULDUTHEL ROAD
RB.

▶‣'OVER & ABOVE',
145 CULDUTHEL ROAD
Donald Fowler of Carruthers-
Ballantyne, Cox & Taylor for Donald
Fowler
c.1936. RB.

▶‣'CLACHNAHARRY',
(NEXT 'DELMORE')
William Taylor of Carruthers-
Ballantyne, Cox & Taylor
1938.

▶ 7 DARNAWAY AVENUE
James Johnson & Rose (?)
1936. RB.

Invermoriston

▶‣'JOHNNIE'S POINT'
PB ‡.

LOTHIAN REGION

Aberlady

▶ LUFFNESS CROFT
J. D. Cairns & Ford (?) for Chairman,
Cement & Concrete Board
1935.

Edinburgh

▶ 4 EASTER BELMONT ROAD
Kininmonth & Spence for Miss Reid
1934.

▶‣'LISMHOR',
11 EASTER BELMONT ROAD
Basil Spence of Kininmonth & Spence
for Dr John King
1932. RB. A&BN, 23 Aug 1935, p.227

▶ 46A DICK PLACE, GRANGE
W. H. Kininmonth of Kininmonth &
Spence for (Sir) Wm. H. Kininmonth
1932. PB. A&BN, 11 Oct 1935, pp.40–41

▶‣'HETHERSETT',
95 WHITEHOUSE ROAD,
CRAMOND
C. F. Reid for Mrs. Frances Haggard
Nov 1932–33. RB.

▶‣'BULNAGARROW',
51 GLEBE ROAD, CRAMOND
James Miller & Partners
Sept 1936 [P]- Sept 1937. RB. [P]

▶ 4 GLENLOCKHART BANK
George Lawrence for Helen Thornton
1938.

▶ 538 QUEENSFERRY ROAD,
BARNTON
W. N. Thomson
1937. RB.

▶ 2 PAIRS HOUSES, EAST CRAIGS
James Miller
1936.

▶ 32 OLD KIRK ROAD,
CORSTORPHINE
James Miller
1936.

▶ RESTALRIG SQUARE &
RESTALRIG CIRCUS
A. H. Campbell (Korrelbeton System)
for Edinburgh Town Council
1925–26. C. Frew, Arch Heritage V (1995),
pp.29–38

Forth

▶ UNKNOWN ADDRESS
Kininmonth & Spence for Scottish
Special Housing Association
1939. TF. RIASD

North Berwick

▶ UNKNOWN ADDRESS
Joe Gleave
1939.

STRATHCLYDE REGION

Ayr

▶‣'WHITE PLAINS',
LONGHILL AVENUE
Alex Mair for Mrs Alexander & Alan
Alexander (nurseryman)
1936.

▶ 151 PRESTWICK ROAD
Percy Hogarth for David Hogarth
(builder)
RB.

Carmunnock

▶ 4 HOUSES AND BUNGALOWS
CATHKIN ROAD

Glasgow

▶ NOS 6, 13, 15 & 17
RODDINGHEAD ROAD,
BROOM, WHITECRAIGS
RB.

▶ 9 LAWERS ROAD, MANSEWOOD
W. E. Gladstone
c.1936. RB.

▶‣'KILMARDINNY', BEARSDEN
J. R. H. MacDonald for J. R. H.
MacDonald
RB. CL, 8 June 1935, pp.604–605

▶ 3 HOUSES, KILMARDINNY
AVENUE, BEARSDEN

▶ 44 PENDICLE ROAD,
BEARSDEN
J. E. Dallachy
RB.

▶ 28 RUBISLAW DRIVE,
BEARSDEN

▶ 15 DOUGLAS PARK, BEARSDEN

▶ NOS 1, 2, 5, 8, 9, 10 AND TWO
OTHERS CARSE VIEW DRIVE,
BEARSDEN
J. R. H. MacDonald
1933–36. RB.

▶ CARETAKER'S HOUSE,
KELVIN COURT
J. N. Fatkin
1939

▶ 2 PAIRS HOUSES,
CARNTYNE ROAD

▶ 16 KIRKVIEW CRESCENT,
MEARNS KIRK

▶ HOUSE, EAGLESHAM CROSS

Helensburgh

▶ 3 KIDSTONE DRIVE

Kilsyth

▶‣'SKYROCK',
HORSBURGH AVENUE
Carmyle Cement Manufacturers
c.1938.

Lanark

▶‣'WINDSOR', CLEGHORN
Stewart Shaw
1934.

Newhouse

▶ BY GRIFFIN MOTEL

TAYSIDE REGION

Arbroath

▶‣'INGLE NEUK'
Gordon & Scrymgeour
1935.

Dundee

▶ 43 FORFAR AVENUE
Gordon & Scrymgeour

▶‣'SUNNINGDALE',
RALSTON ROAD, WEST FERRY
Thoms & Wilkie (Donald Ross)
1933. RB.

▶ 7 BINGHAM TERRACE
Frank Henderson
‡.

▶ 6 ARNDALE DRIVE
Lowe & Barrie
1936. RB.

▶ 5 ARNDALE GARDENS
Lowe & Barrie
1937.

Wales

Aberystwyth

▶ 2 HOLIDAY HOUSES, BORTH
Ronald H. Franks for H. Melen and G.
Fisher
1935. RB. Abercrombie (1939), p.197 [A]

Dinorwic

▶ SIX QUARRYMEN'S HOUSES
David Pleydell-Bouverie for Sir
Michael Assheton-Smith
RB. AJ, 10 June 1937, p.1025

Llandudno

▶‣'VILLA MARINA',
THE PROMENADE, CRAIGSIDE
Harry W. Weedon for Harry Scribbans
1936. RB. [Grade II]. Building, Feb 1937,
p.72 [A]

Marford

▶‣'OLD MOUNT'
Wilfred Beeston for John Bellis
c.1935

Mold

▶ 5 HOUSES,
GWERNAFFIELD ROAD
B.

Penarth

▶ 5 CLIFF PARADE
Gordon Griffiths for Dr & Mrs John
Gibbs
Aug 1938–1939. RB. BofW (1994), p.495.
[O]

Channel Islands

JERSEY

St. Brelade

▶‣'LES LUMIERES',
ROUTE ORANGE, LA MOYE
Arthur B. Grayson for Ernest ('Tony')
Huelin
March 1932–33. RB

▶‣'ROCKFIELD' OR 'ROCKVILLE',
MONT DE LA ROCQUE
Arthur B. Grayson for Mr W. G.
Milne
c.1938. RB. ‡

▶ 3 HOUSES,
MONT DE LA ROCQUE
Arthur B. Grayson
c.1938. RB. ‡

St. Clements

▶‣'FAIRLEA'/'GRANTON',
ST. CLEMENTS INNER ROAD
Arthur B. Grayson
RB

St. Helier

▶‣'GREEN COURT',
GREEN STREET
Arthur B. Grayson
1935. PB

▶ QUEENS ROAD
RB

▶‣'LA VILLETTE'
RB

► 'PRES DE L'EST'
RB

St. Lawrence

► 'BRIMBORION'/'HIGH LEA',
BEL ROYAL
Arthur B. Grayson
1936. RB

► 'TEMPERLEY', MONT COCHON
Arthur B. Grayson
c.1935. RB

► 'LE CLOS' AND 'VILLA DES
VIGNES', MONT DES VIGNES
Arthur B. Grayson
c.1936. RB

St. Peter

► 'RED LODGE' (NOW 'WHITE
LODGE'), MONT DES VIGNES
Arthur B. Grayson for Mr Ballantine
1934. RB

► 'VILLA BONITA',
BEAUMONT HILL
Arthur B. Grayson
c.1935. RB

St. Saviour

► 'SHERINGHAM' LES VARINES
Arthur B. Grayson
1934. RB

Northern Ireland

COUNTY ANTRIM

Belfast

► 5 WATERLOO PARK
R. S. Hill for R. McIntyre
1934. RB. [Grade B1]

► 736 ANTRIM ROAD
Hugh Gault for John Colgan
Dec 1934-. RB. [Grade B1]. Larmour, Belfast:
An Illustrated Architectural Guide (1987), p.90

► 4 CLEAVER GARDENS
Hugh Gault for E. H. Armstrong
1937. RB. Larmour, The Architectural Heritage
of Malone and Stranmillis (1991), pp.42 & 44

► 20 LISMOYNE PARK
Young & Mackenzie for McCune &
Son (Builder)
Aug 1932-. RB. Larmour, Festival of Architec-
ture 1934–1984 (1984)

► 28 LISMOYNE PARK
Hugh Gault for Hugh Gault
1933. RB. Larmour, Belfast: An Illustrated
Architectural Guide (1987), p.90

► HOUSE IN GLENCOE PARK
W. Porte for D. Morrow
March 1935-. RB. Larmour, Belfast: An
Illustrated Architectural Guide (1987), p.90

► 18 COOLDARRAGH PARK
Hugh Gault for H. Yarr
April 1933-. RB

Cushendall

► 'SAN MICHELE' 15 LAYDE ROAD
Unknown architect for Mr Finnegan of
Blackpool
c.1933. RB

Whitehead

► 'WESTBOURNE',
49 CHESTER AVENUE
Adam Dobson for W. Smith
1935. RB

► 'NORWOOD TOWER',
CHESTER AVENUE
Adam Dobson
1935. RB. ‡

COUNTY ARMAGH

Portadown

► 121 MOYALLEN ROAD
Philip Bell for S. Richardson
1938. [Grade B2]. Evans, An Introduction to
Modern Ulster Architecture (1977), p.74

COUNTY DOWN

Bangor

► 20 BEVERLEY HILLS
T. D. Purdy for R. J. Shannon (builder)
1934. RB. ‡. IB&E, 3 Nov 1934, p.938

Belfast

► 23, 25, 27 & 29 OLD
HOLYWOOD ROAD
John MacGeagh
May 1935-. RB. Larmour, Belfast: An
Illustrated Architectural Guide (1987), p.90

► HOUSE IN BELMONT DRIVE
A. F. Lucy for N. Luke
April 1937-. RB. Larmour, Belfast: An
Illustrated Architectural Guide (1987), p.90

► 235 KING'S ROAD
Philip Bell for Ronald Green
1934. RB. ‡

► 9A ASCOT GARDENS
A. F. Lucy for Mrs Selina McKee
Sept 1935-. RB. [Grade B2]

► 15 ASCOT GARDENS
S. Reid for Mrs E. V. Bell
Dec 1938-. RB, B

► HOUSE IN HAMPTON PARK
Unknown architect for W. A. Law
May 1937-. RB

► 98 & 100 KNOCK ROAD
S. Reid for N. Luke
Jan 1939-. RB, B. †

Killinchy

► 135 & 139 WHITEROCK ROAD
Philip Bell
c.1936. RB. [Grade B2]

► 63 BALLYDORN ROAD
Philip Bell
1935. RB. ‡. [Grade B1]

Kircubbin

► 13 ROWREAGH ROAD
Philip Bell
1938. RB

Republic of Ireland

CO. CLARE

Lough Inchiquin

► SHOOTING LODGE
T. P. Kennedy
1937. C. IB&E, 17 April 1937, p.346

COUNTY DONEGAL

Convoy

► ALCOHOL FACTORIES
Eoghan Buckley & John O'Gorman
for Excise Officers
1935-38. RB. Rothery, Ireland 1900–1940,
pp.203–204

Dungloe

► OPPOSITE HOSPITAL
Sean Merry of Clare for Vincent
McElwee
RB. [O]

Labbodish

► ALCOHOL FACTORIES
Eoghan Buckley & John O'Gorman
for Excise Officers
1935-38. RB. Rothery, Ireland 1900–1940,
pp.203–204

CO. DUBLIN

Blackrock

► 'GIRNIEGVE'
(NOW 'STREAMWOOD'),
AVOCA AVENUE
Frederick MacManus for W. N.
Crawford
1936-37. RB. AJ, 22 June 1939, pp.1082–
1083. [A]

Clontarf

► HOUSES IN KINCORA ROAD
McDonnell, Downes & Dixon
1930-31. RB. Advert in IB&E, 26 Sept 1931,
p.859

► HOUSES IN DOLLYMOUNT
John J. Robinson & R. C. Keefe for
P. J. Wallace (contractor)
c.IB&E., 23 April 1932, p.376

Dalkey

► 'BOSULA', SORRENTO ROAD
E. Lionel Crosby
1935. C. Carter (1937), pp.64–65

Dublin

► HOWTH ROAD
Scott & Good for Arthur Shields
1933-34. B. IB&E, 21 Jan 1939, p.47

Foxrock

► 'ARBORES', STILLORGAN
ROAD, WHITECROSS
Frederick MacManus for Mr & Mrs
Edward Jenkins
1937. RB. AJ, 22 June 1939, p.1081. [A]

► UNKNOWN ADDRESS
Joseph V. Downes of McDonnell,
Downes & Dixon for J. V. Downes
1939. B. Advert in IB&E, 26 Oct 1940, p.653

Glasnevin

► 'WENDON', BOITHRIN MOBH
Harold Greenwood for G. M. Linzell
1929-30. RB. IB&E, 13 Aug 1932, pp.735–
737

Killiney

► UNKNOWN ADDRESS
Michael Scott for Col. Fagan
1937. RB. Advert in IB&E, 18 Sept 1937,
p.840

Sandycove

► 'GERAGH'
Michael Scott for Michael Scott
1937. RB. [A]

► 'NEIDIN'
Scott & Good for William Scott
1933-34. RB.

COUNTY LIMERICK

Castletroy

► UNKNOWN ADDRESS
Clifford Smith & Newenham
1937. RB. IB&E, 30 Dec. 1944, p.535

► UNKNOWN ADDRESS
Clifford Smith & Newenham
1937. RB. IB&E, 3 Nov 1945, p.567

COUNTY MAYO

Ballina

► ALCOHOL FACTORIES
Eoghan Buckley & John O'Gorman
for Excise Officers
1935-38. RB. Rothery, Ireland 1900–1940,
pp.203–204

Gazetteer Index

This is an index of architects' names (personal and practice) found in the Gazetteer. Names are given in the fullest form, unless no further information exists. For ease of location, gazetteer columns are referred to as a to d from left to right. Names may appear more than once in a column.

Kennedy, T P, 126b
Kenworthy, W Whiteley, 119c
Kininmonth, William see K & Spence
Kininmonth & Spence, 125ab
Kirby, Reginald Alec, 116d
Knott, Alfred Stocken see K & Moseley
Knott & Moseley, 123b
Kompfner see Keller & K

Lacoste, Gerald Auguste Charles, 120b, 121b, 124b
Lander, Felix James see Welch, Cachemaille-Day & L
Lasdun, Denys, 119d
Lavender, Ernest Clifford see L & Twentyman
Lavender & Twentyman, 124a
Lawrence, George Haslehurst, 125b
le Mare, Bernard Arthur, 115d see also le M & Proskauer
le Mare & Proskauer, 121a
Leete see L & Darby
Leete & Darby, 122bc
Lescaze, William, 116a see also Howe & Lescaze
Lewis, Ernest Wamsley, 117b
Lloyd see Lucas, L & Co
Lock, Max, 120c
Lorne, Francis, 114b see also Burnet, Tait & Lorne
Lowe, Robert William see L & Barrie
Lowe & Barrie, 125c
Lubetkin, Berthold see L & Pilichowski see also Tecton
Lubetkin & Pilichowski, 120b
Lucas, Colin Anderson, 115a see also L, Lloyd & Co and Connell, Ward & L
Lucas, John Archibald see L, Roberts & Brown
Lucas, Lloyd & Co, 116d, 117d, 118d
Lucas, Roberts & Brown, 116b
Lucy, A F, 126b

McAlpine, Messrs (builders), 114c
MacDonald, J R H, 125bc
McDonnell see McD, Downes & Dixon
McDonnell, Downes & Dixon, 126c
MacGeagh, John, 126b
McGrath, Raymond, 115b, 119a, 123a
McIntyre, Donald see Cordingley & McI
Mackellar, Robert Norman see Cackett, Burns Dick & M
Mackenzie see Young & M
MacManus, Frederick Edward Bradshaw, 120b, 126c see also Burnet, Tait & Lorne
Mainwearing, Garry, 124c
Mair, Alexander, 125b
Makins, Clifford C see Bunney & M
Manning, C J, 117c
Marshall, Charles John Evelyn [of Praxis], 117d, 118b
Marshall, Hedley Bernard, 121d
Martin, John Leslie see M & Speight
Martin & Speight, 115d, 118c, 121c
Martin-Kaye, Douglas Niel, 117c
Martindale, P L, 121b
Mason, Hilda, 122d
Maufe, Edward Brantwood, 116d
Mauger, Paul Victor Edison see M & May see also Crowley & M & May
Mauger & May, 118b
May see Mauger & M see also Crowley & Mauger & M
Maynard, J E, 116d
Mayorcas, Elie, 123c
Meen, Frederick J, 122d
Meldrum, Roy, 124d
Mendelsohn, Erich see M & Chermayeff
Mendelsohn & Chermayeff, 114d, 120d
Merry, Sean, 126c
Messenger, Robert see M, Son & Caplat
Messenger, Son & Caplat, 118cd
Miller, James, 117c, 125b
Milne, Oswald Partridge, 119c
Minoprio, Charles Anthony see M & Spenceley
Minoprio & Spenceley, 114c, 118c, 120c
Morgan, Guy Llewellyn, 114c
Moro, Peter see M & Llewelyn Davies
Moro & Llewelyn Davies, 124a
Moseley, Edna see Knott & M

Mullet, Harold Leggett see Mullet & Denton-Smith
Mullet & Denton-Smith, 115b
Muncaster, Joan Elizabeth see Butler & M
Munro, P see M, Son & Pearce
Munro, William Kirkpatrick see M, Son & Pearce
Munro, Son & Pearce, 114a
Myerscough-Walker, Herbert Raymond, 117d, 122a

Napper, Jack Hollingworth, 118c
Nemes, G, 120a
Newenham see Smith & N
Nicholson, Christopher, 114d, 117d
Nissen, P N, 122c
Noller, James E, 122d
Norman, George, 116c
Nunn, John Price, 117d
Nuttall-Smith, George Alexander see N-S & Booth
Nuttall-Smith & Booth, 122a

O'Gorman, John see Buckley & O'G
O'Rorke, Edward Brian, 118d
Osborne, A L, 124a

Pakington, [the Hon] Humphrey Arthur see P & Enthoven
Pakington & Enthoven, 114c, 115d
Palmer, Philip Evans, 120d
Parnacott, Horace Walter, 117a
Parsons, William Michael Tracey, 122b
Patey see Broad & P
Peachey, G Warren, 123b
Pearce see Munro, Son & P
Pearce, Oswald Duncan, 124b
Pepler, Marian see Russell & P
Petter, John see P & Warren
Petter & Warren, 122c
Phillips, Arthur Todd see Cole-Adams, P & Cheriton
Pierce, Steven Rowland, 118a
Pike, Charles William, 116c
Pilichowski, Amnon Vivien see Izod & P see also Lubetkin & P
Pite, Frederick Robert see P & P
Pite, Hugh Stanley see P & P
Pite & Pite, 120c
Pleydell-Bouverie, David, 125d see also Coates & P-B
Porte, W, 126a
Powell, Adrian Evelyn, 114a, 116d, 122b
Praxis see Goddard see also Marshall, C J E
Prentice see White, P & Partners
Pritchard see P, Godwin & Clist
Pritchard, Godwin & Clist, 118a
Procter, John Clifford, 116c, 121d, 124b
Proskauer, A E see le Mare & P
Purdy, T D, 126b

Quennell, Charles Henry Bourne, 117a

Ransom, Geoffrey E, 120c see also Towndrow & R
Reade, W C see Huke & R
Redhouse, H, 115b
Reid, Charles Findlater, 125b
Reid, Robert S, 126b
Roberts see Lucas, R & Brown
Roberts, Arthur Beaver Llewelyn, 121a
Roberts, Gilbert C, 117b
Robertson, Howard Morley see Hall, Easton & R
Robinson, John Joseph see R & Keefe
Robinson & Keefe, 126c
Rodger, Thomas, 124d
Roger Bros (surveyors), 119b
Rolland, Lawrence, 124d
Rolls, Harold Arthur, 114b
Rose, Charles Alexander see Johnson & R
Ross, Donald, 125c
Rothwell, Percy see R & Jones
Rothwell & Jones, 118d
Ruhemann, F A see Dugdale & R
Russell, R D see R & Pepler
Russell & Pepler, 118a

Samuel, Godfrey Herbert, 122c see also Tecton
Samuel & Harding, 114d, 115a, 116d, 119cd, 122a
Sanders, Frank E see S & Smith
Sanders & Smith, 114b
Saunders, George Gerald Girling see Dixon & S
Scarlett, Frank see S & Ashworth
Scarlett & Ashworth, 117a, 118d, 120d
Scatchard, Fred see Blenkinsopp & S
Schultz, Israel Samuel see S & Concannon
Schultz & Concannon, 120d
Scott, Elisabeth Whitworth see S, Chesterton & Shepherd
Scott, Michael, 126cd see also S & Good
Scott, T, 120a
Scott, Chesterton & Shepherd, 120cd
Scott & Good, 126d
Scott-Willey, Hugh Henry see Imrie & Angell & S-W
Scrymgeour, Russell A see Gordon & S
Seal, Arthur John see Seal & Hardy
Seal & Hardy, 116cd, 122d
Selwey, Jasper, 116c
Shaw, Stewart, 120a
Shayler, Frank Hearn see S & Dilkes see also S & Drake
Shayler & Dilks, 122a
Shayler & Drake, 122a
Shepard, Thomas see S, Godman & Kay
Shepard, Godman & Kay, 123c
Shepherd, Alison see Scott, Chesterton & S
Shepherd, C K, 123d
Sherwin, A Glyn, 122d
Simmons, Charles Evelyn see S & Grellier
Simmons & Grellier, 114b, 119b, 124a
Simpson see Duke & S
Simpson, James Roundthwaite Moore, 120cd
Sisson, Marshall Arnott, 115bc, 117b
Skinner, Russell Thomas Francis see Tecton
Smith, Clifford, see S & Newenham
Smith, Edward J see Sanders & S
Smith, M Halliburton, 121b
Smith, Peter, 119d
Smith & Newenham, 126d
Smithells, Roger, 115a
Snailum, Terence see Stafford & S
Speight, Sadie see Martin & S
Spence, Basil see Kininmonth & S
Spence-Sales, Harold John Arthur, 120c
Spenceley, Hugh Greville Castle see Minoprio & S
Squire, Raglan Hugh Anstruther, 114b, 115c, 118a
Stafford, John see S & Snailum
Stafford & Snailum, 116b
Stephenson, Gordon see Holford, S & Yorke see also S & Aldred
Stephenson & Aldred, 121b
Stienlet, Pascal Joseph, 121c
Stocks, John Ellis see Jones & S
Stokes, David, 119d
Stone, Henry Spencer Walcott, 122c see also S & Francis
Stone & Francis, 122c
Sutherland, Thomas Scott, 124d

Tait, Thomas Smith see Burnet, Tait & Lorne
Tall, Marjorie, 118d
Tanner, Douglas see T & Horsburgh
Tanner & Horsburgh, 123d
Tasker see Kemp & T
Tate see Forbes & T & Caldicott
Tatton-Brown, William Eden see T-B & Brett
Tatton-Brown & Brett, 114b
Tayler, Herbert see T & Green
Tayler & Green, 120b
Taylor, Molly, 122b
Taylor, William John see Carruthers-Ballantyne, Cox & T
Taylor, William Robert Hector, 125a
Tecton, 114bd, 119b, 120c, 121b, 123b, 124ab see also individuals: Chitty, Harding, Lubetkin, Samuel
Tewson, Sidney, 116d
Thomas, Hubert Arthur, 115c
Thomas, Mark Hartland, 114a, 122b
Thoms, Patrick Hill see T & Wilkie

Thoms & Wilkie, 125c
Thomson, Stewart Lloyd, 120c see also Connell & T
Thomson, W N, 124c, 125b
Thorne, R, 116c
Towndrow, Frederick Edward, 117c, 118a, 123b see also T & Kaufmann and T & Ransom
Towndrow & Kaufmann, 124b
Towndrow & Ransom, 121a
Townsend, H A, 121a
Tozer, William, 116ab
Tubbs, Grahame Burrell see T, Son & Duncan
Tubbs, Percy see T, Son & Duncan
Tubbs, Son & Duncan, 117b, 119a
Tuely, Richard Clissold see T & Cooper
Tuely & Cooper, 115b
Tuthill, William Francis, 121bc
Twentyman, Alfred Richard see Lavender & T

Uren, Reginald Harold, 120b
Urwin, Samuel Ernest, 115c

Waddington, Frank, 119a
Wadhwa, D C, 119b
Walford (builder), 120a
Walker, Reginald Victor see W & Westendarp
Walker & Westendarp, 119b, 122d
Ward, Basil Robert see Connell & W see also Connell, W & Lucas
Ward, Harry V, 118c
Ward, Horace A, 118b
Warren, Percy Francis see Petter & W
Webster, W W, 121c
Weedon, Harry William, 125d
Welch, Herbert Arthur see W, Cachemaille-Day & Lander
Welch, Cachemaille-Day & Lander, 119ab, 120a
Welch & Lander see W, Cachemaille-Day & L
Westendarp, Rudolf Theodore see Walker & W
Wheatly, Reginald Francis see Cowell, Drewitt & W
White, Margaret Justin Blanco, 115b
White, C Mervyn see W, Prentice & Partners
White, L W Thornton, 120c
White, Prentice & Partners, 115a
Wilford, Charles Edmund, 123d
Wilkie, Alexander Abercrombie see Thoms & W
Williams, [Sir] Owen, 117b
Williams, A E, 122a
Williams, P Wynne, 117c
Williamson, William see W & Hubbard
Williamson & Hubbard, 124d
Winbourne, Goodman George, 119b
Wittet, John see W & W
Wittet, William see W & W
Wittet & Wittet, 125a
Wood, Douglas see W & W
Wood, H S, 121d
Wood, James Douglas see W & W
Wood, William Walter, 116ac, 117a, 121d
Wood & Wood, 120b
Wright, Laurence, 122d
Wyatt, Norman Albert Edward see Jeffrey & W

Yorke, Francis Reginald Stevens, 115a, 117d, 118b, 124b see also Boumphrey & Y and Holford, Stephenson & Y and Y & Breuer and Y & Y
Yorke, Francis Walter Bagnall see Y & Y
Yorke & Breuer, 114ab, 117d 118b, 124a
Yorke & Yorke, 123d
Young, James Reid see Y & Mackenzie
Young & Mackenzie, 126a